CHRIST B.C.

COMMENTARIES BY LLOYD AHLEM

A 13-week course designed to help
young people understand the
significance of the Old Testament as it
relates to God's plan of redemption
through Jesus Christ.

EDITORIAL STAFF
Annette Parrish, Managing Editor
Carol Eide, Youth Editor
Hope Deck, Editorial Coordinator

CONTRIBUTING EDITORS
John Hambrick
Marc Roth
Tim Weir

SENIOR DESIGNER
Ted R. Killian

Published by Gospel Light Publications, Ventura, CA 93006.

Table of Contents

CHRIST B.C.
Course Overview

"How do the Old and New Testaments fit together?" "Why bother reading the Old Testament? It doesn't mean anything now that we have the New Testament." These questions are often asked by Christians. Many are curious about the purpose behind the Old Testament, and many do not understand the significance of the Old Testament as it relates to God's plan of redemption through Jesus Christ. This study of Old Testament types, pictures, symbols and prophecies will help you and your class see God's intervention in and engineering of events in history as well as His promises to be fulfilled in the future. This course will demonstrate that history and God's Word are inspired by His Spirit; that the stories in the Bible are not fairy tales but real-life illustrations of God's involvement in the affairs of humankind; that God's purpose in sending Christ to reconcile the broken relationship between people and Himself was planned from the beginning of the human experience of sin; and that God's future plans for the world are trustworthy and offer hope for our trying times.

Session 1, *The Road to Emmaus.* You and your students will learn that Christ is the key that unlocks full understanding of all Scripture.

Session 2, *God Covers Adam and Eve's Nakedness.* In this session you will discover the futility of people's efforts to cover their sin and that only God's covering for sin through the shed blood of Jesus Christ is sufficient.

Session 3, *Noah Finds Refuge in the Ark.* Just as God provided refuge for Noah and his family in the ark, God has provided Christ as our refuge during stormy experiences.

Session 4, *Melchizedek.* Melchizedek illustrates Jesus' role as our High Priest who is the only one who can offer us complete redemption.

Session 5, *Abraham and Isaac.* Just as God provided a suitable sacrifice to take Isaac's place on the altar, so God provided His own Son, Jesus, through whom all our needs, beginning with the remission of our sins are met.

Session 6, *Joseph.* Joseph, like Jesus, was obedient to God because he knew that God was using his circumstances to accomplish His holy purposes. Today we can be obedient to God with the confidence that God will use our daily experiences to fulfill His ultimate goals.

Session 7, *The Passover.* Just as the Passover reminded the Israelites of how God delivered them from bondage, Jesus' shed blood reminds us that He can deliver us from the bondage of sin.

Session 8, *The Tabernacle Curtain.* The Tabernacle curtain separated an unholy people from God's holy presence. Christ's death on the cross caused the curtain to be torn in two, symbolizing that through Christ sinners are made acceptable to God.

Session 9, *The Ark of the Covenant.* The Ark of the Covenant is a picture of Christ dwelling in our midst, providing atonement and mercy to all who come to Him in faith.

Session 10, *The Bronze Snake.* As the bronze snake lifted up by Moses saved all who looked at it from death, so Jesus offers salvation to all who look to Him.

Session 11, *Prophecies of the Messiah.* The amazing accuracy of prophecies foretelling Jesus' birth, ministry, death and resurrection reaffirms for us that the Bible is trustworthy. The Bible is not just history or literature; it is truth.

Session 12, *The Suffering Servant.* The prophet Isaiah foretold the suffering Jesus would experience. Because Jesus understands pain and suffering, He understands our needs and our suffering.

Session 13, *The Victorious King.* For God's people, the end of history is the beginning of a glorious eternity with Jesus as their Victorious King.

Things You Will Need to Teach These Sessions

Be sure you have in your classroom the following supplies and equipment for every session:

● Extra Bibles
● Pens or pencils
● Scratch paper
● Masking tape or a bulletin board with pins
● A writing surface and something to write with; for example, chalkboard and chalk, or overhead projector with transparencies and pens, or large sheets of butcher paper or newsprint with felt pens.

Individual session plans list the Student Worksheets and any special items needed for the particular session.

This coursebook consists of two parts: the **Leader's Guide** section, which gives you Teacher's Bible Studies and session plans for teaching the thirteen sessions of the course; and the **Student Worksheets,** which include reproducible worksheets and other resources for use with your group in class.

Leader's Guide

KEY VERSES

The **Key Verses** from Scripture focus on the central theme of the session. They are usually among the main verses to be studied in the session.

BIBLICAL BASIS

This heading identifies the Scripture passages to be studied during the session. Carefully read these verses before you look at **This Week's Teaching Plan.** Read them again from a different translation of the Bible and ask the Holy Spirit to guide you as you prepare.

FOCUS OF THE SESSION

The editors have selected one main session theme from several possible themes in the text. This is a brief statement of the theme.

AIMS OF THE SESSION

These aims describe what can be achieved during the session. If you do not feel comfortable with the aims, adapt them or rewrite them to fit the needs of your class. Remember that you are not teaching just to "get through the material" but to move your students toward Christian maturity as they are exposed to God's Word. The **Aims of the Session** will help you do this.

TEACHER'S BIBLE STUDY

Written in everyday language, this Bible study commentary presents background material for you. Study this section with your Bible open and watch for useful information and insights which will further equip you to lead the class session.

SESSION 1

The Road to Emmaus

KEY VERSE

"The secret things belong to the Lord our God, but the things revealed belong to us and to our children forever." Deuteronomy 29:29

"And beginning with Moses and all the Prophets, he explained to them what was said in all the Scriptures concerning himself." Luke 24:27

BIBLICAL BASIS

Mark 16:19,20; Luke 18:35-43; 19:1-10; 24:13-15,25-27,29-35; John 3:1-21; 8:31,32; 14:26; Acts 6:8-10; 8:34-38; 11:19-24; 15:30-35; 16:11-15,40; 17:1-4,11,12; 18:24-28; 1 Corinthians 2:9-14; 10:32—11:1; 15:3-5; Ephesians 1:9,17; Hebrews 4:12,13; Revelation 3:20

FOCUS OF THE SESSION

Jesus is the key that unlocks full understanding of all Scripture.

AIMS OF THIS SESSION

You and your students will have accomplished the purpose of this Bible study session if you can:

- DISCUSS Jesus' use of the Old Testament to teach that He is the Messiah;
- EXAMINE ways Christians best learn about and understand Scripture;
- IDENTIFY the fact that truly understanding Scripture begins with faith in Jesus Christ and EVALUATE your relationship with Him.

Teacher's Bible Study

Unlocking the Scriptures Today

This course is a study of Old Testament Scriptures that reveal God's historical and eternal plan for salvation through... Some have already been fulfilled; some are yet to be fulfilled.

Although looking for references to Jesus in the Old Testament is not a new way to study the Bible, it may be new to some of your students. Reassure them that it is a method that has the New Testament's stamp of approval (see Luke 24:27; 1 Cor. 10:1-4; 1 Pet. 3:18-22). It is a faith-building exercise that strengthens the Bible student's belief in the divine inspiration of God's Word and points again and again to God's plan of salvation through Jesus Christ. Jesus truly is the key that unlocks all Scripture.

A Long Walk Home

The story in Luke 24:13-35 has been described by scholars and critics as one of the immortal short stories of the world. Within a single page, the minds of two devout Jews are moved from utter confusion to a clear understanding of Christ's purpose as described in Scripture to total enthusiasm and immediate action. The Jews had recently witnessed a crucifixion—dirty work done at the hands of religious leaders who represented the belief system in which they placed their faith. The victim was a prophet whose deeds and words carried love and authority and compelled their confidence. A good man had died, horribly punished by men who claimed to be doing God a favor. The two travelers on the road to Emmaus were at a loss to understand what had happened. Either they had to believe in the utter wrongdoing of the authorities or in the righteousness of their act, in the complete innocence of the victim or in his guilt as a blasphemer. There was no middle ground, no comfortable explanation for the sentence. Their confusion was evident by the downcast expressions on their faces and the intensity of their discussion of what had just taken place in Jerusalem (see vv. 13-18).

Have you ever witnessed the examination of a pastor who was accused of unprofessional conduct. I had known him and his examiners for many years. Both the accused and the accusers were men whose credibility I had never doubted. But their testimonies were completely contradictory. I could not sort out the facts. I had no key, no clue, no one with inside information to relieve my conflict.

The evening following the formal questioning I tried to sleep but could not stop the questions that kept jabbing me awake. Someone I trusted was letting me down. That was many years ago, and to this day I do not know who was right and who was wrong. I know what the panel of church leaders decided, but that did not put the matter to rest. Time has healed the memory, but my trust in some friends has been lessened as a result. So it must have been with the travelers from Emmaus. They were hungry to resolve their conflict and reestablish their faith on trustworthy grounds. What they had based their trust on in the past seemed to be faltering.

Sense Out of Confusion

In the midst of their discussion, Cleopas and his companion were joined by Jesus, whose identity was divinely hidden from them until the time was right (see Luke 24:16,31). Jesus' simple questions concerning the travelers' discussion revealed the depth of their struggle with understanding what they had experienced. When Jesus asked, "What are you discussing together as you walk along?" (v. 17), they answered, "About Jesus of Nazareth ... The chief priests and our rulers handed him over to be sentenced to death, and they crucified him; but we had hoped that he was the one who was going to redeem Israel" (vv. 19-21). They were struggling to make sense out of what they had expected of Christ as Messiah and the reality of the events they had witnessed. With Jesus' help their minds were brought into a new understanding of all they held dear concerning the Scriptures and God's plan to provide a Messiah.

Have you ever witnessed the changes that take place when someone makes sense out of confusing feelings or experiences? I once counseled with a teenager who was perpetually in trouble with his parents, school authorities and the law. In three years of high school he had acquired little more than one semester's credits. He was the product of a divorced family, a Christian mother, a strained family economy and some badly chosen friends. A juvenile officer told me that this boy would end up either shooting or being shot by a police officer.

"I'm stupid!" he would bark, as we talked. "Let's test that out," I replied. "Your believing you're stupid doesn't make it so!" So we administered an intelligence test to get insight into the truth. The result? the boy's IQ was in the superior range, similar to that of college professors and physicians. I explained this to my client and he would not believe it—at first. But as the truth of the matter sank in, he realized this information explained his intense interest in reading. It also clarified other things about himself he could not explain while at the same time believing that he was stupid. Eventually, his self-image changed and became more positive. The reason for the change? Sense and hope had come out of confusion.

The Emmaus story demonstrates the ability of Jesus to bring sense out of confusion. The travelers had "hoped that he was the one who was going to redeem Israel" (Luke 24:21). Before Jesus enlightened the travelers' understanding, their dreams had seemed shattered. They admitted this to Jesus in regretful, bewildered tones. Emotionally, they had played for high stakes and were experiencing the pain of loss.

They had expected Jesus, as the Messiah, to bring a great political victory for Israel over her oppressors. Messiah, you see, was more than just a religious idea to devout Jews. The rabbis of Jesus' day (and many today) were teaching that the Messiah would come and overturn the existing political and military order. Jews were taught four characteristics of Messiah's coming: (1) He would come cataclysmically—that is, His coming would be dramatic and bring about great change; (2) Jerusalem would be the seat of His power; (3) Israel would be restored to full political and military dominance in the world; and (4) the essential character of Messiah's reign would be full justice with retribution for all Israel's enemies. The hopes of Jews who expected Jesus to fulfill this image of the Messiah were dashed in the Crucifixion.

Jesus responded to the disappointment of His companions by cutting through the misconceptions of rabbinic teaching and opening their eyes to the insight of the ages! "Beginning with Moses and all the Prophets, he explained to them what was said in all the Scriptures concerning himself" (v. 27). We do not know the particular points Jesus made. But the phrase "Moses and all the Prophets" has been taken by many Bible scholars to indicate that all of the Old Testament not only records the history of God's interaction with His people but also testifies concerning His Son. From Genesis to Malachi the Old Testament cannot be fully understood without using God's key: Jesus Christ.

Jesus brings order out of chaos. Cleopas and his friend did not at first know that it was Jesus who was teaching them, but they were greatly impressed by His words. In retrospect they observed, "Were not our hearts burning within us while he talked with us on the road and opened the Scriptures to us?" (v. 32).

After this time of enlightenment concerning the Scriptures, the story takes a new turn. Jesus acted as if He would go on, not obligating His companions to extend hospitality on His behalf. Obviously

11

(sidebar, middle column)

"The secret things belong to the Lord our God, but the things revealed belong to us and to our children forever." We are to study and understand the Scriptures; God...

which we can understand Jesus' substitutionary sacrifice. As God provided a ram as a substitute for Isaac, He also provided His only Son as a substitutionary payment...

THIS WEEK'S TEACHING PLAN

The step-by-step session plan presented here is based on a minimum of 45 minutes of class time, but with enough material for more than 60 minutes. Select and adapt the suggested activities to meet the specific needs of your class and the class time available.

APPROACH

Each session plan includes a learning activity designed to capture the interest of your class and introduce the session theme. Your **Approach** is successful if it whets your students' learning appetites in preparation for the **Bible Exploration**.

BIBLE EXPLORATION

The **Bible Exploration** is the heart of your class session because it involves each student directly in the study of God's Word. It is during this period that you will invite your students to explore and discover both what the Bible says and what it means for their lives today.

CONCLUSION AND DECISION

This important section is designed to help your students appropriate the truths of Scripture for themselves and assume responsibility for altering behavior in their own lives. Here they will deal with the question, "What does the Bible mean to me and how can I put it into practice in my own life?" Be sure to leave enough time for the **Conclusion and Decision** in each session.

Student Worksheets

These reproducible pages are designed to involve your students in searching the Scripture, thinking about it, interpreting it and applying it to their personal lives. Think of the **Student Worksheets** as a resource to make your job easier and more effective. The **Student Worksheets** are designed so you can simply pop them out of the book (they are perforated) and make the necessary number of copies on the copy machine. Prepare enough for your students and a few for visitors.

Something Extra

In the **Clip Art** section at the back of this manual you will find a number of pages you can use to enhance your study. Included in these pages is a time line showing the events covered in this study as well as Bible story clip art relating to the Bible content you will be exploring. Use this art to advertise your Bible study in your church's bulletin or newsletter, or as visual aids during class time.

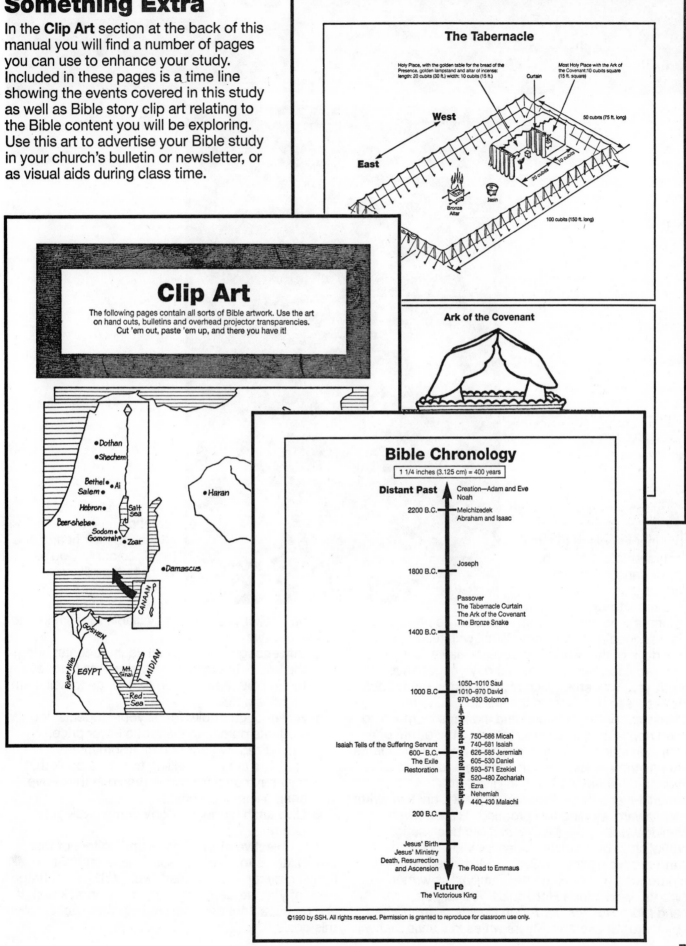

The Tabernacle

Holy Place, with the golden table for the bread of the Presence, golden lampstand and altar of incense: length: 20 cubits (30 ft.) width: 10 cubits (15 ft.)

Most Holy Place with the Ark of the Covenant:10 cubits square (15 ft. square)

Curtain

West

East

50 cubits (75 ft. long)

20 cubits

10 cubits

Bronze Altar

Basin

100 cubits (150 ft. long)

Clip Art

The following pages contain all sorts of Bible artwork. Use the art on hand outs, bulletins and overhead projector transparencies. Cut 'em out, paste 'em up, and there you have it!

Dothan
Shechem
Bethel • Ai
Salem
Hebron
Beer-sheba
Sodom • Gomorrah • Zoar
Salt Sea
Haran
Damascus
CANAAN
GOSHEN
River Nile
EGYPT
Mt. Sinai
MIDIAN
Red Sea

Ark of the Covenant

Bible Chronology

1 1/4 inches (3.125 cm) = 400 years

Distant Past — Creation—Adam and Eve
Noah

2200 B.C. — Melchizedek
Abraham and Isaac

1800 B.C. — Joseph

Passover
The Tabernacle Curtain
The Ark of the Covenant
The Bronze Snake

1400 B.C.

1050–1010 Saul
1000 B.C — 1010–970 David
970–930 Solomon

750–686 Micah
740–681 Isaiah
Isaiah Tells of the Suffering Servant — 626–585 Jeremiah
600– B.C. — 605–530 Daniel
The Exile — 593–571 Ezekiel
Restoration — 520–480 Zechariah
Ezra
Nehemiah
440–430 Malachi

Prophets Foretell Messiah

200 B.C.

Jesus' Birth
Jesus' Ministry
Death, Resurrection
and Ascension — The Road to Emmaus

Future
The Victorious King

A paperback book titled *Christ B.C.* is the companion piece to this coursebook. It gives both leader and student an opportunity between class sessions to explore the key themes presented in each session. The paperback is designed as a daily devotional with readings for six days of the week. The seventh day a reading is not provided because on that day you will meet with your students. Each chapter of the paperback takes a key theme from the session, such as "redemption" or "mercy," and explores its meaning and application in a personal way. The format of a daily devotional will also help you and your students build stronger Bible reading habits and personalize your time spent with God in His Word.

Bill Myers, the author, is a popular Christian writer and award winning film producer. His achievements include writing the *McGee and Me* book series (published by Tyndale House) as well as cocreating and producing the *McGee and Me* video series (produced by Focus on the Family). His written works also include *Hot Topics, Tough Questions* and *More Hot Topics, Tough Questions* (published by Victor Books). Bill Myers writes in a style that will grab your students' attention as well as challenge their hearts and minds to apply God's Word to their lives.

Your students will be more likely to obtain and use the book if you make it available to them in one of these ways:

● Buy enough books for all your students; bring the books to class and let students purchase them. (You may be able to arrange to sell them on consignment.)
● Buy enough books for all your students; let students purchase them at a lower price, subsidized by your church. (Sometimes students are more willing to read a book that they have paid for rather than one they have been given at no cost.)
● Give each student a copy of the book at no charge.

The objective of the writers and editors of this curriculum is to help the teacher and student "in all things grow up into...Christ" (Eph. 4:15). Encourage each of your students to use the paperback text. It is a practical tool designed to help them accomplish this goal.

Presenting Christ to High School Students

How do you present Christ to high school students? Here are some suggestions.

1. Pray. Ask God to prepare each young person to receive the message of salvation and to prepare you to present it.

2. Lay the foundation. High school students are evaluating you and the Lord you serve by everything you do and say. They are looking for people who show a living, growing relationship with God. They are looking for people in whose lives knowing God makes a noticeable difference. And they are looking for people who love them and listen to them as God loves them and listens to them.

Learn to listen with your full attention. Learn to share openly both the joys and the struggles you encounter as a Christian. Be honest about your own questions and about your personal concern for students. Learn to accept teenagers as they are. Christ died for them while they were yet sinners. You are called to love them as they are.

3. Be aware of opportunities. Students *might* come forward after a lesson that deals with salvation, or ask for an appointment to talk after class. However, it is more likely that they will wait for *you* to suggest getting together. Try inviting a student out for a soft drink; you will then have some time alone together in which you can share what Jesus means to you.

4. Don't buttonhole students. Don't lecture them or force the issue. Here are some tips to keep in mind:

a. Put the student at ease. Be perceptive of his or her feelings. Remember that the student is probably nervous. Be relaxed, natural and casual in your conversation; don't be critical or judgmental.

b. Get the student to talk while you listen carefully. Young people will sometimes throw out superficial or shocking statements just to get your reaction. Don't begin lecturing or problem solving. Instead encourage the person to keep talking.

c. Be gently direct. Do not overpower the student with demands from the gospel. But make no apologies either. God does not need to be defended and neither does His truth. Remember that students may have trouble bringing up spiritual matters. If you sense this, a simple question like, "How are you and God getting along?" can unlock a life-changing conversation.

d. Using a booklet that outlines the plan of salvation can be helpful. Move through the points slowly enough to allow time for the student to think and comprehend. But do not drag out the presentation unnecessarily.

e. Make sure the student understands how to accept Christ. If you feel that he or she understands, ask if he or she would like to accept Christ now. If the answer is affirmative, ask the student to pray with you. Explain that praying is simply talking to God. We can be natural with Him and simply tell Him our needs and our thoughts. In this case the student may tell God of his or her need for Christ and desire to have Him as Lord and Savior.

Suggest that the new Christian begin growing in the faith. You may wish to suggest some Scripture in an easy-to-read translation of the Bible or a study manual suited to the age and maturity level of the student. (You may want to visit your local Christian supplier to see what is available.)

If the student is not ready to make a decision to accept Christ, suggest some passages of Scripture to read, such as John 14–16; Romans 3–8; or the brief Gospel of Mark. Make sure the student has a Bible or New Testament in an easy-to-read translation. (If he or she does not, you might want to lend or give an appropriate copy.) Remember to pray for the student as he or she gives further consideration to the gospel message.

5. Remember: Your responsibility is simply to present the gospel and to be able to explain the hope that is within you. It is the Holy Spirit who makes the heart ready for a relationship with God.

The Road to Emmaus

KEY VERSE

"The secret things belong to the Lord our God, but the things revealed belong to us and to our children forever." Deuteronomy 29:29

"And beginning with Moses and all the Prophets, he explained to them what was said in all the Scriptures concerning himself." Luke 24:27

BIBLICAL BASIS

Mark 16:19,20; Luke 18:35-43; 19:1-10; 24:13-15,25-27,29-35; John 3:1-21; 8:31,32; 14:26; Acts 6:8-10; 8:34-38; 11:19-24; 15:30-35; 16:11-15,40; 17:1-4,11,12; 18:24-28; 1 Corinthians 2:9-14; 10:32—11:1; 15:3-5; Ephesians 1:9,17; Hebrews 4:12,13; Revelation 3:20

FOCUS OF THE SESSION

Jesus is the key that unlocks full understanding of all Scripture.

AIMS OF THIS SESSION

You and your students will have accomplished the purpose of this Bible study session if you can:
- DISCUSS Jesus' use of the Old Testament to teach that He is the Messiah;
- EXAMINE ways Christians best learn about and understand Scripture;
- IDENTIFY the fact that truly understanding Scripture begins with faith in Jesus Christ and EVALUATE your relationship with Him.

Teacher's Bible Study

Unlocking the Scriptures Today

This course is a study of Old Testament Scriptures that reveal God's historical and eternal plan for salvation through His Son, Jesus. A study of types, symbols and prophecies of Christ in the Old Testament can unlock the Scriptures for us. Jesus used the Old Testament to explain "what was said in all the Scriptures concerning himself" to the two travelers He met on the road to Emmaus following His resurrection (Luke 24:27). This is the theme of today's study. Each of the succeeding sessions in this course will explore a specific Old Testament prophecy, symbol or event that points to Christ. But before we begin this study, a good understanding of what types and symbols are and how they function is necessary.

Types and Symbols

Augustine said, "The New is in the Old contained; the Old is by the New explained." Jesus is the key to the riddle of the Old Testament; the translator for the code. Many Old Testament events, although impressive in their own right, have spectacular meaning and bring us light when we see them as types of Christ and His work. Deuteronomy 29:29 tells us that,

"The secret things belong to the Lord our God, but the things revealed belong to us and to our children forever." We are to study and understand the Scriptures; God has revealed His plan for a Savior and has given this knowledge to us as a gift.

The types of Christ in the Old Testament have several characteristics. A type is a person, thing or experience that is symbolic of the nature of Christ and His Work. It represents Him accurately with respect to some important character trait or deed. It will not represent every aspect of His character or purpose. When the Israelites painted blood on their doorposts so the angel of death would not enter their households, it was symbolic of the fact that salvation comes only by the shedding of blood (see Exod. 12:13; Lev. 8:14,15; Heb. 9:22).

A type is usually symbolic of God's initiative to reconcile man to Himself. God always makes the first move. God commanded Abraham to sacrifice his son Isaac—an event that is a test of Abraham's obedience until we see that it was a picture of the sacrifice of Christ (see Gen. 22:2,7-14; Heb. 10:1,5-10). Man would never initiate such a thing, but God, in His divine wisdom, created a foundation upon

which we can understand Jesus' substitutionary sacrifice. As God provided a ram as a substitute for Isaac, He also provided His only Son as a substitutionary payment for our sins.

A type may be symbolic of revelation yet to be realized. As such, the typical characters became creatures of faith and not just performers of ritual. Hebrews 11 is a great litany of heroes of faith, who having not seen, believed and had their faith regarded by God as righteousness.

Prophecies

One of the strongest arguments for the validity of the Word of God is the numerous incidents of fulfilled prophecies concerning the birth, death, resurrection and ascension of Christ. The Old Testament is replete with prophecies concerning Christ, foretold not only by the prophets, but by King David as well (see Ps. 22). A prophecy could foretell (predict) a future event, or counsel or warn concerning a present situation. In both cases the Old Testament prophets were speaking for God, declaring His divine will and purpose. The prophecies concerning Jesus recorded in the Old Testament are all foretelling in nature.

Some have already been fulfilled; some are yet to be fulfilled.

Although looking for references to Jesus in the Old Testament is not a new way to study the Bible, it may be new to some of your students. Reassure them that it is a method that has the New Testament's stamp of approval (see Luke 24:27; 1 Cor. 10:1-4; 1 Pet. 3:18-22). It is a faith-building exercise that strengthens the Bible student's belief in the divine inspiration of God's Word and points again and again to God's plan of salvation through Jesus Christ. Jesus truly is the key that unlocks all Scripture.

A Long Walk Home

The story in Luke 24:13-35 has been described by scholars and critics as one of the immortal short stories of the world. Within a single page, the minds of two devout Jews are moved from utter confusion to a clear understanding of Christ's purpose as described in Scripture to total enthusiasm and immediate action. The Jews had recently witnessed a crucifixion—dirty work done at the hands of religious leaders who represented the belief system in which they placed their faith. The victim was a prophet whose deeds and words carried love and authority and compelled their confidence. A good man had died, horribly punished by men who claimed to be doing God a favor. The two travelers on the road to Emmaus were at a loss to understand what had happened. Either they had to believe in the utter wrongdoing of the authorities or in the righteousness of their act, in the complete innocence of the victim or in his guilt as a blasphemer. There was no middle ground, no comfortable explanation for the sentence. Their confusion was evident by the downcast expressions on their faces and the intensity of their discussion of what had just taken place in Jerusalem (see vv. 13-18).

Have you ever been in a place of such mental conflict? I witnessed the examination of a pastor who was accused of unprofessional conduct. I had known him and his examiners for many years. Both the accused and the accusers were men whose credibility I had never doubted. But their testimonies were completely contradictory. I could not sort out the facts. I had no key, no clue, no one with inside information to relieve my conflict.

The evening following the formal questioning I tried to sleep but could not stop the questions that kept jabbing me awake. Someone I trusted was letting me down. That was many years ago, and to this day I do not know who was right and who was wrong. I know what the panel of church leaders decided, but that did not put the matter to rest. Time has healed the memory, but my trust in some friends has been lessened as a result. So it must have been with the travelers from Emmaus. They were hungry to resolve their conflict and reestablish their faith on trustworthy grounds. What they had based their trust on in the past seemed to be faltering.

Sense Out of Confusion

In the midst of their discussion, Cleopas and his companion were joined by Jesus, whose identity was divinely hidden from them until the time was right (see Luke 24:16,31). Jesus' simple questions concerning the travelers' discussion revealed the depth of their struggle with understanding what they had experienced. When Jesus asked, "What are you discussing together as you walk along?" (v. 17), they answered, "About Jesus of Nazareth . . . The chief priests and our rulers handed him over to be sentenced to death, and they crucified him; but we had hoped that he was the one who was going to redeem Israel" (vv. 19-21). They were struggling to make sense out of what they had expected of Christ as Messiah and the reality of the events they had witnessed. With Jesus' help their minds were brought into a new understanding of all they held dear concerning the Scriptures and God's plan to provide a Messiah.

Have you ever witnessed the changes that take place when someone makes sense out of confusing feelings or experiences? I once counseled with a teenager who was perpetually in trouble with his parents, school authorities and the law. In three years of high school he had acquired little more than one semester's credits. He was the product of a divorced family, a Christian mother, a strained family economy and some badly chosen friends. A juvenile officer told me that this boy would end up either shooting or being shot by a police officer.

"I'm stupid!" he would bark, as we talked. "Let's test that out," I replied. "Your believing you're stupid doesn't make it so!" So we administered an intelligence test to get insight into the truth. The result? the boy's IQ was in the superior range, similar to that of college professors and physicians. I explained this to my client and he would not believe it—at first. But as the truth of the matter sank in, he realized this information explained his intense interest in reading. It also clarified other things about himself he could not explain while at the same time believing that he was stupid. Eventually, his self-image changed and became more positive. The reason for the change? Sense and hope had come out of confusion.

The Emmaus story demonstrates the ability of Jesus to bring sense out of confusion. The travelers had "hoped that he was the one who was going to redeem Israel" (Luke 24:21). Before Jesus enlightened the travelers' understanding, their dreams had seemed shattered. They admitted this to Jesus in regretful, bewildered tones. Emotionally, they had played for high stakes and were experiencing the pain of loss.

They had expected Jesus, as the Messiah, to bring a great political victory for Israel over her oppressors. Messiah, you see, was more than just a religious idea to devout Jews. The rabbis of Jesus' day (and many today) were teaching that the Messiah would come and overturn the existing political and military order. Jews were taught four characteristics of Messiah's coming: (1) He would come cataclysmically—that is, His coming would be dramatic and bring about great change; (2) Jerusalem would be the seat of His power; (3) Israel would be restored to full political and military dominance in the world; and (4) the essential character of Messiah's reign would be full justice with retribution for all Israel's enemies. The hopes of Jews who expected Jesus to fulfill this image of the Messiah were dashed in the Crucifixion.

Jesus responded to the disappointment of His companions by cutting through the misconceptions of rabbinic teaching and opening their eyes to the insight of the ages! "Beginning with Moses and all the Prophets, he explained to them what was said in all the Scriptures concerning himself" (v. 27). We do not know the particular points Jesus made. But the phrase "Moses and all the Prophets" has been taken by many Bible scholars to indicate that *all* of the Old Testament not only records the history of God's interaction with His people but also testifies concerning His Son. From Genesis to Malachi the Old Testament cannot be fully understood without using God's key: Jesus Christ.

Jesus brings order out of chaos. Cleopas and his friend did not at first know that it was Jesus who was teaching them, but they were greatly impressed by His words. In retrospect they observed, "Were not our hearts burning within us while he talked with us on the road and opened the Scriptures to us?" (v. 32).

After this time of enlightenment concerning the Scriptures, the story takes a new turn. Jesus acted as if He would go on, not obligating his companions to extend hospitality on His behalf. Obviously they had spent a long time discussing the Scriptures, and the time was ripe for His companions to extend themselves to Jesus personally, not just academically. Jesus' attitude was truly characteristic of the Holy Spirit—never coercive, never pounding His way into lives. Instead Jesus makes Himself available. He creates the opportunity, engineers the circumstances, prepares minds and hearts but does not force a response. This attitude is illustrated by His words in Revelation 3:20: "Here I am! I stand at the door and knock. If anyone hears my voice and opens the door, I will come in and eat with him, and he with me." Jesus creates the opportunity, but we must open the door.

Sudden Insight

The Emmaus travelers did not know Jesus' identity but felt in their hearts the authority of His words. As a result they were hungry to hear more and they urged Him to stay the night (Luke 24:29). They listened to the voice and opened the door. In doing so they were confronted with Christ, the true Messiah.

This confrontation took place through the breaking of bread. Once Jesus had entered the house and the bread had been brought to the table, He assumed the role of master or father of the household. Jesus did this by performing the tasks of blessing and breaking the bread for His hosts. Something clicked in Cleopas and his companion's minds when they saw Jesus in this role. "Their eyes were opened and they recognized him" (v. 31). Their enlightenment was complete and Jesus' purpose for that situation was fulfilled. At this point Jesus "disappeared from their sight" (v. 31).

It was an ordinary meal, in an ordinary home, with common bread being divided. This situation reminds us that He is Christ in very common, ordinary situations to very common, ordinary folks. Most of us, I fear, prefer persuasion in spectacular settings, with great miracles and stereophonic sound announcing the Christ. No quiet, noncoercive voices for us. Deafening noise, rhythmic pounding and a star-studded performance by folk heroes making Him known is our style. No wonder we often miss Him!

The Emmaus travelers didn't miss Him. Their experience stirred an excitement in them that, despite the late hour, they had to share with the disciples back in Jerusalem. Jesus had personally unlocked all the Scriptures and had shown how they all pointed to Him. Cleopas and his companion had vaulted from utter disappointment to utter elation. No wonder

they hurried back to Jerusalem to share their excitement with the disciples and those gathered with them (see v. 33).

The understanding of Cleopas and his companion contained that wonderful "Aha!" that comes when something begins to make sense. Educational psychologists call this kind of understanding insight learning. It is that sudden burst of comprehension that comes when you finally have figured out the answer to a difficult math problem or the moral to a complex story. The solution is obvious when it appears. As such it is almost immune to forgetting. Cleopas and his friend, in their old age, would have no trouble recalling their encounter on the Emmaus road. It was sudden, dramatic and made sense of their confusion. Furthermore, it was life-changing, and such an event is never forgotten.

Emmaus and Principles of Learning

We, like the Emmaus travelers, will benefit from searching the Word of God "beginning with Moses and all the Prophets" to discover "what was said in all the Scriptures concerning himself" (v. 27). The result of our study might be like that of the Emmaus travelers. We may see God's plan of salvation woven throughout Scripture, have our faith strengthened and experience an excitement to share what Christ has done with others.

Before you begin unfolding the story of Jesus told throughout the Scriptures, consider the following principles of Bible learning and understanding, some of which were displayed in the experience of Cleopas and his companion. Use these principles to prepare yourself, as a teacher and as a student, to make the most of your opportunities. Then use these principles to foster growth in your students' lives.

1. Jesus did not leave His followers alone in their struggle for deeper understanding. Although He is no longer physically present to teach us as He did Cleopas and his companion, Christians do have the Holy Spirit present in their lives to teach them all things (see John 14:26; 16:13; 1 Cor. 2:9,10). As Jesus unlocked the Scriptures to Cleopas and His friend, the Holy Spirit continues to illuminate the Word of God to us today. The Holy Spirit enables us to make right decisions and to realize growth in our Christian experience.

The travelers on the Emmaus road were taught by the greatest Teacher the world has ever known. The interpretation of the Old Testament Scriptures that they received from Jesus was a correct one. When Jesus ascended into heaven, He did not leave the Church without teachers

but placed gifted teachers in the Church (see Eph. 4:7,11-14). As we consistently come under their teaching, we receive a steady and healthy diet of God's Word that results in spiritual maturity. This maturity protects us from "every wind of teaching" (v. 14). It is then that we are assured of receiving sound doctrine (see Titus 1:9; 2:1).

2. Significant and helpful learning is most often tutored learning. This is learning in a one-to-one relationship, close up, directly given. It is why Barnabas took the recently converted Paul under his wing (see Acts 9:27,28). In turn Paul served as mentor to Timothy (see 1 Tim. 1:1,2,18). This is why doctors complete internships and residencies. This is the reason prospective teachers are assigned to student-teaching roles, or why apprentices learn their trades from master craftsmen. Was there tutorial teaching in the Emmaus experience? Of course. It was short, but divine energy was present and the result was lasting. In the same way, you and your students can benefit from a tutorial relationship. Seek out people whose knowledge of the Scriptures and personal maturity you respect. Ask those persons to interact with you and work through questions you have as you study the Bible. Share truths being discovered and discuss applications of those truths. This personal discipling will enrich your life and will spur you on to growth beyond that which can be accomplished in the classroom.

3. Learning achieved in a social situation stays with us longer. Remember that Jesus not only taught but also lived with His disciples (see Luke 8:1-3). This involvement in His disciples' lives created an atmosphere conducive to learning. We learn better in the presence of others. Truth can not only be taught, it can also be modeled in the lives of mature Christians (see 1 Cor. 11:1). Others keep an eye on us and we feel accountable to each other.

4. Sharing reinforces our beliefs. I have often said that I learned more psychology in my first year of college teaching than I did in all the years of my graduate and undergraduate study. As a teacher, have you ever felt that you were learning more from the lessons you taught than the students? This is a common occurence.

The scriptural idea that what we believe with our hearts we need to confess with our lips is a great and valid learning principle (see Rom. 10:9,10). Once we have shared our learning we imply that we are ready to defend what we have said. Look again at the Emmaus travelers. Once the great insight had occurred, they rushed back to Jerusalem to share what they had learned (see Luke 24:33-35). They were no longer passive about their knowledge, for they had found the answer to their lives' greatest question, and were not going to sit and wonder. Their doubts were overcome and they went public with their information. Your students can do the same with what you share in the classroom. Convey to them the excitement you feel when sharing God's truth with others and ask them to share their experiences of telling others about Christ.

Also emphasize that by sharing what they have learned about Jesus they will affect change in the lives of others (see John 4:4-39). Our learning of faith is a personal experience of insight. But faith moves from the one to the many. The travelers to Emmaus become examples for us of those who, upon finding faith, allow it to regenerate their lives and others'. So may it be with us.

5. Meaningful learning often comes at the end of times of pondering, after many trial answers to problems, after much wondering and committed study. Then the great "Aha!" happens. In the case of our Emmaus folks, insight was preceded by lengthy training in the Scriptures. It is a very safe bet that when Jesus opened the Scriptures to them, they knew what He was referring to. These companions had probably been through years of instruction. Similarly a Bible passage that has been read often will sometimes "open up" revealing deeper truth or understanding of divine principles. The work of the Holy Spirit, our reading and applying knowledge from other points of Scripture and our pondering the meaning of the passage all contribute to this common experience.

6. Don't hold back on presenting the truth; it does a remarkable job of defending itself from its opponents without our arguments. God's truth has great capacity to survive manipulations and it is highly reinforcing. Jesus said, "If you hold to my teaching, you are really my disciples. Then you will know the truth, and the truth will set you free (John 8:31,32). The more we immerse ourselves in the Word, the more clearly truth will reveal itself to us. Note how Jesus based His teaching to the Emmaus travelers on Scripture (see Luke 24:27). So bare the truth; unsheathe the Word; let God's truth do its own arguing in the hearts of men (see Heb. 4:12).

7. In the experience of faith it is always God who takes the initiative. Our coming to faith is not some original adventure or great human mental invention. It is our response to a thrust already made (see Luke 19:10). God has been at work before we ever dreamed He existed (see 1 Pet. 1:2). Faith is our expression of trust in a loving Father who is tenderly seeking His children. So it was at Emmaus. It was not the travelers who overtook Jesus while looking for an answer to their quandry. It was the Savior coming to those whose minds were prepared to believe His Word (see Luke 24:13-15).

In contrast, all other religions are man's attempts to find God. As such, they become the extension of man's intellectual futility. Human thought systems are always limited to man's imagination and do not flourish with the glory of God-given revelation. When Jesus revealed Himself to Cleopas and his partner, their hearts warmed strangely within them—a common experience of those who have come to salvation.

This Week's Teaching Plan

APPROACH TO THE WORD

APPROACH (5-10 minutes)

Materials needed: Large index cards.

Preparation: Before class letter the following words on index cards—one word on each card (the definitions are for your use as indicated in the game.)

1. *Foreshadow*—To represent or indicate beforehand.
2. *Prefigure*—To show, suggest or announce by an image or likeness.
3. *Type*—A person, thing or event believed to foreshadow another.
4. *Prophecy*—The inspired announcement of God's will or purpose.
5. *Symbol*—Something that associates one thing with another.

Move students into five groups. Give each group an index card you have prepared. Instruct each group to read the word they were given. Then instruct each group to write on the index card a definition they have made up for their word.

When groups have finished writing, have a representative from one group read his or her group's word and definition. The members of the class (minus the members of the group that is sharing) vote true or false for the accuracy of the definition. Then read the correct definition. Repeat this process until each group has shared. Move to the Exploration by saying, **Each of these terms can be used to describe how an Old Testament Scripture foretells or illustrates a New Testament event from Jesus' life, death and future reign at the end of history. Today's study will reveal how Jesus, after His death, explained these Old Testament illustrations to two of His followers.**

ALTERNATE APPROACH (5-8 minutes)

Materials needed: Large sheet of paper taped to the wall, felt pens.

Preparation: Before class, letter the heading "Symbols Associated with Jesus" at the top of the sheet of paper.

As students arrive, ask them to write about or draw on the paper symbols or events that remind them of Jesus. Their responses may include: cross, lamb, shepherd, crown, dove, rock, Bible, miracles of healing, empty tomb, second coming, fish. Refer to students' work and say something like, **Many of these New Testament symbols and events have Old Testament counterparts. These Old Testament counterparts were engineered by God to point people to Jesus Christ who was to come. For example, the lamb sacrificed at the Passover during Moses' day illustrates for us the sacrifice of Christ for our sins. Some of these Old Testament illustrations are called "types"; others are called "symbols" or "prophecies."** Add that today's study will reveal how Jesus, after His death, explained these Old Testament illustrations to two of His followers.

EXPLORATION (30-40 minutes)

Materials needed: Session 1 Student Worksheet for each student.

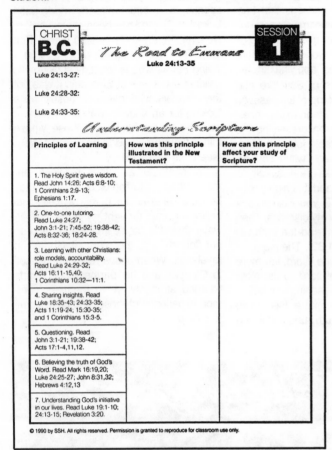

Step 1 (15-20 minutes): Distribute Student Worksheets and direct students to open their Bibles to Luke 24. Ask volunteers to share in reading aloud the verses listed on their worksheets. As each group of verses is read, lead a discussion of the verses using the following outline and information from the Teacher's Bible Study. Encourage students to take notes on their worksheets as the discussion progresses.

Luke 24:13-27

- **Why were the two travelers feeling downcast?** (See vv. 17-24.)
- Share the rabbinic teaching about the Messiah that Cleopas and his companion may have believed concerning Jesus (see the Teacher's Bible Study section titled "Sense Out of Confusion" for more information). Point out that this teaching was not in line with what Old Testament teaches about the Messiah.
- **What did Jesus criticize the travelers for not doing?** (See v. 25.) **Why do you think they should have continued to believe that Jesus was the Messiah?** (They should have examined what the Scriptures said about Jesus and seen that He is the promised Messiah.)
- **What did Jesus do to encourage their faith and prove that He was the Messiah promised in the Old Testament?** (See v. 27.) Mention that the words "Moses and all the Prophets" imply the whole Old Testament.

Luke 24:28-32

- Have a student read aloud Revelation 3:20. Ask, **How does this verse describe the way Jesus related to His two com-**

panions in Luke 24:28,29? (Jesus provided an opportunity for them to respond to Him; He did not coerce them into accepting Him, but waited for their invitation.)

- **How did the travelers respond when Jesus acted as if He was going to travel further?** (See v. 29.)
- **When they realized who Jesus was, what did they say to each other about their experience?** (See v. 32.)
- **What do you think the words "our hearts burning within us" (v. 32) mean?** Share Lloyd Ahlem's comments from the Teacher's Bible Study concerning the "Aha!" experience (see the section titled "Sudden Insight").

Luke 24:33-35

- **Why do you think Cleopas and his companion went at once to Jerusalem?**
- **What effect do you think the telling of their experience had on their faith? On the faith of the Eleven? Why do you think it is important for Christians to tell others about what Jesus has done?**

Move to Step 2 by stating, **Let's focus on how the learning experience of Cleopas and his companion can help us in understanding God's Word and strengthen our faith in Jesus Christ.**

Step 2 (10-12 minutes): Move the class into groups of three to four students each. (Note: When moving students into groups, use a variety of techniques such as color coding their worksheets so that each color represents a group or grouping them by birthdays or maybe shoe sizes.)

Introduce this activity by saying, **There are several basic principles that describe how Christians best learn about and understand Scripture. Many of these principles are illustrated in the story of Jesus and the Emmaus travelers and can enhance our own study of Scripture.** Assign each group at least one principle listed on the chart in the "Understanding Scripture" section of the Student Worksheet. Direct each group to look up the verses listed for its principle then answer the questions in the other two columns of the chart. Allow 5-8 minutes for students to work.

Step 3 (5-8 minutes): Ask a representative from each group to share his or her group's findings. Add any additional information from the Teacher's Bible Study to clarify or complete students' responses. As needed to enhance students' understanding of the material ask the following questions: "How would having the wisdom of the Holy Spirit make your study of Scripture more meaningful?" "What kind of person might you choose to tutor you as you study the Bible?" "How can other Christians help you obey God's Word and mature in your faith?" "Why do you think sharing what you have learned with others strengthens your own understanding of Scripture?" "How can asking questions and searching the Scriptures yourself for answers protect you from false teaching?" "How might knowing that God's Word can defend itself affect your willingness to share your faith with non-Christians?" "How does knowing that Jesus takes the initiative in building a relationship with you make you feel toward Him and the Bible?"

Move to the Conclusion by saying, **The understanding of God's Word begins with faith in Jesus Christ as Savior and Lord. When we put our faith in Christ, we have access to the Holy Spirit's help and wisdom to understand God's Word and how God wants us to live. Without Christ, you will never really know God's plans for your life. Let's examine our personal relationships with Christ.**

CONCLUSION (8-10 minutes)

Materials needed: Index cards.

Say, **When we put our faith in Christ as our Lord and Savior, we establish a personal, intimate relationship with Him.** Then list on the board or overhead student's responses to this question: "What are the benefits of having a personal relationship with Jesus Christ?" Responses should include: going to heaven, having my sins forgiven, having someone who knows me and always loves me, never being alone, having help in making decisions and choices. Distribute index cards and direct each student to write on his or her card a one sentence description of his or her relationship with Jesus Christ. Emphasize that you will not collect their cards, and encourage them to be as honest as possible. Then say, **Write one sentence describing how studying God's Word can help build your relationship with Christ.** Close by saying, **If you are interested in knowing more about establishing a personal relationship with Jesus Christ or strengthening your relationship with Him, I will be glad to talk to you after class.** Pray, thanking God that He cares about each person and that He wants each person to know Him personally. Be available after class to talk with students. (For help in explaining the gospel to your students refer to the article, "Presenting Christ to High School Students," on p. 9.)

Encourage students to read chapter 1 of the student paperback *Christ B.C.* The chapter contains a devotional reading for each of the six days following this Bible study session. Each reading is based on the theme "understanding."

NOTES:

God Covers Adam and Eve's Nakedness

KEY VERSE

"Blessed is he whose transgressions are forgiven, whose sins are covered." Psalm 32:1

"The law requires that nearly everything be cleansed with blood, and without the shedding of blood there is no forgiveness." Hebrews 9:22

BIBLICAL BASIS

Genesis 2:16,17,25; 3:1-21; Matthew 4:1-3; 26:27,28; John 8:44; Romans 3:23; 5:8; 2 Corinthians 4:4; 11:14; 2 Timothy 2:26; Hebrews 9:22; 1 Peter 5:8; 1 John 1:9; 3:8

FOCUS OF THE SESSION

Adam and Eve's attempt to cover their nakedness was insufficient; only the animal skins provided by God were adequate. In the same way, our attempts to cover our own sinfulness are insufficient, God provides the covering for sin through the shed blood of His Son, Jesus Christ.

AIMS OF THIS SESSION

You and your students will have accomplished the purpose of this Bible study session if you can:

- EXPLORE Adam and Eve's sin and their inadequate attempt to cover it.
- EXAMINE how the covering God provided Adam and Eve foreshadowed the covering of Christians' sins by the shed blood of Jesus Christ;
- IDENTIFY ways you try to cover your own sins and why only God's covering is adequate.

Teacher's Bible Study

This session examines a familiar Bible event—the Fall. Pay special attention to the element of the story that foreshadows Christ: The animal skins God provided to cover Adam and Eve's nakedness.

Back to the Beginning

Upon completion of creation it was as if God had written a beautiful symphony; trees, animals, resources, scenic wonders were all waiting in harmony to be explored and were placed under the stewardship of man. God said to Adam and Eve, "Be fruitful and increase in number; fill the earth and subdue it. Rule over the fish of the sea and the birds of the air and over every living creature that moves on the ground" (Gen. 1:28). All that God required of Adam and Eve was obedience to one simple requirement: "You are free to eat from any tree in the garden; but you must not eat from the tree of the knowledge of good and evil, for when you eat of it you will surely die" (2:16,17). God's generosity to Adam and Eve and the freedom He allowed them were beyond compare. Their innocence was complete; there was no blemish of sin in their lives. Their innocence is symbolized by the fact that in their nakedness "they felt no shame" (v.

25). God made them like Himself—independent in will, capable of loving relationships and in perfect harmony with all of creation.

But having been made free, Adam and Eve were also given the opportunity to obey or disobey God. They could experience the fulfillment of divine design, or they could choose to play the symphony their own way, concentrating on their own selfish interests and ignoring the wishes of God. God made them free to rebel, and this they chose to do.

Satan's Methods

In Genesis 3:1 we discover several lessons about Satan's character and methods. Satan, or the serpent (see Gen. 3:1; Rev. 12:9), is described as very crafty—more so than any other wild creature (see Gen. 3:1). This fact is a good warning to us to remember our limited awareness and gullibility in spiritual matters.

Our first clue revealing how Satan works comes with his twisting and questioning of God's command. Satan asked, "Did God really say, 'You must not eat from any tree in the garden'?" (v. 1). That question was enough to catch Eve's attention.

Satan subtly twisted a truth that Eve knew came from God (see 2:16,17) and placed a big question mark after it. It was enough to plant a seed of doubt in Eve's mind. Then Satan presented Eve with a reasonable-sounding half-truth. "'You will not surely die,' the serpent said to the woman" (3:4). Cunningly, the serpent blended the lie that Eve would not die with a twisted version of God's Word that really says, "For God knows that when you eat of it your eyes will be opened, and you will be like God, knowing good and evil" (v. 5). Satan always appeals to human reason and pride and makes his suggestions seem plausible, even if they conflict with God's Word. After giving ear to Satan's words, Eve, looking at the tree in a new light, "saw that the fruit of the tree was good for food and pleasing to the eye, and also desirable for gaining wisdom" (v. 6). She was sold. She yielded to Satan's reasoning and "took some and ate it" (v. 6).

Who wouldn't want to learn and understand? Who isn't mystified by the hidden, tantalized by the unseen? On the basis of Satan's half-truth, Eve allowed herself to ponder the possibilities. The tree was, after all, pleasant to the eye, would make one wise and was good for food. The most basic needs and wants of mankind were dangled before her, packaged in a way that told her she could meet these needs and wants in her own power.

We also find that Eve did not sin alone. "She also gave some to her husband, who was with her, and he ate it" (v. 6). Adam had heard God's command and he was present during Satan's dialogue with Eve. The temptation and opportunity to sin was fully shared.

We may feel sympathy for Adam and Eve when we recognize our humanness in them. We may even desire to justify what they did. Shared disobedience makes sin feel safer, much more acceptable. Your students are struggling with sin. Some of the black and white dos and don'ts of their childhood are beginning to grey. Many students will base their judgments solely on the approval of their peers. Some will turn to God's Word and try to apply its teachings on obedience to their daily experience. Others will try to straddle the fence between God's Word and the world. Now is an important time for them to know what God's Word says about sin so they can walk in obedience rather than waver and drift on the world's values.

Sin is almost always shared, and its effects ripple through relationships. But sin is a faulty element in relationships. It does not build; it destroys. The results are aloneness and isolation.

Loss of Innocence

Adam and Eve lived physically to experience the eye-opening that Satan had promised. But they died spiritually, and eventually physically, as God had promised. Innocence was lost. For the first time in their experience they perceived evil. It is also likely that for the first time they perceived the character of Satan as well. God had made everything good and Adam and Eve had been shielded from the only evil that existed by the command not to eat (see 2:16,17). God wanted to continue to shield them, but Adam and Eve bolted from behind His protection and faced evil on their own. Immediately their disobedience ushered in shame and they became aware of their need for covering. "Then the eyes of both of them were opened, and they realized they were naked; so they sewed fig leaves together and made coverings for themselves" (3:7).

Genesis 3:7 strikes me as one of the most ludicrous, ineffectual and stupid efforts of mankind. Adam and Eve had broken a perfect relationship with a perfect God. They had exposed themselves to Satan whose wisdom and power is totally devoted to evil. And then Adam and Eve

tried to cover themselves and their shame with fig leaves. Their efforts were hopelessly inadequate. Imagine yourself getting caught, stark naked, while stealing the choicest fruit from the finest garden in your city. Your nakedness would become upmost in your mind; you would probably run for the nearest fig tree and try to cover yourself, too. But how can the guilty fend off the indignation of an insulted God with only fig leaves as covering?

One way people try to avoid confronting their sinfulness and need for repentence is rationalization. The great rationalization for man's sin is that he is just acting the way "nature" made him, and therefore is not to be blamed. Sinful actions are dubbed as "impulses that evolved over time." They are even given the positive tone that sometimes they serve as healthy self-protective devices. When man acts out these impulses he is merely doing what nature intended, or so goes the argument. You will see this tendency in your student's noncommittal attitudes toward their own and their friends' sins. For example drinking alcohol, which is prohibited by law for minors, is not often objected to by teenagers—unless perhaps a person is planning on driving. Whether or not they drink responsibly, the fact remains that it is against the law and God's Word commands us to obey those in authority over us (see Rom. 13:1).

The language of the *New Bible Commentary* clarifies this human tendency to rationalize sin. "The Bible nowhere provides a philosophical or speculative account of the ultimate origin of evil. As the book of redemption, it describes the mode by which sin made its entry into the sphere of human experience. This is an historical account of the fall of man . . . . temptation came from without and sin was an intruder into the life of man. Sin cannot be regarded, therefore, as 'good in the making': rather did it spoil a world made 'good'".[1] Evil exists because two free people made a terrible choice: to play God for themselves, to determine good and evil for themselves and to exempt themselves from the need for God's loving protection. Evil did not just happen to them without their consent.

Lost Bearings

In Genesis 3:8 the story takes an interesting turn. Adam and Eve hear a familiar, once welcome, but now fearful sound. "Then the man and his wife heard the sound of the Lord God as he was walking in the garden in the cool of the day" (v. 8). Their response? "They hid from the Lord God among the trees of the garden" (v. 8).

Then God called out what seems to be a strange question: "Where are you?" (v. 9). Doesn't it seem that God should have asked, "What have you done?" In a sense, these questions are one in the same. God knew where Adam and Eve were. He was simply confronting them with the result of their sin: their lostness. This is how sin works. When we sin, we lose our bearings. We lose our sense of place and rootedness. We become disoriented as to where we are and where we belong. Adam illustrates this point in his response to God's question. He said, "I heard you in the garden, and I was afraid because I was naked; so I hid" (v. 10).

Before Adam and Eve's experience with sin, they belonged in God's presence, walking in the garden with Him during the cool of the day. After they sinned they did not know where they belonged. Their relationship with God had been redefined and they were confused. They were afraid; they were not willing to take responsibility for their sin so they hid.

Along with covering their nakedness with fig leaves, Adam and Eve tried to cover their guilt with excuses. Both attempts were inadequate. God questioned them further and their responses became more desperate. "Who told you that you were naked? Have you eaten from the tree that I commanded you not to eat from?" God asked (v. 11). Adam, unwilling to admit his sin, passed the buck to Eve—and to God as well: "The woman you put here with me—she gave me some fruit from the tree, and I ate it" (v. 12). God questioned Eve and she also denied responsibility saying, "The serpent deceived me, and I ate" (v. 13).

Following this interrogation, the judgment of God upon Adam and Eve and Satan is described. All of Adam and Eve's attempts to cover their guilt did not shield them from experiencing the consequences of their sin. Creation is cursed, their sorrows multiply and life becomes a sweaty struggle for existence ending in death (see vv. 16-19). This is a clear signal that our attempts to cover and justify ourselves on our own are inadequate. Yet like Adam and Eve, people still try.

During the 1960s I was a member of an academic senate in a system of colleges and universities. Campus disturbances were common, sometimes violent. One of my colleagues on the senate, a political moderate in those days, was badgered by professional radicals to join in a destructive demonstration on his campus. The consequences of not joining would be injury to his family and home. He thought it easier to go along with the idea than to risk these losses. So he participated, only to be shown on television while engaging in very stupid, unprofessional behavior.

When the melee subsided, he had to explain his foolish actions. But he had no way to cover himself; his misbehavior was a matter of public record. Instead of apologizing and risking further threats from the radicals, he began to rationalize his behavior. In a few weeks he became a ranting revolutionary, more out of the need to cover himself than from any well-thought-out change of philosophy. He needed forgiveness, but he knew no way to obtain it except to embarrass himself in public and risk further threat. He was not willing to do this, so he altered his belief to match his behavior. His new belief made his behavior seem acceptable and his conscience was temporarily salved.

To those who saw through his experience he was merely doing a fig-leaf job on a bad act. And like Adam he lost his place and his bearings about life. He became a campus sorehead and shortly gave up his professorship to follow radical causes. I don't know where he is today, but he is probably wandering a good deal and doing a lot of repair on his apron of fig leaves.

Our own efforts to cover our sin aren't much better. Like Adam, Eve and my former colleague, we are equally ludicrous when we cover ourselves with silly rationalizations and maskings. The greatest self-deception is a belief that we can shield ourselves from the consequences of knowing evil and experiencing sin. Yet social science textbooks and self-help literature encourage us to attempt just that. Popularized religion (Science of Mind, Dianetics, EST), humanistic philosophy and cult ritual still sell the theory that some form of fig leaves will take care of our need for forgiveness and our relationship problem with God. Teenagers are especially susceptible to avoiding facing their need for forgiveness. Often they feel they are invincible; they feel that the need to worry about consequences doesn't apply to them. Teenagers are also impressionable and are ready bait for those who peddle everything but repentance.

God's Covering Forshadows Jesus

In Genesis 3:21 God addresses man's lostness and his need for adequate covering or forgiveness. God did not abandon the man and woman, leaving them alone in their struggle with guilt and shame. "The Lord God made garments of skin for Adam and his wife and clothed them" (v. 21). There are two characteristics of the covering God provided for Adam and Eve that are significant. The first is the fact that

God provided it. This presents a picture of God's grace toward all humanity. The initiative God took to reach out to Adam and Eve as sinners foreshadowed another event in which God reached out to all the people of the world: "But God demonstrates his own love for us in this: While we were still sinners, Christ died for us" (Rom. 5:8; also see John 3:16).

The second significant characteristic of the covering God provided for Adam and Eve is the nature of it: skins. There is no cost involved in using fig leaves as a covering. A fig tree can simply grow new leaves to replace those taken. A covering of skins, however, involves the death of an animal; it involves the shedding of blood. This is the beginning of the sacrificial system among God's people. The shedding of blood is the only means by which man's sins can be covered and forgiveness can be obtained. As Hebrews 9:22 says, "the law requires that nearly everything be cleansed with blood, and without the shedding of blood there is no forgiveness."

The story of Cain and Abel presenting their sacrifices to the Lord illustrates this point. Abel brought an acceptable sacrifice to the Lord because he "brought fat portions from some of the firstborn of his flock" (Gen. 4:4). But Cain's sacrifice, "some of the fruits of the soil" (v. 3), was rejected by God. Although the text does not refer to a sin offering that required an animal sacrifice, most commentators feel that Abel's sacrifice was accepted because it represented an attitude of one needing forgiveness for his sins. Forgiveness of sins could only come through a blood sacrifice. Hebrews 11:4 supports their position by stating, "By faith he [Abel] was commended as a righteous man, when God spoke well of his offerings." Abel's sacrifice was therefore based on some knowledge of what God required of those seeking forgiveness (see Rom. 10:17). Cain was not commended and therefore must not have offered his sacrifice in the right spirit—faith—as Abel did. Cain demonstrated this by his choice of a sacrifice from *among* the fruits of the soil rather than bringing an offering of the firstfruits or the best he had.

Leviticus describes in more detail God's requirements concerning sacrifices. Those sacrifices whose purposes include atonement or forgiveness of sins require the shedding of blood of some animal (see Lev. 1:1-17; 4:1—6:13). The shedding of blood, or death, of the animal symbolizes its substitution in making payment for the sins of the person offering it. As part of the sacrificial system, the high priest was instructed to make a sacrifice for the sins of

himself and his household and then to sacrifice for the sins of the Israelite people (see Lev. 16:1-34). Yet this means of obtaining forgiveness was imperfect. This shedding of blood had to be repeated "again and again, the way the high priest enters the Most Holy Place every year with blood that is not his own" (Heb. 9:25).

In putting the sacrificial system in place, God did more than provide a temporary means by which people, like Adam and Eve, could receive cleansing from sin (see v. 13). God had created a picture, a reference point, from which His obedient people could recognize His provision of an eternal, once-for-all sacrifice of atonement—Jesus Christ. "We have been made holy through the sacrifice of the body of Jesus Christ once for all" (10:10). This picture has been displayed for us to see throughout history and the means of receiving forgiveness through Jesus Christ's sacrifice is now available to everyone. Unlike the sacrifices of animals, Jesus' shed blood offers us complete forgiveness by which we are made righteous in God's eyes (see vv. 12-18; 2 Cor. 5:21).

Fig Leaves or Forgiveness?

So where does this leave those of us who are disoriented and lost in sin? We must recognize that we have fallen short of God's expectations. At this point we have two choices: forgiveness or fig leaves. We can receive genuine forgiveness for our mistakes and straighten out our relationship with God, or we can dress in elaborate gowns and robes of fig leaves, deceiving ourselves into believing nothing has gone awry. When I meet older people who have opted for a lifetime of fig leaf covering, I discover whole gardens and arboretums of clipped, shaped, trellised and fertilized fig leaves. The path to repentance for these people is so difficult. It takes major stress or even catastrophe for them to uncover themselves, admit their sin and receive forgiveness. Young people have the advantage that change is a constant part of their lives. They may find it easier (but not necessarily easy) to break from their old ways and turn to Christ for forgiveness.

We all have a tendency, like Adam and Eve, to run for the fig tree rather than seek God's forgiveness. Our personal bouquets of fig leaves consist of all our excuses, rationalizations, blaming of others or any other device we may use to cover a sin. Or our fig-leaf arrangements may be elaborately constructed philosophies of self-fulfillment or fun-seeking that keep us from yielding to God's direction for our lives. When we hide behind a brand of psychology, philosophy or an alteration of God's truth, we are investing in fig leaves.

Our society is drenched in the human potential movement, in self-actualization psychology, even moral legalism and reinforcement. These movements prevent people from dealing with their spiritual need for genuine, complete forgiveness. These philosophies are subtly supported on high school campuses through special speakers invited into the classrooms, curriculum and films used and handouts distributed by different organizations to students. All of these serve to confuse students' values and blur their understanding of their need to deal with sin. Anything less than submitting to God's provision of forgiveness through Jesus Christ will not produce justification and eternal life for us. Only Christ, through His death and resurrection, can adequately cover us.

Notes

1. Davidson, Stibbs and Kevan, eds., *The New Bible Commentary* (Grand Rapids: Wm. B. Eerdmans Publishing Co., 1965), p. 79.

This Week's Teaching Plan

APPROACH TO THE WORD

APPROACH (5-8 minutes)

Ask students to help you write a short definition for "sin." Your definition might read, "Any thought or action that goes against the teaching of God's Word and/or interferes with building a person's relationship with God." Then write the following on the chalkboard or overhead: "True or False: The effects of sin are almost always shared." Ask students to respond to the statement then explain why they think the statement is true or false. Optional: Students who feel the statement is true may move to one side of the room while students who feel it is false move to the other. Allow time for each side to try to convince the other to accept its viewpoint. Students may change sides at any time during the discussion.

Say, **Today we will examine how the first sin resulted in consequences that have been felt by all people. We will also see how only God could provide an adequate solution for this sin and the sins of people today.**

ALTERNATE APPROACH (3-5 minutes)

Materials needed: Piece of shelf paper approximately five feet long, felt pens.

Preparation: On shelf paper draw at least one conversation balloon for each student you expect in class. At the top of the paper letter the words, "Excuses we make to cover the wrong things we do." Tape the shelf paper to a wall where students can easily reach it.

As students arrive have them write in the conversation balloons common excuses people make to cover the wrong things they do. When all students have had a chance to participate, read each excuse aloud. (Dramatic gestures, facial expressions and voice inflections will make this activity more fun while at the same time stress the shallowness of inadequate excuses.) Optional: Ask individual students to role-play people making the excuses listed, or have students read the excuses in unison as you point to each one. (Again, encourage students to ham it up.)

Move to the Exploration by saying, **This week's lesson will show us that our attempts to cover our sins are inadequate. We will also discover God's solution to our problem of dealing with sin.**

BIBLE EXPLORATION

EXPLORATION (40-50 minutes)

Materials needed: Post-it Notes, Session 2 Student Worksheet for each student.

Preparation: On Post-it Notes letter the Bible verse references listed in Step 1—one reference on each note.

Step 1 (6-8 minutes): Give the Post-its you have prepared to students who feel comfortable reading aloud. Tell them to be ready to read their verses when you direct them to do so. Then say, **Satan, also called the devil, played a key role in influencing the first sin that people ever committed. Satan continues to pressure people today to sin. Let's find out more about who Satan is and what he is like.** Ask students to read their assigned verses: (1) John 8:44; (2) 1 Peter 5:8; (3) 2 Corinthians 11:14; (4) 2 Corinthians 4:4; (5) 2 Timothy 2:26; (6) 1 John 3:8; (7) Matthew 4:1-3. List on the chalkboard or overhead the characteristics and activities of Satan mentioned in the verses. The list should include: murderer; liar; seeks to devour people; masquerades as something good; tries to keep unbelievers from hearing the gospel; traps people and makes them obey him; sinner from the beginning; tempter.

Move to Step 2 by stating, **In our Bible study we will see Satan in action. As we go through the Scriptures, watch for any of the traits and actions I've listed.**

Step 2 (20-25 minutes): Direct students to turn in their Bibles to Genesis, chapter 2. Give a brief summary of this chapter. Mention that at this point Adam and Eve lived in complete freedom from sin and enjoyed a perfect relationship with God and each other. Say, **Their innocence is evident in the fact that they were not ashamed of their nakedness** (see v. 25). Ask a volunteer to read verses 16,17. State that Adam and Eve were given a free will to obey or disobey God.

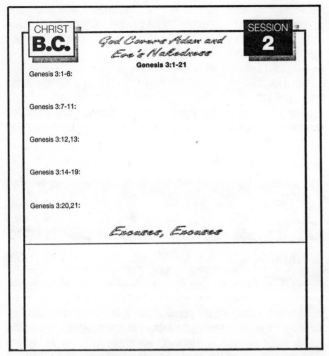

Distribute the worksheet and direct students to turn in their Bibles to Genesis, chapter 3. Ask volunteers to share in reading aloud the verses listed on their worksheets. As the verses are read, lead a discussion using the following outline and information from the Teacher's Bible Study. Encourage students to take notes on their worksheets as the discussion progresses.

Genesis 3:1-6

• **What characteristics or actions of Satan do you recognize in these verses?** Refer to the list made in Step 1. Responses may include: tempter, liar, sinner, deceiver.

• **How did Satan undermine the command God gave Adam and Eve to obey?** (He questioned God—see v. 1; he quoted God's words incorrectly—compare 2:16,17 with 3:1; he planted a seed of doubt in Eve's mind—see vv. 3,4.)

• **How did Satan appeal to Eve's pride?** (See v. 5.)

• **What did Eve consider as good reasons to eat the forbidden fruit?** (See v. 6.)

Genesis 3:7-11

• **What did Adam and Eve lose by disobeying God?** (Freedom from sin; innocence; a perfect relationship with God.) Mention that their shame points to their lost innocence.

• **How did they try to cover their nakedness?** (See v. 7.)

• **What did Adam and Eve gain because of their sin?** (The knowledge of good and evil; a broken relationship with God

resulting in physical and spiritual death; shame; guilt because of sin—see 2:17; 3:7,22)

• **Why do you think Adam and Eve hid when they heard the sound of God walking in the garden?** (See vv. 8-10.)

Genesis 3:12,13

• Say, **Adam and Eve tried to cover their sin physically with fig leaves. What verbal excuses did they give?** List student's responses on the chalkboard or overhead.

• **Do you think their efforts to cover their sin were adequate? Why or why not?**

Genesis 3:14-19

• Briefly summarize the consequences of Adam and Eve's sin. Emphasize that they illustrate that the most important thing in their lives—their relationship with God—had been broken.

Genesis 3:20,21

• **After pronouncing strong words of judgment against Adam and Eve's sin, God clothed them with garments of skin. How were God's garments of skin better than Adam and Eve's coverings of fig leaves?** (See v. 21.)

• Share Lloyd Ahlem's comments from the Teacher's Bible Study under "God's Covering Foreshadows Jesus" where he describes two characteristics of the covering God provided.

• Read Hebrews 9:22 to your students. Then ask, **What does this verse say is necessary for a person to receive forgiveness?** (The shedding of blood.) Then read Matthew 26:27,28. Ask, **Whose blood was shed so that we can receive forgiveness for our sins?** (Jesus' blood.)

Step 3 (10-12 minutes): Move the class into groups of four to five students. Ask volunteers to suggest sins that are common among their peers. Then say, **Within your group, choose one of the sins we have listed. Then, in the "Excuses, Excuses" section of your worksheets, work together to write a short story or dialogue illustrating what a person who committed that sin might say or do to cover him- or herself.** (If completed, refer to the Alternate Approach activity.)

After 5-8 minutes ask a representative from each group to read its scenario. Optional: Those groups that feel comfortable doing so may act out their scenarios. Then ask, **Why is it impossible to hide our sins from God?** (He knows our hearts and sees through or excuses.) **How does sin affect our relationship with God?** (It breaks the relationship and creates a gap between us and God.) **Is it possible to live without sinning? Why or why not?** Read Romans 3:23.

Step 4 (4-5 minutes): Ask a student to read aloud Romans 5:8. Ask, **How would you describe God's provision of a covering for our sins?** Then say, **Just like the covering God provided for Adam and Eve, God has provided a covering for our sin through the shed blood of Jesus Christ.**

CONCLUSION & DECISION

CONCLUSION (2-5 minutes)

Ask, **What excuse to cover sin are you most tempted to use? Write it on your worksheet. Now write a reason why that excuse is inadequate to cover your sin.** Then say, **God has provided an adequate covering for our sin through the death of Jesus Christ. But because we were created with free wills, like Adam and Eve, we must choose to accept God's covering in order to find forgiveness. God promises that when we don't try on our own to cover our sins but

confess them to Him, we will be completely forgiven.** Read 1 John 1:9. Then close in prayer thanking God for making it possible for our sins to be forgiven and for our relationship with Him to be repaired. Be available after class to talk further with students about forgiveness.

Encourage students to read chapter 2 of the student paperback *Christ B.C.* Each of the daily readings will explore the theme "righteousness."

Noah Finds Refuge in the Ark

KEY VERSE

"You are my hiding place; you will protect me from trouble and surround me with songs of deliverance." Psalm 32:7

"'Come to me, all you who are weary and burdened, and I will give you rest. Take my yoke upon you and learn from me, for I am gentle and humble in heart, and you will find rest for your souls. For my yoke is easy and my burden is light.'" Matthew 11:28-30

BIBLICAL BASIS

Genesis 6:1—8:22; Deuteronomy 7:25; Psalm 32:6,7; 57:1-3; 89:32; 91:2,4,5; Proverbs 3:31-35; 6:16-19; Isaiah 40:28-31; Zechariah 8:17; Matthew 11:28-30; Luke 12:15; 1 Corinthians 6:18-20; Philippians 4:6,7; 2 Timothy 4:17,18; 1 Peter 5:8; 2 Peter 2:1-3,17-19; 1 John 5:3-5

FOCUS OF THE SESSION

Just as God provided refuge for Noah and his family in the ark, God has provided Christ as our refuge during stormy experiences.

AIMS OF THIS SESSION

You and your students will have accomplished the purpose of this Bible study session if you can:

- DISCUSS how God provided refuge for Noah and his family during the Flood;
- LIST ways a person can take refuge in Christ;
- CHOOSE steps you will take to prepare for stormy experiences.

Teacher's Bible Study

The story of Noah and his family finding refuge in the ark is a symbol of God's grace extended to humankind in many ways. In this session we will focus on a few of the many types and pictures from this narrative that were fulfilled in Christ.

The Days of Noah

From the day that Adam and Eve were denied residence in Eden, the character of humankind declined into moral and spiritual bankruptcy; Genesis 6:1 through chapter 8 tells the story. Genesis 6:5 declares that the evil among people was great; it had saturated their thoughts and hearts: "The Lord saw how great man's wickedness on the earth had become, and that every inclination of the thoughts of his heart was only evil all the time." People's behavior had become so bad that God was sorry for having made them: "The Lord was grieved that he had made man on the earth, and his heart was filled with pain" (v. 6). Such language does not indicate that God made a mistake (see Gen. 1:27,31).His perfect creation had gone foul by the free will of man and God was repulsed by it. The following words of Scripture express the response of an insulted God: "I will wipe mankind, whom I

have created, from the face of the earth" (v. 7). Only a new start would be sufficient to renew hope for people and their relationship with God.

But even when insulted by sin, God gives grace. One man found favor in God's eyes. One man had not surrendered to all the evil impulses in which others indulged. This man was Noah (see vv. 8,9). Noah's character was above reproach. He was not sinless, but he sought to do God's bidding and was regarded as righteous. Because of this Noah would be preserved from the deluge God had planned for the destruction of the human race (see Heb. 11:7).

The Ark Is Built

Upon choosing Noah, God told him of His plan "to put an end to all people, for the earth is filled with violence because of them" (Gen. 6:13). Then God gave Noah specific instructions to build an ark (see vv. 14-16). God told him what size to make it, where to put the door, how to lay out the interior and what materials to use. Finally God told Noah exactly what to put in the ark. There would be a plentiful supply to begin again—both physically and spiritually. Noah's immediate family would be in-

cluded (see 6:18), as well as animals for repopulating the earth and for burnt offerings and enough food for all (see vv. 19-21; 7:2,3; 8:20).

Noah's response to God's instructions stresses his obedience and faith in God. Genesis 6:22 states, "Noah did everything just as God commanded him." Noah's response also set him further apart from the rest of his generation. His construction project must have boggled the minds of most who watched him. Imagine seeing a huge boat being built, without a sail or rudder, on dry land so far from the water you could never haul it to sea. Furthermore, it had no prow or stern; it was just a big box made of wood sealed up tight with pitch. This was no Chriscraft for waterskiing. This was a barge designed with only one purpose in mind: To protect as much cargo as could be loaded aboard. No provisions were made for navigation or for seaside loading or docking. Noah's neighbors must have laughed at him.

The Preacher of Righteousness

During this time Noah was occupied with more than building. He spent some time preaching also. He wasn't very successful, apparently, for the apostle Peter says that nobody listened (see 2 Pet. 2:5; also see 1 Pet. 3:18-20). The ancient historian Josephus says that he prodded his audience so insistently that they wearied greatly and he was afraid that they would kill him if he didn't stop.[1] Jesus experienced this when He preached to the people in His hometown (see Matt. 13:53-58). I wonder how many times Noah went back to his work of building the ark just to get away from surly audiences.

But Noah was a man of character. God said of him, "I have found you righteous in this generation" (Gen. 7:1). Only a man of character could have persisted in such a mission. Noah lived out the purpose for which he was intended. If we live as God intends, we can persist through rejection. And we can find our way in God's will without a lot of cheering or back-patting.

In evil times such as Noah's, evil people are unable to see their sin. So long have excuses been made, motives rationalized and consequences overlooked that the mind can no longer comprehend the evil done. This is evident in the fact that no one listened to Noah. Satan influenced people's reasoning in those times just as he did in Eden. His purpose is to undermine and create doubt concerning what God has established (see Gen. 3:1-6). It is clear that Satan is just as active in pursuing his evil interests in the world today as he was in the days of Adam and Eve and Noah (see 1 Pet. 5:8,9).

I remember counseling a young college student who was feeling terribly depressed. His moods were starting to interfere with his studies as well as his social life. As we unraveled his story, some reasons for his depression became obvious. He had been raised on good moral principles, but without the structure and reinforcement of sound biblical understanding. Since he didn't have a solid base, he began to think he could make up his own standards. He decided he would not do anything that was without his or his friends' consent. He entered into a lifestyle of pleasure and sexual indulgence that he and his friends condoned. But when his girlfriend became pregnant and badgered him for a promise of support, he could not understand why the problem was being handed to him. It wasn't really his fault, he thought; she had consented to being sexually involved. She did not protect herself and therefore she could just as well face the consequences on her own.

But those old standards he had been raised with were gnawing at him. Although he could not understand why, his conscience had long ago been formed by these standards and now they were telling

him he was a moral failure. As with most failure, depression was the result. The solution to resolving his depression was to face up to his sin and find the biblical basis behind the moral standards imprinted on his conscience. But he would have none of it. The pleasure of his indulgence was too gripping. Instead, he began an intellectual assault upon his conscience, rationalizing his impulses as good in themselves and his behavior as in keeping with modern standards. Furthermore, he had plenty of help from teachers who saw him as a youngster liberating himself from old strictures that hampered his freedom. But his depression remained. He was being devoured by his rationalizations (with Satan's help, I'm sure). His situation was probably similar to the hardheartedness of the people to whom Noah preached.

Noah Finds Refuge in the Ark

The trying days of preaching to spiritually deaf ears and the physical toil of building ended with the completion of the ark. "The Lord then said to Noah, 'Go into the ark, you and your whole family'" (Gen. 7:1). And Noah, still persisting in obedience to God, "did all that the Lord commanded him" (v. 5). After Noah and his family entered the ark, the famous parade of animals began. It is interesting to note that Noah may not have rounded up the animals on his own. "Pairs of clean and unclean animals . . . came to Noah and entered the ark" (vv. 8,9). When all were in the ark, "the Lord shut him in" (v. 16). God closed the door of the ark.

Then God unleashed the forces of nature. The restraints imposed on the waters in the second and third days of creation were relaxed for the destruction of sinful man (see 1:7-10,13). The earth cracked open and sealed waters gushed out. Rain came and drenched the earth from above. For approximately one year's time Noah and his family survived in the ark, and only because God had provided a refuge for them (see 7:6; 8:13).

Finally, in accordance with God's timing, the waters receded. "God remembered Noah . . . and he sent a wind over the earth, and the waters receded" (8:1). God's last words to Noah had been, "Go into the ark" (7:1). Now God said to Noah, "Come out of the ark" (8:16). Noah would now begin the human story again. And he began by giving honor to the Lord. "Noah built an altar to the Lord and . . . sacrificed burnt offerings on it" (v. 20). God was pleased by Noah's act of worship, and following the sacrifice God established this covenant with Noah and with "all life on the earth" (9:17).

Genesis 9:8-17 describes a covenant between God and man. A covenant is an agreement, a pledge irrevocably taken and marked by a sign. The sign God provided for Noah was the rainbow (see v. 13). The agreement God made was, "Never again will all life be cut off by the waters of a flood; never again will there be a flood to destroy the earth" (v. 11).

Noah and Types of Christ

The story of Noah is much more than an account of a catastrophic event. It is a collage of pictures that illustrates God's grace and salvation through Jesus Christ. Let's isolate the individual pictures and see what they teach us about Jesus.

First we see Noah as a singular, righteous person. He was the only one through whom God could redeem humankind from the judgment of the Flood. This points to Christ as the only means God has provided by which we can be saved from our sin. "Salvation is found in no one else, for there is no other name under heaven given to men by which we must be saved" (Acts 4:12).

Second, Noah's character illustrates an important point concerning Christ's character. Only a righteous individual could be God's agent of salvation. Likewise, only a clean, unblemished animal could be offered as a sacrifice by the priests for sin (see Lev. 4:3). Christ, the offering God used to make atonement for man's sin, was clean and unblemished. Peter describes Christ in this way: "For you know that it was not with perishable things such as silver or gold that you were redeemed from the empty way of life handed down to you from your forefathers, but with the precious blood of Christ, a lamb without blemish or defect" (1 Pet. 1:18,19). Peter goes on to say in verse 20, "He was chosen before the creation of the world, but was revealed in these last times for your sake." God had planned a way of salvation for people from the very beginning. It isn't by chance that He chose Noah to save humankind from the flood; it was by design and for our sake so that we could understand God's way of salvation in Christ.

The third picture we will examine is one of God's grace and provision through Jesus Christ. It is this picture that will be the focus of your time with your students. In this picture we see that God provided a refuge for Noah during the flood. Having heard God and obeyed Him, Noah was exempted from the judgment that befell his unrepentant generation. In the midst of the upheaval when "all the springs of the great deep burst forth, and the floodgates of the heavens were opened" (Gen. 7:11), Noah was preserved by God. Like Noah we are provided a refuge during times of turmoil if we obey and believe God's Word. This refuge is found in a right relationship with Jesus Christ. Psalm 32:7 declares, "You are my hiding place; you will protect me from trouble and surround me with songs of deliverance." Psalm 91 is a beautiful hymn that further describes God's gracious provision for the godly, "I will say of the Lord, 'He is my refuge and my fortress, my God, in whom I trust' . . . . He will cover you with his feathers, and under his wings you will find refuge; his faithfulness will be your shield and rampart. You will not fear the terror of night, nor the arrow that flies by day" (vv. 2,4,5). The Old Testament is full of descriptions such as these. Take time to read Psalm 57 as well. As you do, notice that it is in the *midst* of disaster and distress that God provides refuge; He does not always remove disaster from around us. Like Noah, He often provides a way for us to survive, protected by our trust in Him, in spite of the storms of life.

In the New Testament Jesus identifies Himself as the one who can provide rest and rejuvenation. Matthew 11:28-30 is Jesus' invitation to share our burdens in life with Him. It says, "Come to me, all you who are weary and burdened, and I will give you rest. Take my yoke upon you and learn from me, for I am gentle and humble in heart, and you will find rest for your souls. For my yoke is easy and my burden is light." It is by coming to Christ, submitting to Him, learning from Him and sharing our burdens with Him that our souls can find rest.

The biblical message is generously punctuated with promises of rest, refuge and peace for children of God who seek solace in Him (see Ps. 23; Isa. 43:1,2; Phil. 4:7). There is no man-made belief system or philosophy that is as personal and mindful of individual human needs as the gospel of Christ.

Considering the many invitations in Scripture to enter into the peace of God and find refuge in Him, I wonder at my efforts to go it alone and take all the bruises I do when I'm in trouble. I also wonder at the places of refuge chosen by so many that only add to their troubles. I am thinking of a college freshman who was in my class in introductory psychology. She was cute, verbal, intelligent and experimenting with all the nonsensical ideas and activities the world made available to her. As I got to know her, I found the force of guilt was heavily upon her. She had been molested by her father, introduced to drugs by her high school English teacher and scolded by her priest for not taking her religion seriously. Furthermore, she felt helplessly guilty for having allowed herself to be exploited and abused by all these people. The refuge she chose was the deadening numbness of alcohol and deceptive euphoria of drugs.

Happily not every person's search for refuge manifests itself in this way. On Monday evenings my wife and I began opening our living room to students who wanted to talk about personal concerns. No agenda was necessary; there was no admission charge and no barriers restricting any subject. My wife and I simply listened. We listened from about 8:30 p.m. when our small children went to bed until about 10:30 p.m. when we served refreshments. Most of them went home then, but some had not completed their agendas. So we sat up longer, often past midnight, with one or two who carried burdens they could hardly bear. Then we gently tried to point them to Christ, not coercively or with guilt, but with the message of the refuge God wanted to provide for them. By the time the last of them left, the coffee cups had been filled many times, then stuffed with ashes from innumerable cigarettes. The house stunk and our clothes smelled like a tobacco bonfire, but peace began to come and over a couple of years we were heartened by a number of students who found peace and refuge in Christ.

In time we left that area of the country for other duties in the midwest. As we were leaving, one young woman who had spent many evenings with us but who had shared little of herself came and said, "I'm sorry you are going. Your living room is the safest place I have ever known in my life. No one accused me, and I could think through the assaults made upon my weak values. God was there with me. Thank you for making me feel safe." I felt more than paid for all the long nights we had spent.

But if the needs of these students were so great, so are the needs of so many others. What is happening to those who have no refuge in Christ and no home to enter to feel a small sensation of His comfort? What is your favorite refuge that you run to? Is it to the loving arms of Jesus and His followers or some self-chosen substitute? Are you facing the world without the help of God's protection? Even though I have known the good news of God's comfort for many years, I am still constructing little refuges that fall short of the grace of God. I would still rather rationalize certain of my errors rather than seek forgiveness and peace in Christ. But when the heat is on and my stress is high, I run quickly to the presence of God. It's the little things that still tempt me to "go it alone." It's the tiny arenas of struggle where pride wants a foothold and I want to dictate the outcome and settle the issues. But I am learning that I don't have the power to effectively protect myself. I've discovered that Jesus is more able than I.

A final lesson we can learn from Noah is this: In seeking refuge in God we, like Noah, are provided with an opportunity to begin again. This is like the experience of people newly regenerated in Christ (see 2 Cor. 5:17). Noah was an old man in his new beginning. This illustrates that there is always hope, no matter what your age or your circumstances. In Christ it is never too late for a new beginning. In Christ there is always relief from spiritual debt and moral fault (see 1 John 1:9). In Christ there is rest for your souls. For many this comes in the form of forgiveness. People, by their own resources and wits, accumulate debts they cannot pay and sins they cannot forgive or have forgiven on their own. They wonder if there is any way out. Not until they come to terms with their sin and seek refuge and forgiveness through Christ will they be set free to begin again.

Note

1. *The Works of Josephus* (Peabody, MA: Hendrickson Publishers, 1987), p. 32.

NOTES:

APPROACH TO THE WORD

APPROACH (3-5 minutes)

Materials needed: Session 3 Student Worksheet titled "Stormy Times" for each student. Note: The "Stormy Times" worksheet appears on the top half of the page, so after you make photocopies cut copies in half. Distribute the top halves to volunteers during the Approach. Save the bottom halves for use in Step 2 of the Exploration.

When students have gathered, distribute worksheets. Direct students to complete the worksheet as directed on the page. After a couple of minutes ask students to share the experiences they rated as the most and least stressful or difficult. Invite them to share the reasons behind their choices. Then ask, **What are some ways people respond when they encounter difficult circumstances?**

CHRIST **B.C.**

Stormy Times

SESSION **3**

On a scale of 1 to 5, rate each experience listed according to how stressful or difficult an experience it would be.

		A breeze				Very difficult
		1	2	3	4	5
1.	Pressure to drink, take drugs or have sex.					
2.	A family member or close friend dying.					
3.	Wearing the wrong thing to a social gathering.					
4.	Being abused.					
5.	Deciding what to do after graduation.					
6.	Developing a serious health problem.					
7.	Having a pet named Fred.					
8.	Being criticized behind your back by a friend.					
9.	Parents divorcing.					

BIBLE EXPLORATION

EXPLORATION (35-45 minutes)

Materials needed: Session 3 Student Worksheets titled "Noah Finds Refuge in the Ark" and "Refuge in Christ" (photocopied with the worksheet used in the Approach), large sheets of paper and felt pens. Optional—poster board, magazines and glue for use in Step 2.

CHRIST **B.C.**

Noah Finds Refuge in the Ark
Genesis 6:1—8:22

SESSION **3**

Genesis 6:1-7,11-13:

Genesis 6:8,9:

Genesis 6:14-22:

Genesis 7:1—8:22:

It Pays to Prepare

Step 1 (15-20 minutes): Distribute the "Noah Finds Refuge in the Ark" worksheet. Direct students to turn in their Bibles to Genesis, chapter 6. Introduce this portion of the study by saying, **As we look at these verses, look for ways God reached out to**

Noah and the people living around him. Then ask several volunteers to share in reading aloud the verses listed on the worksheet. As the verses are read, lead a discussion of the verses using the following outline and material from the Teacher's Bible Study. Encourage students to take notes on their worksheets as the discussion progresses.

Genesis 6:1-7, 11-13

- **How would you describe the morals of the people of Noah's day?** (See vv. 5,11.) Avoid a discussion of "the sons of God" marrying the "daughters of men." This is a difficult passage and it is not the focus of the session. You may suggest to any curious students that they make an independent study of the passage then share their findings with you later.
- **What was God's response to the people's corruption?** (See vv. 6,7,13.) Ask several volunteers to read the following verses: Psalm 89:32; Proverbs 3:31-35; 6:16-19; Zechariah 8:17. Then ask, **How does God feel about sin? Why do you think He hates sin?**

Genesis 6:8,9

- Also read Hebrews 11:7 and 2 Peter 2:5. **Why did Noah find favor with God?** (See Gen. 6:9) Responses to this question may include: he did not walk in the ways of the sinful world; he preached righteousness; he walked with God.
- **Why would being righteous be an especially difficult task for someone living in Noah's day?** Responses may include: he had no one supporting him in his walk with God; he didn't have any godly examples to follow.
- Share Lloyd Ahlem's comments from the Teacher's Bible Study in the section titled "The Preacher of Righteousness" concerning the stresses Noah probably faced as a preacher of righteousness.

Genesis 6:14-22

- Say, **These verses describe what happened from the time Noah and his family entered the ark until the time they left the ark (about one year).**

Genesis 7:1—8:22

- Instead of reading every verse, ask volunteers to read only the following verses: 7:2,3,16,23; 8:1,15,16. Then ask, **How did God provide for Noah and His family during the flood?**
- Read Genesis 8:20-22. **What was the first thing Noah did when he left the ark? How did God respond? How would you discribe the relationship between God and Noah?**

Step 2 (12-15 minutes): **Let's take a second look at the story of Noah in terms of how it presents for us a picture of Jesus Christ as a refuge in stormy experiences.** Move the class into three groups (or a multiple of three). Give each group a large sheet of paper and felt pens. Then distribute the "Refuge in Christ" worksheets to students. Give each group one of the following assignments from the worksheet:

Group 1

Write a newspaper article describing a person who can find refuge in Christ. Use these verses as a basis for your article: Genesis 6:9,22; 7:5; Psalm 32:6; 91:14; 1 John 5:3-5.

Group 2

Write slogans or one-word descriptions that illustrate what refuge in Christ is like. Use these verses as a basis for your descriptions: Genesis 6:21; 7:11-13,16,23; Psalm 32:7; 57:1-3; 91:2,4,5; Isaiah 40:28-31; Matthew 11:28-30; Philippians 4:6,7.

Group 3

List the "top ten" influences in the world from which you need protection. Use these verses as a basis for your list: Deuteronomy 7:25; Luke 12:15; 1 Corinthians 6:18-20; 2 Timothy 4:17,18; 1 Peter 5:8; 2 Peter 2:1-3,17-19. Optional—provide poster board, glue and magazines for this group to use to illustrate its list.

Allow 5-8 minutes for each group to complete its assignment. Then ask each group to share the results of its efforts. As Group 3 shares, mention that God does not promise to remove stormy experiences from our lives, although He may chose to do that. God does promise that in the *midst* of disaster and distress He will provide refuge. To many non-believers the mark of a Chris-

tian is often the way in which he or she deals with and perseveres through hardship.

Step 3 (8-10 minutes): Say, **Now let's discuss specific ways a person can take refuge in Christ.** As a group list as many ways as possible by which a person can strengthen his or her faith and find refuge during difficult experiences. State that the steps a person takes today to strengthen his or her faith will help that person weather a storm tomorrow; the key is preparation. Make sure your list includes the following points:

1. Become a Christian (stress that without a relationship with Christ, refuge in Christ is impossible);
2. Ask Christ for forgiveness for sin in your life;
3. Nurture your relationship with Christ through prayer and Bible study. This will help you develop the Christian maturity to persevere in hard times (share any programs your church offers to help them in this area, or recommend resources you feel would enrich their prayer lives and personal Bible study—starting a prayer journal is one suggestion you may want to offer);
4. Build relationships with other Christians. Share your struggles and pray together;
5. Identify situations that can lead you into danger or weaken your faith. Avoid them if possible and pray for strength should you encounter such an experience. Plan ahead of time how you will respond to these situations.

As each point is made ask, **Why do you think this point is important? How would applying it help a person in his or her daily life?** Move to the Conclusion by saying, **We can try to find refuge without Christ's help, but He is the only refuge that can adequately help us deal with any crisis we may experience.** Or move to the Optional Step 4.

Optional Step 4 (3-5 minutes): Write on the board or overhead the words, "Places People Run for Refuge." Ask students to suggest places people their age look for refuge instead of turning to Christ. Responses may include: drugs or alcohol, isolation, friends, anger, leaving home. Move to the Optional Conclusion by saying, **Some of these refuges are dead ends. Some may be of help. But without Christ's protection all of them are inadequate.**

CONCLUSION & DECISION

CONCLUSION (3-5 minutes)

Use this Conclusion if students did not complete the Optional Step 4. Ask, **What are some steps you need to take to prepare for stormy experiences?** Refer to the list made in Step 3 of the Exploraton. Say, **If you are not a Christian, the first step to take if you want to have access to refuge in Christ is to put your faith and trust in Him. If you are a Christian, consider what steps you need to take to strengthen your relationship with Christ.** Direct students to write in the "It Pays to Prepare" section of their worksheets what step(s) they want to take to prepare for stormy experiences. Lead students in silent prayer. Close by asking God to strengthen each one in his or her relationship with Christ.

Be available after class to talk to any students who express an interest in becoming a Christian or to counsel any students who are struggling with a difficult circumstance.

OPTIONAL CONCLUSION (3-5 minutes)

Use this Conclusion if students completed the Optional Step

4. Ask, them to consider this question: **Where do you run first when you experience troubles?** Then say, **If you are not a Christian, the first step to take if you want to have access to refuge in Christ is to put your faith and trust in Him. If you are a Christian, consider what steps you need to take to strengthen your relationship with Christ.** Direct students to write in the "It Pays to Prepare" section of their worksheets what step(s) they want to take to prepare for stormy experiences. Refer to the list made in Step 3 of the Exploration. Lead students in silent prayer. Close by asking God to strengthen each one in his or her relationship with Christ.

Be available after class to talk to any students who express an interest in becoming a Christian or to counsel any students who are struggling with a difficult circumstance.

Encourage students to read chapter 3 in the student paperback *Christ B.C.* The readings in this chapter will explore the theme "refuge."

Melchizedek

KEY VERSE

"The Lord has sworn and will not change his mind: 'You are a priest forever, in the order of Melchizedek.'"
Psalm 110:4

"Therefore, since we have a great high priest who has gone through the heavens, Jesus the Son of God, let us hold firmly to the faith we profess." Hebrews 4:14

BIBLICAL BASIS

Genesis 14:1-20; Matthew 16:21; John 14:27; 16:33; Hebrews 7:1-3,11-25; 1 John 2:1; Revelation 21:2-4

FOCUS OF THE SESSION

Jesus is our High Priest in the order of Melchizedek. As such only He can offer us complete redemption.

AIMS OF THIS SESSION

You and your students will have accomplished the purpose of this Bible study session if you can:

- DISCUSS how Melchizedek is a type of Christ;
- DEFINE redemption and IDENTIFY Jesus as the only means of obtaining forgiveness of sins;
- EVALUATE where you tend to seek redemption and accept Christ as your Savior as the Holy Spirit leads.

Teacher's Bible Study

Melchizedek's appearance in the Old Testament has the air of mystery about it. Only a couple of verses are devoted to him, but within these verses a clear type of Christ emerges. We also find reference to Melchizedek in Psalm 110 and throughout Hebrews, chapters 5 through 7.

The Setting

Genesis, chapters 12—14 describe the circumstances in which Abraham (at this time he was called Abram) and Melchizedek met. Abraham had followed God's call to leave his home in Ur of the Chaldeans and go to Canaan (see Gen. 12:1,5). Abraham's nephew Lot accompanied him. Because of the severe famine afflicting Canaan, Abraham decided to proceed to Egypt where he set up temporary residence. While in Egypt his wealth and numbers increased greatly. "Abram acquired sheep and cattle, male and female donkeys, menservants and maidservants, and camels" (v. 16).

(Note: Because of the focus of this study, we will not explore the circumstances surrounding Abraham's stay in Egypt. Read Genesis 12:10-20 and be prepared to answer any questions, should they arise. Notice that God's call to Abraham in vv. 1-9 did not include Abraham traveling to Egypt, and it is significant that

his relationship with God is not mentioned during his stay there.)

From Egypt Abraham traveled back toward the land of Canaan (see 12:20—13:4). Abraham had prospered and his entourage was so large that it could have been considered a small nation on the move. Abraham had the ability to maintain an army of "318 trained men born in his household" (14:14) and compete with hostile forces (see vv. 13-16).

Abraham had the opportunity to use these resources to deal with a situation concerning his nephew Lot. Genesis 13 tells us that in order to resolve bickering among their herdsmen over grazing land, Abraham and Lot parted ways. "Abram lived in the land of Canaan, while Lot lived among the cities of the plain and pitched his tents near Sodom" (v. 12). It is obvious that, despite the fact that the land around Sodom was fertile, Lot had made a bad choice. "The men of Sodom were wicked and were sinning greatly against the Lord" (v. 13). Also, Bera the king of Sodom and the kings of neighboring cities had many enemies. The cities of Sodom, Gomorrah, Admah, Zeboiim and Bela were conquered during a battle in the Valley of Siddim. The cities were ransacked and Lot and his possessions were carried off among the plunder (see 14:8-12). When

Abraham heard the news, he gathered his trained men and conducted a nighttime raid to rescue Lot. The Bible says that Abraham "brought back his relative Lot and his possessions" (v. 16).

Abraham Is Greeted by Melchizedek

Upon returning from battle, Abraham was greeted by Melchizedek, the king of Salem, who brought bread and wine for refreshment. Melchizedek blessed Abraham and gave praise to "God Most High, who delivered your enemies into your hand" (v. 20).

Melchizedek, was probably king over the area that is now Jerusalem. Language scholars suggest that the name Salem is a derivative of Ursalim, which is also the basis of the name Jerusalem. The name "Melchizedek" has significant meaning. First it means "king of righteousness," and secondly it means "king of Salem" which means "king of peace" (see Heb. 7:2). First John 2:1 calls Jesus "the Righteous One." John 14:27 and 16:33 both describe Jesus as the agent of God's peace. Thus, even the name of Melchizedek testifies that he is a type of Christ.

Melchizedek was king over the region that was to be the center of the Promised Land of Israel. It would become the site of God's Temple and the center of worship. It would be many years before this promise would be realized, but the story provides us with a glimpse of the kingdom that would be built. Melchizedek was a godly king, ruling where the King of kings was to be crucified and where prophecy concerning Christ and the New Jerusalem is yet to be fulfilled (Rev. 21:2).

Melchizedek served as both king and priest, probably presiding over a large household much like Abraham's. As king he had authority to set guidelines for his subjects and carry out judgment when needed. He was also responsible for their welfare. Melchizedek's role as king provides us with a picture of Christ that points to Jesus' role as our King, Judge, Lord, Provider and Protector.

Although Melchizedek was a Canaanite king, he was a servant of the one true God. As "priest of God Most High" (Gen. 14:18) Melchizedek was able to offer sacrifices and thereby advocate atonement for the sins of his people. Abraham saw in him the character and nature of the one true God and honored Melchizedek by paying tithes to him (see v. 20).

Jesus and the Order of Melchizedek

This is where the mystery of Melchizedek presents itself. The Jews have long based their claim as a blessed people upon the importance of the covenant relationship between God and Abraham (see 12:2,3). It is through Abraham that the Levitical order of priests would be established and it is through this order that the Jews might expect a redeemer to come. Yet Abraham, in paying tithes to Melchizedek, acknowledged him to be of a higher order than himself. Hebrews 7:4 describes this honor given to Melchizedek: "Just think how great he [Melchizedek] was: Even the patriarch Abraham gave him a tenth of the plunder!" The superiority of the priestly order of Melchizedek over the order of Levi is reemphasized in Hebrews 7:9,10. "One might even say that Levi, who collects the tenth, paid the tenth through Abraham, because when Melchizedek met Abraham, Levi was still in the body of his ancestor."

Why do these two orders exist? What is it about Melchizedek that makes his order of priesthood so important? These questions can only be answered when we look at Melchizedek as a type of Christ. Christ is described as a priest in the order of Melchizedek (see 5:5,6). Priesthood in the order of Levi was inherited by members of the tribe of Levi (see Num. 3:1-13; Heb. 7:16). Jesus' earthly genealogy places Him as a member of the tribe of Judah (see Heb. 7:14). Priesthood in the

order of Melchizedek is "not on the basis of a regulation as to his ancestery but on the basis of the power of an indestructible life" (v. 16). Jesus' resurrection gives evidence of His fulfillment of this requirement (see Luke 24:1-8).

There are other evidences that point to the necessity of a priesthood that is superior to that of Levi. Hebrews 6:20 and 7:3 both describe the order of Melchizedek as an eternal priesthood. The Old Testament story of Melchizedek does not mention his death. Many commentators feel that the Bible does this to illustrate that he is consistent with the eternal Christ whose kingdom has no end. Hebrews describes the Christlike attributes of Melchizedek in chapter 7, verse 3: "Without father or mother, without genealogy, without beginning of days or end of life, like the Son of God he remains a priest forever." This clarifies that Melchizedek is a clear type of Christ. He is not simply a pawn of chance circumstance, but part of history designed and directed by God. Jesus was without an earthly father; He existed before the creation of the world (see 1 Pet. 1:20); He conquered death and He continues to act as the eternal High Priest. "Because Jesus lives forever, he has a permanent priesthood. Therefore he is able to save completely those who come to God through him, because he always lives to intercede for them" (Heb. 7:24,25).

Because the priesthood of Jesus is eternal and perfect, the sacrifice of Christ is final (see v. 27). In contrast to the day-to-day offerings by the Aaronic priests, Christ's giving of Himself was a once-and-for-all accomplishment. He was the sinless one giving Himself once for the sinful. There is no need for anyone else to repeat Jesus' sacrifice of atonement, try to improve upon it or add anything to it. By His sacrifice Jesus opened the only way by which people can be reconciled to God. Atonement means that God and people can be reunited through Christ. Through the Aaronic order the priests had to be cleansed before they could offer sacrifices for the people (see Heb. 5:1-3). They bore the same sinful tendencies and blemishes we all do. This is not so with Christ; He is the lamb without spot or blemish and the perfect sacrifice that needed no cleansing (see Heb. 7:26).

Complete Redemption

This picture of Jesus as our High Priest is one of redemption. Very simply, redemption means to buy back something that is already our own.

When I was a boy, a teacher of mine illustrated this word with a simple story

adapted from *Little Boat Twice Owned*. A young lad built a beautiful model boat. He took care to make every part a perfect replication of a well-known sailing vessel. When he had finished it, his friends admired it greatly and were surprised at the great skill he had demonstrated in building the boat. It was as fine a model as they had ever seen. But it did not seem appropriate to have it sit on a shelf in his home. It should be sailed, as boats were meant to do. So he carried it to the nearby brook and set it free to be carried by the winds. The currents of air and water caught it and since it was so beautifully made and balanced, it rushed out beyond the reach of its maker. The boy chased along the water's edge, trying to find a way to recover his treasure. But he could not. He watched it disappear downstream as it went its unfettered way.

Some weeks later the lad, still sorrowing for his loss, was walking along a street leading to his home. He chanced to pass a hardware store and stopped to look into the window. Something caught his eye. There was his boat! The store was now closed, but early the next morning he rushed down to the shopkeeper and asked to have his boat returned. The shopkeeper could see that he was very determined to get his treasure back, but the man replied, "I paid good money for that boat and I'll have to get my price for it. It is well made and should attract any number of interested customers."

"But it's mine!" responded the boy.

"I won't sell it for awhile," said the shopkeeper. "I'll save it for you. See if you can get the money."

The boy hurried off and gathered all he had ever saved and brought it to the store. It was just enough, so the shopkeeper handed over the beautiful treasure, the boat. "First I made you; then I bought you, now I'll keep you safe forever!" pledged the lad as he left the store.

In spiritual terms this is a good illustration of redemption. First God made us; then He gave us a free will. We took our own course and lost track of the One who designed and created us. When we became entangled in sin, we were purchased with all that God could give—His only Son, Jesus Christ.

But the story of the boat fails at one important point. Unlike the boat which is carried by the wind rather than by its own will, we have all set sail upon life under our own will. We chose to get away from our Creator and we must choose to be returned to our rightful owner. Nevertheless our redemption has been provided for. God has given us a way to return to Him through the final sacrifice of Jesus Christ, the great High Priest (see John 3:16; Heb. 10:12-14). But our way of return to God must be accepted by us. We are His, but our choice is vital (see Rom. 10:9). God made us free and does not violate our freedom. As God has given us the gift of His Son, we must make a gift of ourselves to Him to experience His redemption. And what a marvelous redemption it is!

Our redeemer is Jesus Christ, "very God of very God," as one of the great creeds so elegantly states. Abraham knew of him, in a sense, through Melchizedek who was a type of Christ. Old Testament saints had faith in a coming Christ whom they could know, in a limited sense, through spiritual types God had provided for them. They saw more dimly than we, for in our time we have been privileged to know the person of Jesus Christ, both experientially and historically. The ancients were commended for their faith in what they hoped for and what they knew to be true but could not see (see Heb. 11:1,2).

What Redeemer Do You Seek?

Consider the three following statements. Put a "True" or "False" by each statement as it expresses your present belief.
1. Every person needs a savior whether he or she knows it or not.
2. Every person seeks redemption, whether he or she understands it or not.
3. Every person worships something, whether he or she realizes it or not.

The response to each of these statements, I believe, is true. People choose interesting saviors as objects of worship. Worship and the choice of a savior is a worldwide personal and cultural activity. That is, everyone, everywhere, in all times, regardless of background chooses a savior and an object of worship. Not only do people do so individually, but they do it corporately or nationally.

Arnold Toynbee, the British historian, says that every civilization that has ever existed has grown up, integrated itself, then chosen a savior to prevent its decline. In choosing a savior, Toynbee says, each civilization has picked one of four possibilities. The first is the savior he calls the *philosopher king*. This savior is a statement of belief and commitment to a high and lofty value that people have derived apart from God. Plato, the ancient philosopher, believed that such a savior was necessary to preserve ancient Greece. He thought that unless all people gave themselves seriously to philosophy of a humane sort, the state could not be preserved.

The second savior people seek is the *sword*. History is full of the terrors of people who have chosen the sword as their means of self-preservation. The Roman Empire, Hitler's Third Reich, Napoleon of France, to name a few, have lived and died by the sword.

The third savior is the *creative genius*. Nations have believed that by their power of inventiveness they can overcome both nature and their enemies and thus be able to preserve themselves. This is perhaps the savior chosen by highly technological societies, although one might think that the savior of the sword has been chosen as well in such cases.

The fourth is a *spiritual savior*. More than twenty major civilizations have come and gone in the known history of man. Most have chosen one of the first three saviors. Probably the longest continually surviving entity that has the basic characteristics of a civilization is the Christian Church. It has survived all its historical peers and is surviving yet. Although Toynbee apparently was not sure whether he prefered Buddhism or Christianity, he recognized the need of nations for a savior and that only a spiritual savior could fill this need.

People, like nations, are driven by their very natures to seek redemption in some form. No person goes merrily through life devoid of the impulse to seek a savior. The question is not whether people will or won't seek saviors, but whether they will choose the only one that can truly save, the eternal High Priest, Jesus Christ.

We all seek to be redeemed from our lostness. We have an innate need to find some organizing center for our lives. We are all keenly aware—unless we have been subjected to so much academic rationalization that we can't see our need—that we need someone or something greater than ourselves to find us, help us with our problem with guilt, give us meaning and justify our existence.

For some years, as a psychologist, I have been a student of personality organization. One of my favorite courses to teach is "Theory of Personality." Today there is no formal theory of personality that does not place ego at the center of human existence and experience. Self is king. Self can deal with guilt. Every theory constructs the personality so that the enhancement of self, of ego, is the primary psychological task of man. Self is god, and a poor and diminutive god it is. In the process of making ego god, every form of self-justification, self-gratification and self-enhancement has been tried. But failure is the inevitable result. Human life was made to organize itself around the person of Christ, empowered by the Holy Spirit, with ego as orbital and secondary. This is the reason the Bible describes Jesus by such terms as High Priest, Lord and King. He is primary; only He can save us and give our lives meaning. Why else do we have the scriptural admonition to "seek first his kingdom and his righteousness, and all these things will be given to you as well" (Matt. 6:33). By choosing Christ as Savior our needs are met completely. Because He is King and High Priest only He can accomplish our complete redemption.

The human drive for redemption of some sort, for some organizing center to worship is so dominant it consumes most of the energies of humankind. Current psychology has promoted the idea of the self-fulfilled, self-actualized life as the goal of human effort. This is clearly the god of the humanist and of those following New Age religions who have discarded any notion of a god outside of human invention. But the fact is that when a person puts God, in Christ, into the center of his or her life and experience, that person finds more fulfillment than if fulfillment is sought as an end in itself. Thus it is strange to an unbeliever that "whoever loses his life for my [Christ's] sake will find it" (Matt. 10:39). In contemporary psychological theory, and practice in secular society, this makes no sense whatsoever.

Some have tried to make moral uprightness their god and their redemption. Like the efforts of the Levitical and Aaronic priests their efforts fall short. They do not count for eternity (see Heb. 7:11,23,24). I once studied under a professor who as a youngster confessed Christian belief. But when he had received a generous humanist education, he set out to be as great a moral specimen as any Christian might be, but without the help of God. He discovered that he could be as good as any Christian in moral terms without going through the necessity of surrendering his life to the great High Priest. The result was that this professor was one of the most upstanding and truly caring men I have ever known. But his effort will fail when he meets the King. He cannot present himself as a worthy substitute for Christ (see John 14:6). He has chosen to play god in his own life and his morality has become a form of idolatry. He will have to say to God that he figured out his salvation his own way. But God is sovereign; He will have neither peer nor competitor. My professor will be a lost soul because he would not submit and accept the sacrifice God has provided by which he may be saved.

As you consider this lesson, think about the gods you may have sought in the past. Consider how they fell short of the sacrifice of Christ. What gods are your students being pressured to seek? Is it the god of fun, of fortune, sex, drugs, music, self-importance, Satan? God has gone to great lengths to assure us that only His redemption through Christ is sufficient. Through the ages God has made His redemption known through types and pictures in the Old Testament and completed that redemption through the sacrifice of His Son Jesus, our eternal High Priest. We are without rationalizations or excuse.

This Week's Teaching Plan

APPROACH TO THE WORD

APPROACH (3-5 minutes)

Materials needed: Coupons from your local newspaper (2 for 1 yogurt, discount off at a record store).

When students have gathered show the coupons and ask, **What do I need to do in order to use these coupons?** Allow responses from several students then say, **The process by which I exchange a coupon for a product or a service is called "redemption." Today we are going to talk about a different kind of redemption; we are going to look at how Jesus has made it possible for our lives to be redeemed from sin.**

ALTERNATE APPROACH (5-8 minutes)

Materials needed: Slips of colored paper—three pieces for each student; two different snacks such as doughnuts and fruit or popcorn; drinks.

Preparation: Set up a snack/drink table so that snacks are labeled with a price marked "2" and drinks are labeled with a price marked "1." Ask an adult leader to be in charge of accepting payment from students for snacks and drinks.

As students arrive, give each one three slips of colored paper. Direct students to the refreshments where they can redeem their slips of paper for munchies (snacks are worth two slips; drinks are worth one slip). Allow students to mingle until everyone has had a chance to redeem his or her slips of paper. Then gain students' attention and say, **The process by which you purchased your snacks is called "redemption." You exchanged or redeemed your slips of paper for the munchies. Today we are going to talk about a different kind of redemption; we are going to look at how Jesus has made it possible for our lives to be redeemed from sin.**

BIBLE EXPLORATION

EXPLORATION (30-40 minutes)

Materials needed: Session 4 Student Worksheet for each student, Post-it Notes.

Preparation: Write the following Scripture references on Post-its—one reference per note: Matthew 16:21; John 14:27 and 16:33; Hebrews 7:3,24; 1 John 2:1.

Step 1 (1-3 minutes): Introduce today's Bible study by briefly summarizing Genesis, chapters 12 and 13. Mention the following points:

- God directed Abraham to leave his home and travel to a land He set aside for Abraham and his family. God also promised to make Abraham's descendants into a great nation, blessed by Him. When Abraham left his nephew Lot went with him.
- During his travels Abraham went to Egypt to avoid a famine.
- When Abraham's household left Egypt, he was quite wealthy and his household was quite large. Later, Abraham and Lot parted ways and Lot settled near the city of Sodom.

Step 2 (10-12 minutes): Direct students to open their Bibles to Genesis, chapter 14. Distribute the Session 4 Student Worksheets and ask volunteers to share in reading the verses listed on their worksheets. As the verses are read, lead a discussion of the verses using the following outline and material from the Teacher's Bible Study. Encourage students to take notes on their worksheets as the discussion progresses.

Genesis 14:1-16

- Give a brief review of the events surrounding Lot's capture and subsequent rescue by Abraham.
- Mention that Abraham's household included 318 trained fighting men who protected the large number of livestock and peo-

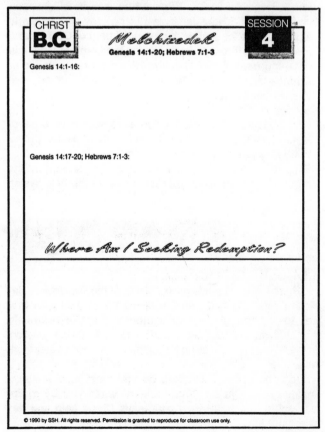

CHRIST **B.C.**

Melchizedek
Genesis 14:1-20; Hebrews 7:1-3

SESSION **4**

Genesis 14:1-16:

Genesis 14:17-20; Hebrews 7:1-3:

Where Am I Seeking Redemption?

ple. In a sense, Abraham's household was a wandering nation with sufficient influence to command respect from neighboring kings.

Genesis 14:17-20; Hebrews 7:1-3

• **What do these verses tell us about Melchizedek?** List students' responses on the board or overhead. Responses should include: king of Salem (later called Jerusalem), priest of God Most High, king of righteousness, king of peace, honored by Abraham, no known genealogy, a priest forever.

• Mention that there are varying opinions about whether Melchizedek was an actual historical person or a manifestation of Jesus Christ in human form. (This type of manifestation is called a "theophany." God's appearance to Abraham in Gen. 18:1-15 is considered as a theophany.)

Step 3 (12-15 minutes): Say, **Let's compare what we know about Melchizedek with what the Bible says about Jesus.** Ask the students to whom you gave references written on Post-its to read their verses as you direct. Discuss each passage as it is read using the following outline. As appropriate, refer to the list of Melchizedek's characteristics on board or overhead.

1 John 2:1

• Compare this verse to Hebrews 7:2 and Genesis 14:18. Ask, **How does Jesus fulfill the meaning of Melchizedek's name?** Then say, **To be righteous means to be without sin.**

John 14:27; 16:33

• Compare the meaning of Melchizedek's name in Hebrews 7:2 to these verses. **What things trouble people's hearts and prevent them from experiencing peace?** (Sin, pain caused by other's sin.) **Why is Jesus able to provide people with peace?** (He is stronger than sin; He has conquered death and is more powerful than anything in the world.)

Matthew 16:21

• **In what city was Melchizedek king? What happened to Jesus in Jerusalem?**

• Read Revelation 21:2-4. **What future events will happen concerning the New Jerusalem?** Then say, **Jerusalem is significant as the setting for the fulfillment of God's plans for the world through Jesus Christ, the Lamb of God. It is only appropriate that Melchizedek—a represenatative of Christ—be the king of Salem, the Old Testament city that later became Jerusalem.**

Hebrews 7:3,24

• **God declared that Jesus is a "priest forever in the order of Melchizedek" (v. 17). What characteristic of Jesus' priesthood is given in this verse?** (It is forever, eternal.)

• Explain the difference between the Levitical priesthood and the order of Melchizedek by reading verses 11-25. Ask, **Which priesthood is superior? For what reasons?** (Melchizedek's order is powerful, eternal, perfect, permanent, able to save those who come to God through Jesus; the Levitical priesthood is imperfect, weak, useless and unable to save anyone.) (Note: If you do not choose to complete the Optional Step 4, move to Step 5.)

Optional Step 4 (3-5 minutes): Share Lloyd Ahlem's comments from the Teacher's Bible Study section titled "Complete Redemption" that Jesus as our High priest is a picture of redemption. Explain this picture by telling the *Little Boat Twice Owned.* Summarize the application of the story by saying, **God created us and cares for us. Because we were given free wills, we chose to run away from God and become separated from Him. Then we become bound by sin. God, through the death of His Son Jesus, paid the price to redeem us from our bondage to sin. The Bible says all people have sinned and need redemption** (see Rom. 3:23).

Step 5 (7-10 minutes): If you did not complete the Optional Step 4 say, **Jesus as our High Priest is a picture of redemption. Jesus paid the price to purchase us from sin by sacrificing His life.** Then reread Hebrews 7:25. **Who does this verse say can take advantage of the redemption Jesus has already purchased?** (Those who come to God through Christ.)

Move the class into groups of three to five students each. Say, **Even though Jesus has provided a complete, perfect way to clean sin out of our lives, some people try to find salvation from sin in other ways. As a group, list on the backs of your worksheets ways people try to escape sin without Christ's help.** Allow 3-5 minutes for groups to work. Then compile a master list of students' ideas on the board or overhead. The list may include: doing good or being moral, perfect church attendance, numbing guilt with drugs, using money to buy acceptance of your sins from others, expect others to straighten out your life for you, seek a religion or philosophy of life that will say your sin is acceptable or not your fault, fight with people who criticize your actions, have good academic performance to look acceptable to yourself and others.

Summarize students' work by saying, **Every person seeks to escape the sin in his or her life in some way. Some turn to Christ; others don't. What is it about these ways of escape you've listed that don't measure up to the redemption Jesus offers?**

Move to the Conclusion by saying, **Just as the Levitical priesthood's attempts to save the Israelites were weak, and inadequate, so our attempts to save ourselves do not take away our problem with sin. Jesus' priesthood is eternal and is based on "the power of an indestructible life" (Heb. 7:16). Because of this Jesus is able to save us from sin.**

CONCLUSION & DECISION

CONCLUSION (3-5 minutes)

Refer to the list made during Step 5 of the Exploration. Say, **Both Christians and non-Christians try to deal with their day-to-day struggle with sin without asking Christ for help.** Ask students to write their responses to the following questions in the "Where Am I Seeking Redemption?" section of their worksheets (emphasize that you will not be collecting their papers): **Which one of these escapes do you most tend to run to instead of to Christ? What happens when you try to find escape in that way? How can Jesus Christ help you deal with your sin?**

Close in prayer asking God to help each student in his or her struggle with sin. Pray that those who are Christians will rely on their relationship with Christ to deal with sin. Ask that those who are not Christians will consider asking Christ to come into their lives and deal with their sin. Be available after class to talk with students who want to find out more about redemption in Christ.

Encourage students to read chapter 4 in the student paperback *Christ B.C.* The readings in this chapter explore the theme "redemption."

Abraham and Isaac

KEY VERSE

"The angel of the Lord called to Abraham from heaven a second time and said, 'I swear by myself, declares the Lord, that because you have done this and have not withheld your son, your only son, I will surely bless you.'" Genesis 22:15,16,17

"He who did not spare his own Son, but gave him up for us all—how will he not also, along with him, graciously give us all things?" Romans 8:32

BIBLICAL BASIS

Genesis 12:1-4; 18:9-14; 21:5; 22:1-18; Luke 2:30-35; John 3:16,17; 19:17; Romans 5:6-8; 6:23; 8:32; Hebrews 4:14-16; 9:14; 11:17-19; 10:21,22

FOCUS OF THE SESSION

Just as God provided a suitable sacrifice to take Isaac's place on the altar, so God provided His own Son Jesus through whom all of our needs, beginning with the remission of our sins, are met.

AIMS OF THIS SESSION

You and your students will have accomplished the purpose of this Bible study session if you can:
- IDENTIFY God's provision of a ram as a substitutionary sacrifice for Isaac;
- DISCUSS how Jesus' sacrifice on the cross is God's provision of forgiveness for sin;
- WRITE your personal response to Jesus' sacrifice for your sins.

Teacher's Bible Study

The Significance of the Improbable

My graduate training emphasized the study of statistics and probability. Our professors asked us to calculate the chances of the occurrence of specific human events and behaviors. When behavior deviated from normal probability, we then ventured to explain its occurrence. Improbable behavior was seen as significant and therefore meaningful.

One evening a fellow student in a graduate seminar told of a highly improbable student he had taught in an American military academy. My colleague described a young man who was the most accomplished member of his high school class. He could play football with the best of athletes and was eventually given the distinction of All-American for his athletic achievements in college. To be appointed to a military academy meant that he had the recommendations of mentors who knew him well. They described him as highly gifted in a number of ways. He was an excellent musician. He could play several instruments with sufficient proficiency to qualify for a chair in a symphony orchestra. He was also socially adept. He was elected commandant of the corps— the equivalent to student body president. After four years of military school he graduated as the top academic student. He

was then selected as a Rhodes Scholar and studied in England. (A Rhodes scholarship is an honor only conferred upon the highest achievers.) While in England he distinguished himself as a rugby player, a game he had not played much previously. Later, while on active military duty in Southeast Asia, he was decorated for valor while in combat. His outstanding record earned him a command post in the Pentagon. In the late 1950s a national magazine recorded his story and he became one of America's heroes.

When the story was finished, we were sitting in amazement at what we had just heard. Such an improbable human being had to be regarded as significant. We began calculating the chances that another person with as many aptitudes could emerge in a country the size of the United States. Knowing the approximate rarity of several of the aptitudes this man possessed, we could do some reasonable guessing. Our estimate, as a class, was that only once in about 300 years could a person with as many superior gifts appear in an American university. No wonder his story received our undivided attention!

An Improbable God

When I apply my mathematical mind to the great events of Scripture, I find that

God has made Himself known in most improbable ways. No man, however gifted, could duplicate what God has done. His actions, therefore, are significant and noteworthy.

The selection of the experiences of Abraham to serve as typical of the salvation story is a significant, improbable act of God. Most of us begin our careers in our 20s. We prepare ourselves by schooling and by the normal processes of maturing. Then we set out, having first assessed what our most likely chance of success will be in a given endeavor. Extremely rare is the individual who begins when life is well advanced. True to God's character, He uses an improbability such as this to get our attention, making it clear that only He is directing events. Look at Abraham. In Genesis 12:1-4 we learn that Abraham was 75 years old when God first promised to make him the father of a great nation. What a time to set out to become a great nation! Although Abraham would live another hundred years, one of his age was usually well-established in life with a household of children. Yet Abraham was childless, and a man without descendants would not seem to be a likely candidate for fathering a great nation.

But the improbabilities continue. Perhaps God had a sense of humor to tell

Sarah, who "was past the age of child-bearing" (18:11), that she was going to have her first child. Furthermore, God allowed 25 years to pass from the time of His first promise in Genesis 12:2 to the birth of Isaac in Genesis 21:5. (Sarah was ninety years old when Isaac was born, see 17:17). Imagine how she felt during all those years. When she heard the news in Genesis 18:10-12 she was so surprised she could only laugh. How ridiculous it seemed that an old woman was going to have a baby!

I worked for a number of years in a retirement center and I can just imagine one of our residents coming to breakfast and announcing that the first baby ever born in our facility was on its way. There wouldn't be a believer in the dining room. Her announcement would be chalked up as a goofy symptom of senility!

But God is improbable. His work is characterized by serendipity. No one duplicates God. He has no peer. Abraham in all his improbable experiences was encountering the nature and character of God. And true to that nature and character, God provided Abraham with the promised son. Abraham named his son Isaac (see 21:3), which means, "he laughs"—perhaps a warm reflection upon the improbability of his existence.

At this point God's immediate promise of a son had been fulfilled. It seemed that now nature could take charge and eventually the promised nation would be procreated. Yet that would be too predictable; it would push the evidence of God's sovereignty into the background. So God commanded that Abraham's son of promise be sacrificed as a burnt offering on an altar on a particular mountain (see 22:1,2).

Immediately Abraham responded to God's command. "Early the next morning Abraham got up and saddled his donkey. He took with him two of his servants and his son Isaac. When he had cut enough wood for the burnt offering, he set out for the place God had told him about" (22:3). Abraham moved decisively and obediently. In spite of the apparent conflict between God's promise that was to be fulfilled in Isaac and God's command to sacrifice Isaac, Abraham trusted that God knew what He was doing. Hebrews 11:19 states, "Abraham reasoned that God could raise the dead, and figuratively speaking, he did receive Isaac back from death." Another reason God's command must have seemed odd to Abraham was that it was out of character for God. God had never called for a human sacrifice. In Leviticus 20:2 and Deuteronomy 18:10-13 we learn that the practice of sacrificing

children to the pagan god Molech was detestable to God. Yet Abraham, knowing God's true character, trusted that God's purpose was holy.

I have two fine sons, both now adults and men of faith in Christ. They are a joy to me as a loving father. I can scarcely imagine committing such an act as God commanded Abraham to carry out. It is absolutely beyond my comprehension. I am most certain that I could never bring myself to Abraham's position, to the point of raising his knife over his beloved son of promise. When my human senses react to the story, I conclude that either Jehovah is a God beyond my comprehension or He is the most despotic and unfair being I can imagine. There is no middle ground. My lack of comprehension is the obvious answer to this dilemma. Yet Abraham did not rely on a common-sense analysis of God's command. Abraham saw God's command through the eyes of faith and not knowing the outcome reasoned that God's command would not cancel His promise that would be fulfilled through Isaac.

A Type of Christ

The element that gives purpose to God's seemingly absurd command to sacrifice Isaac is Christ. When we see these events as typical of God's sacrifice of His only beloved Son, our understanding of God's ways is enriched. It is possible that God uses improbable means such as types so that we will not rationalize that His actions are just another invention of the religious minds of groping people. No mere man could have claimed to be God in ways Christ has done. The odds are beyond possibility. The venture into Christian faith is a way unlike any other because it is orchestrated by God, not man. To ultimately believe in Christ is an adventure and a continuing intellectual and spiritual experience different from any other you have had or ever will take.

Abraham's experience is evidence of the remarkable way in which God works. Let's consider how Abraham, an improbable progenitor, is chosen by God who in turn chooses to work in unsuspecting ways to accomplish an absolutely remarkable purpose. Abraham's experience is presented by God as an Old Testament prototype of a New Testament Christ. Let's enumerate the ways in which Abraham's story is like the Savior.

1. Abraham was chosen by God (see Genesis 12:1-4); God initiated the action. Just as God freely chose to provide His own Son, He freely chose Abraham to model the gift of salvation to come through Christ. God initiated His covenant with

Abraham and He initiates reconciliation with sinful man through His Son (see 2 Cor. 5:18).

In human relationships we do just the opposite. If a breach of trust has come between one of us and another, it is assumed that the offending party will initiate the reconciliation. The offended one waits for the other to move. This is also the case in many other religions as well. Most religions believe that man has morally and spiritually offended their deities. These religions require some move on the part of the offender to initiate reconciliation. Thus we have the motive behind the sacrifices, rituals, prayer wheels, superstitions, self-abasement and atonement efforts these religions promote. But in Christian faith, God does the unusual. He makes the move toward reconciliation. Romans 5:8 illustrates this by saying, "But God demonstrates his own love for us in this: While we were still sinners, Christ died for us." Many of us have thought of ourselves as hunting for God, only to discover that He has already found us and is waiting for our response of obedience (see Luke 19:10).

2. Abraham received the promise from God, but he had to act upon it to personally experience its fulfillment. If Abraham had not willingly obeyed and acted upon God's command to sacrifice Isaac, God's promise to make Abraham's decendants into a great nation would still stand. But by obeying, Abraham was able to enjoy first-hand the fulfillment of that promise. God's personal response to Abraham's trust was, "I will surely bless you . . . . all nations on earth will be blessed, because you have obeyed me" (Gen. 22:17,18). Abraham also had the privilege of seeing Isaac married to Rebekah (see Gen. 24). Through this union, which was also engineered by God, Abraham had the assurance in his final days that God would continue to be faithful to His promise.

We, too, have received a promise. It is the promise that God's grace, His sacrifice of Jesus for our sins, is adequate for our need for reconciliation with God (see John 3:36). If we ignore the promise, God does not withdraw the opportunity to experience His grace, but we cut ourselves off from personally experiencing the fulfillment of His promise in our lives.

3. Abraham and Sarah learned that God's agenda cannot be rushed or manipulated by human efforts. When the years began to pass without a son arriving, Sarah tried to help matters along. As was common practice in her day, she arranged for Abraham to father a son by another woman, then claimed that son as her own (see Gen. 16:1-4). But this was not the

son of promise (see Gal 4:22,23); this was the son resulting from human efforts to make God look good and probably to spare herself some embarrassment. In the same way, redemption cannot be provided by human effort (see Eph. 2:8,9). We cannot improve on God's sacrifice of Jesus and find salvation by any other means than through Christ (see Acts 4:12). No human effort, no matter how noble, will replace divine action. God is totally responsible for providing for our redemption. We cannot earn it by our efforts, we must accept it by submitting in repentance and faith to Jesus (see Acts 3:19). Hebrews 12:2 describes Jesus as "the author and perfecter of our faith."

4. The place God directed Abraham to take Isaac is typical of Calvary where God's own Son was sacrificed. We know that the region of Moriah (see Gen. 22:2) is in the same vicinity as Calvary. Second Chronicles 3:1 indicates that the location of Solomon's Temple in Jerusalem is on Mount Moriah. The Temple and the traditional location of Calvary are fairly close in proximity. The point is that Moriah, like Calvary was a place of promise. It was located in the heart of the land that was promised to Abraham's decendants. As such the location is an indication that God fulfills His promises to His people. God provided a substitute for Isaac (see Gen. 22:13), and for us on Calvary God provided a Lamb that can remove all the moral and spiritual blemishes in our lives (see John 1:29; Rev. 5:9,12). For those who accept God's provision of Jesus, God regards us as whole and clean, with the status of "son" (see Gal. 3:26). His own provision makes up for our lack of ability to call ourselves members of His family.

5. God's covenant with Abraham is typical of the new covenant He has made with us through Christ (see Heb. 10:15-18). A covenant is a promise that is valid and exists whether the other party or person keeps the agreement or not. In a contract, the agreement ends when one party does not honor the contract. Christians hopefully live in covenant with one another. Christian marriage is a covenant, not a contract. Church fellowship and membership is a covenant, not a contract. Thus God's covenant with Abraham is a model both for the relationship of Christ to His Church and our relationships with each other.

6. Abraham's story is a type of Christ in many ways. The type that you will be focusing on with your students describes how God's provision of a substitute for Isaac on the altar is like God's provision of His own Son on the cross. Abraham did not withold his only son from God (see Gen. 22:12). In the same way God gave His only Son for our sake (see John 3:16). God provided a ram as a substitute for Isaac on the altar. "Abraham looked up and there in a thicket he saw a ram caught by its horns. He went over and took the ram and sacrificed it as a burnt offering instead of his son" (Gen. 22:13). God also provided a substitute for us—His Son Jesus Christ (see Rom. 8:32). Because of our sins a penalty must be paid. "For the wages of sin is death," states Romans 6:23. We deserve death as a result of our rebellion against God. But God, in His grace, provides a way for us through faith in Him to have our death sentence turned into a sentence of eternal life. Verse 23 also states how God has made this possible for us: "But the gift of God is eternal life in Christ Jesus our Lord." Because of His great love, God gave His Son to die on the cross in our place.

Related to this illustration of God's love is the illustration of how Abraham and Isaac's faith is typical of the person who puts his or her trust in God's promise fulfilled through Christ. Faith in Christ trusts before it has full understanding. We trust in advance of understanding. In western schools we are taught to believe only after we have experimented and figured things out. Not so with Abraham and Isaac. Isaac participated in the preparation of the offering of himself without knowing the personal consequences. He willingly carried the wood for the burnt offering (see Gen. 22:6), and when he asked where the lamb was that was to be sacrificed and Abraham responded, "God himself will provide the lamb for the burnt offering, my son" (Gen. 22:8). This was enough for Isaac. He trusted without fully understanding.

There is much about the nature of God and His will that I don't understand. But to some degree I have learned to let my intellect catch up with my faith. When I am short of answers I can say with confidence, "God will provide." If I wait until all the evidence is in before I believe, I will never believe. So it was with Abraham and Isaac. They acted ahead of God's provision. In fact, the Hebrew name for God, *Jehovah-Jireh*, used in Genesis 22:14 means "the Lord will provide." When you and I follow Abraham's example, we stop painting ourselves into intellectual corners limited to our meager mental aptitudes.

We have seen that Abraham's experience is typical of many aspects of the salvation story fulfilled in the New Testament through Jesus' death. These parallels between the Old and New Testaments are amazing. They can serve to strengthen the faith of your students in a God who is actively pursuing a relationship of reconciliation and trust with each one and who is able to meet their individual needs.

This Week's Teaching Plan

APPROACH TO THE WORD

APPROACH (4-5 minutes)

Materials needed: Index cards.

Distribute index cards then say, **If God were to ask you to give up three things (possession, person, activity), what three things would be the most difficult for you to part with?** Direct students to write their responses on index cards. After 2-3 minutes ask volunteers to share any or all of the things listed on their cards.

Move to the Exploration by saying, **In today's Bible study we will look at an event in which God asked Abraham to give up something that was very important to him. We will also look at how this event is a picture of an other event that would happen more than 2,000 years later.**

BIBLE EXPLORATION (35-45 minutes)

Materials needed: Session 5 Student Worksheet for each student.

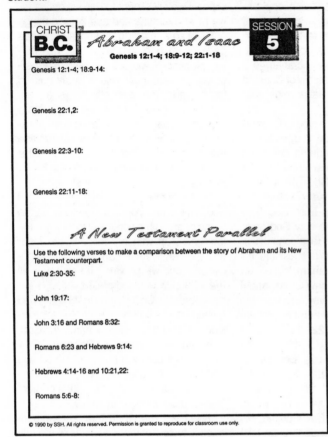

Preparation: Letter the question and assignment from Step 3 on the chalkboard or on an overhead transparency. Cover them from students' view until you reach Step 3.

Step 1 (3-5 minutes): Share the story about the national hero from the section of the Teacher's Bible Study titled "The Significance of the Improbable." Also mention the estimate by Lloyd Ahlem and his classmates of the probability of such a person appearing again in an American university. Allow a minute or two for students to share improbable events from their own experience or that they have heard about.

Move to Step 2 by saying, **Improbable or impossible-seeming events grab our attention and are looked upon as significant. Scripture is filled with improbable things God has done. God often uses the improbable as a means to get us to pay attention to what He has to say. Let's look at God's improbable actions in the life of Abraham.**

Step 2 (12-15 minutes): Distribute the Student Worksheets and direct students to open their Bibles to Genesis, chapter 12. Ask volunteers to share in reading aloud the verses listed in the "Abraham and Isaac" section of their worksheets. As the verses are read, lead a discussion of the verses using the following outline and information from the Teacher's Bible Study. Encourage students to take notes on their worksheets as the discussion progresses.

Genesis 12:1-4; 18:9-14
- What did God promise Abraham and Sarah?
- Mention that Abraham was 75 years old when God made these promises.

- Read Genesis 21:5. Ask, **What is improbable about this event? What does this improbability tell you about God's involvement in what happened?** (Only God could have caused it to happen; it was beyond man's capabilities.) Mention that Sarah was past the age of child bearing (see 18:11).

Genesis 22:1,2
- **According to common sense, why would Abraham have reason to question what God asked him to do?** (Isaac was his only son through whom God had said He was going to keep His promise to Abraham; Isaac's death would seem contradictory to God's promise; also mention that sacrificing human beings is detestable to God—see Deut. 18:10-13.)

Genesis 22:3-10
- **How did Abraham respond to God's command to sacrifice Isaac?** (He immediately obeyed the command.)
- Read Hebrews 11:17-19. Ask, **Why wasn't Abraham hesitant to obey God?**

Genesis 22:11-18
- **Why did God test Abraham?** (See v. 12.)
- **What did God provide on the mountain?** (See vv. 13,14.)
- **What promises did God make to Abraham in verses 17,18?**
- **What was God's response to Abraham's actions?** (God commended Abraham for his obedience and God reaffirmed His promise to make Abraham's descendants into a great nation—see vv. 16-18.)

Step 3 (10-12 minutes): Move the class into groups of four to five students. (If you have a small number of students in your class, group them in pairs or trios.) Reveal the following question and assignment you wrote on the board or overhead before class and read them out loud.
1. The story of Abraham offering Isaac as a sacrifice is a picture of what New Testament event?
2. List the details from the story of Abraham and Isaac that foreshadow New Testament events.

Direct groups to answer the question and complete the assignment using the verses listed in the "A New Testament Parallel" section of their worksheets and the story in Genesis 22:16-18 as a basis for their comparison of the two events.

Step 4 (5 minutes): Regather into the larger group and ask for responses from groups. List the details students identified. Be sure the list includes the following: Isaac's birth was engineered by God/Jesus' birth came about by God's acting; Isaac carried the wood for his own sacrifice/Jesus carried the cross; Abraham willingly offered Isaac as a sacrifice to God/God willingly offered Jesus as a sacrifice for our sins; God provided the ram as a substitute for Isaac on the altar/God provided Jesus to die in our place on the cross; through Isaac all nations would be blessed/through Jesus all people can approach God and find forgiveness; God initiated His covenant with Abraham/He initiates our reconciliation with Him through Jesus' death on the cross. Share any additional information from the Teacher's Bible Study section titled "A Type of Christ."

Step 5 (5-8 minutes): Say, **The Hebrew name used for God in this story of Abraham and Isaac is** *Jehovah-Jirah* **(Gen. 22:14). This name means literally, "the Lord will provide." Our study of this event has shown us that it is typical of Jesus' sacrifice on the cross. What does Jesus' sacrifice tell us about God's concern for our needs? What basic need**

of ours can be met through Jesus' death? Allow time for students to share their responses to these questions. Point out that Jesus' death on the cross shows us that God cares enough about us to sacrifice His best, His only Son Jesus, to provide for our need for forgiveness of sin. It also shows that He is individually concerned about every need in our lives.

CONCLUSION & DECISION

CONCLUSION (8-10 minutes)

Materials needed: Stationery, envelopes.

Read John 3:16,17 and Romans 5:8 to your students. Then distribute stationery and envelopes. Say, **Write a letter to God telling Him how you feel about His provision of His only Son, Jesus Christ, as a sacrifice for our sins. Then tell Him one thing you would like to do to express your feelings to Him about this sacrifice.** Give students several minutes to write their thoughts. If students need help thinking of actions, suggest some of the following: write a song of praise to Him for His provision; accept His provision by asking forgiveness for your sins; consider becoming a Christian; show love to others who need to know about Jesus. Say, **Keep your letter in your Bible as a reminder of Jesus' sacrifice for your sins and of your response to His sacrifice.** Encourage students to follow through on the response they have planned.

Close in a prayer of thanks for Jesus' sacrifice on the cross. Optional: Close by singing an appropriate song of praise. Be available after class to talk with any students who want to know more about Jesus' sacrifice for our sins. For help in presenting the gospel to your students refer to the article "Presenting Christ to High School Student" on p. 9.

Encourage students to read chapter 5 of the student paperback *Christ B.C.* The readings in this chapter explore the theme "provision."

NOTES:

Joseph

KEY VERSE

"Joseph said to his brothers . . . 'God sent me ahead of you to preserve for you a remnant on earth and to save your lives by a great deliverance.'" Genesis 45:4,7

"For God so loved the world that he gave his one and only Son, that whoever believes in him shall not perish but have eternal life. For God did not send his Son into the world to condemn the world, but to save the world through him." John 3:16,17

BIBLICAL BASIS

Genesis 37:1-36; 39:1–50:26; Matthew 3:17; 4:1; 26:14-16; 28:18; Luke 23:20-25,32,33,39-43; John 3:16,17; 6:35; 12:27,28; 18:37; Acts 2:24; 4:12; Colossians 1:22; Hebrews 4:14,15; 1 John 1:9

FOCUS OF THE SESSION

Joseph, like Jesus, was obedient to God because he knew that God was using his circumstances to accomplish His holy purposes. Today we can be obedient to God with the confidence that God will use our daily experiences to fulfill His ultimate goals.

AIMS OF THIS SESSION

You and your students will have accomplished the purpose of this Bible study session if you can:
- COMPARE Joseph's obedience to God to Jesus' obedience to God;
- IDENTIFY the results or rewards of being obedient to God, especially in difficult or hard to understand circumstances;
- PLAN one way to respond obediently to God in a specific situation you may encounter this week.

Teacher's Bible Study

One fascinating story in the Old Testament is that of Joseph (see Gen. 37—50). It can be read easily in one sitting and I strongly suggest that you do so. This story is a picture of the grace of God operating in spite of, and because of, circumstances. Neither the conditions of the day, nor the politics of the time, nor the unruly behavior of individuals could thwart the will of God in carrying out His purpose in this segment of history or in any period of time.

Joseph and His Brothers

Joseph and his brothers each had personality traits that, in certain circumstances and relationships, would cause trouble for them. Yet God used the conflicts between these personalities to accomplish His will. We can gain some insight into these traits by reading about Jacob's last hours when he described his sons and gave his last blessing and inheritance to them (see Gen. 49).

Jacob described Reuben as "turbulent as the waters" (v. 4). He demoted Rueben from his position as firstborn because he had slept with one of his father's wives. Simeon and Levi were two of a kind; Jacob described them as "violent" and as men

who "have killed men in their anger and hamstrung oxen as they pleased . . . their anger, so fierce, and their fury, so cruel!" (vv. 5-7). When one of their sisters was raped by a son of a neighboring king, the brothers took vengeance into their own hands, entered the king's city and slaughtered every man there (see Gen. 34). On the other hand, Joseph is described as "a fruitful vine near a spring" (Gen. 49:22) and Judah as one who will be praised and honored by his brothers (see v. 8). Here Judah was given the position of firstborn that was previously held by Reuben. Issachar was described as a strong beast who willingly served with vigor (see vv. 14,15). The story of Joseph illustrates the explosive, unpredictable combination this melting pot of personalities made.

Joseph, the Improbable Survivor

Like the story of Abraham and Isaac, we learn about the improbability of God who likes to do impossible things. God took the unstable environment in which Jacob's family members coexisted and gave glory to His name as Sovereign Lord. The key in this story that illustrates God's sovereignty is Joseph.

In some ways Joseph seems to have been an unlikely candidate to survive all that befell him. Genesis 37:3 says that Jacob "loved Joseph more than any of his other sons, because he had been born to him in his old age." Joseph was the favorite son, with 10 jealous older brothers (see v. 4). He was doted upon by his father and given a "richly ornamented robe" (v. 3) as a sign of his father's favor—a sign that evoked spite from his brothers. He was also the son of Jacob's favorite wife, Rachel (see 29:30; 30:22-24).

We see in chapter 37 of Genesis that Joseph had the habit of irritating his brothers, and even his father, by sharing his dreams with them. In each of the dreams Joseph shared, he was placed in a position of authority over them. In his first dream, Joseph told his brothers that all of them "were binding sheaves of grain out in the field when suddenly my sheaf rose and stood upright, while your sheaves gathered around mine and bowed down to it" (v. 7). As a result of Joseph's tactlessness, his brothers hated him all the more. And as if his brother's hatred did not convince him to hold his tongue, Joseph shared a second dream that even earned a rebuke by his father (see vv. 9,10). Although Joseph's dreams accurately described his future, his lack of tact in sharing his dreams simply made his home situation more unstable.

One day Joseph was sent by his father to see how the sheep tending was going (see vv. 12-14). Unfortunately he was wearing the special coat given him by his father Jacob (see v. 23). His brothers saw him coming in the distance, and by the time Joseph reached them, they had formulated a plan to get rid of him (see v. 18). They grabbed him, threw him into a dry cistern and when a caravan came by, they sold him as a slave (see vv. 24-28). The brothers reported to Jacob that Joseph had been killed by wild animals and Jacob mourned Joseph for many days (see vv. 31-34).

Now what are the chances that a protected child, beloved by his father and mother, can survive as a slave sold to travelers going to a strange land? Humanly speaking, we can doubt that any chance exists at all—at least not without leaving deep emotional scars. Yet we learn through Joseph's many experiences in Egypt that he prospered materially as well as emotionally and spiritually.

Upon reaching Egypt, Joseph was sold to Potiphar, who was one of Pharaoh's officials (see 39:1). Many would have been paralyzed by the adjustment to life as a slave, but "the Lord was with Joseph and he prospered" (v. 2). Verse three says that Potiphar recognized that the Lord was with Joseph, giving him success. As a result, Potiphar put Joseph "in charge of his household, and he entrusted to his care everything he owned" (v. 4).

While in Potiphar's service, Joseph was repeatedly tempted sexually by Potiphar's wife (see vv. 6,7,10). Joseph honored God through his actions and words by resisting her and acknowledging her proposition as a sin against God (see v. 9). Joseph's obedience landed him in the king's prison (see v. 20)—a risk he was willing to take to remain faithful to God. At this time Joseph's circumstances seemed grim. But God used—engineered—Joseph's circumstances in several ways. First, by removing Joseph from Potiphar's service, God opened the way for greater responsibility and blessing for Joseph in the service of Pharaoh. Word of Joseph's gift of interpreting dreams, which he exercised in prison, would earn him an audience with Pharaoh. After interpreting Pharaoh's dream concerning a coming famine in the land, Joseph was installed as second-in-command over Egypt (see 41:9-45).

Through Joseph's new position, God provided a way for the preservation of the lives of those who came to Egypt for help during the predicted famine. Among these people would be Joseph's brothers (see 42:1-3). God used this situation to set the scene for reconciliation and reunion between Joseph and his family.

Eventually, Joseph's family would join him in Egypt (see 46:5,6). During these years we see Joseph as the leader of the family. His high level of maturity is evident when we look at the conversation between Joseph and his brothers following Jacob's death. The brothers were still worrying that Joseph would someday take revenge upon them for their past cruelty. They had not matured to a point that they could accept Joseph's forgiveness and see God's working in all of their circumstances. "When Joseph's brothers saw that their father was dead, they said, 'What if Joseph holds a grudge against us and pays us back for all the wrongs we did to him?'" (50:15). The brother's sent word to Joseph, expressing their fear. Joseph's response to his brothers illustrates his maturity: "When their message came to him, Joseph wept . . . . Joseph said to them, 'Don't be afraid. Am I in the place of God? You intended to harm me, but God intended it for good to accomplish what is now being done, the saving of many lives. So then, don't be afraid. I will provide for you and your children.' And he reassured them and spoke kindly to them" (vv. 17,19-21). Joseph spoke to them as a parent calming the fears of a child.

What made the difference? Why did Joseph prosper in so many ways instead of perishing? The answer lies in Joseph's faithfulness to God and trust in God's sovereignty. Joseph knew, at each step in his life, that God would use his circumstances to accomplish His purposes. We find an illustration of this when we read in Genesis 45:7 about Joseph's reunion with his brothers: "God sent me ahead of you to preserve for you a remnant on earth and to save your lives by a great deliverance."

Joseph as a Type of Christ

It is in Joseph's obedience to God and God's engineering of his circumstances that we also see a type of Christ. Joseph is probably the most Christlike of any Old Testament personality. The parallels between the two are too numerous to go into detail on all points, but as you spend time studying Joseph with your students, encourage them to suggest as many points of comparison as they can. Let's survey several of these points:

1. Joseph was loved by his father and lived in fellowship and a position of honor with his father in Hebron (see Gen. 37:3). Jesus was beloved by God the Father and lived in heaven in a position of honor and fellowship with God before being sent to earth. (See Matt. 3:17; John 17:5.)

2. Joseph declared openly his brother's sins, then shared his dreams declaring his future exalted position over them. In response, he received hate from his brothers. (See Gen. 37:2,5-11.) Jesus testified against the sins of men and declared His future exaltation. In response many of His listeners hated Him (see Matt. 23:30,31; Mark 8:31; John 15:18).

3. Joseph's brothers plotted against him and sold him for 20 pieces of silver. (See Gen. 37:19-28.) The Jewish leaders plotted against Jesus and Judas betrayed Jesus to them for 30 pieces of silver (see Matt. 26:14-16; Luke 20:19).

4. While serving in Potiphar's house, Joseph did not yield to Potiphar's wife's temptations and was obedient to God (see Gen. 39:7-10). He said to her, "How then could I do such a wicked thing and sin against God?" (v. 9). Jesus was tempted by Satan in the wilderness. Jesus did not yield to Satan but rather used God's Word in resisting him (see Matt. 4:1-11).

5. Joseph was wrongly accused by Potiphar's wife and thrown into a dungeon. There he counseled two other prisoners. One prisoner died, the other lived (see Gen. 39:19,20; 40:1-22). Jesus was falsely sentenced then nailed to a cross between two criminals. One criminal gained eternal life through Christ; the other cursed Him and died (see Matt. 26:59-65; Luke 23:32,33,39-43).

6. Joseph was raised from the dungeon of death by Pharaoh and was given all power in Egypt. Throughout his time in the dungeon, Joseph was helped by God and he prospered (see Gen. 39:20b-23; 41:14,41-43). Jesus was raised from the dead by the Lord Almighty. He was then given all power in heaven and earth (see Matt. 28:18; Eph. 1:18-23).

7. Joseph was acknowledged as savior and ruler over his brothers (see Gen. 47:25). Jesus is acknowledged as Savior and Lord by his followers and will someday be acknowledged as Lord by all people (see Luke 24:50-53; John 20:24-28; Acts 2:36; Phil. 2:9-11).

8. Joseph sustained the physical lives of the people who came to him for food (see Gen. 41:55-57). Jesus provides eternal life to all people who come to Him in faith (see John 3:16; 6:35; Acts 4:12; 1 John 5:11,12).

9. When Joseph's brothers admitted their sin against him and humbled them-

selves before him, Joseph forgave them and joyfully received them back into relationship with him as brothers (see Gen. 44:16—45:14). To all who confess their sins to Christ, He provides forgiveness. We then become members of His family (see Colossians 1:22; 1 John 1:9; 3:1).

Such a strong parallel between Joseph and Christ could only be from God's hand. God took a pampered, immature boy whose heart was obedient and, through difficult circumstances, prosperity and testings of his faith, produced a mature example of Christlikeness. Genesis tells us repeatedly that God was with Joseph. Knowing this, Joseph faithfully and obediently trusted God—even when his circumstances called for discouragement (see Gen. 39:2,9,21,23; 40:8; 41:16,28,32, 38,51,52; 45:5-8).

God Uses Our Obedience and Circumstances

We also are called to be like Christ. Jesus said, "I have set you an example that you should do as I have done for you" (John 13:15; also refer to 1 Pet. 2:21). This is an easy task when we clearly sense God's presence with us and when we see prosperity in our circumstances. It is a different thing to obey and submit to God when sacrifice is involved. Yet consider the anguish of Christ as He prayed in the garden of Gethsemane: "And being in anguish, he prayed more earnestly, and his sweat was like drops of blood falling to the ground" (Luke 22:44). Christ knew the cost of obedience. He willingly endured the pain of crucifixion in order to be obedient to God and fulfill God's purpose for the world. Paul described this attitude of Christ when he wrote, "Let us fix our eyes on Jesus, the author and perfecter of our faith, who for the joy set before him endured the cross, scorning its shame, and sat down at the right hand of the throne of God" (Heb. 12:2). Unlike Christ, we do not often know where God is leading us through His will. We, like Joseph during his days in prison, need to realize God is with us and then ask Him to work through us—even when we can't see an end to our difficulties. Joseph didn't sit around waiting for times to get better. Wherever he was he acted, he was productive and he trusted God.

I have a daughter who experienced great difficulty and attack on her self-esteem during her early adolescence. Her peers, for reasons we still do not understand, labeled her as an outcast, an untouchable. Many nights her mother sat with her trying to soothe the pain she was feeling. Often my daughter asked if God was listening or if He even cared. Not knowing if God would improve her circumstances, she took a step in trust that set the course for her walk with Christ. She trusted that God was with her and cared for her even though she couldn't "feel" His presence. She chose to persevere in faith, to listen to the voices of family who told her she was valuable to them and to God rather than to her peers who tore at her self-respect. With this new perspective on her circumstances, her faith has matured and her difficult experiences have allowed her to encourage others. In her obedience and trust in God, God has used her in ways that only she could serve.

This is true for all of us. We are all different members of one body (see 1 Cor. 12:12-27). Each of us plays a unique part in God's purpose. If we respond to God with obedience, we will see Him use us as examples to others. The Thessalonian Christians were commended by Paul for such obedience: "You became imitators of us and of the Lord; in spite of severe suffering, you welcomed the message with the joy given by the Holy Spirit. And so you became a model to all the believers in Macedonia and Achaia" (1 Thess. 1:6,7). As Christians we can walk through life blind to God's working around us or we can, through our obedience to Him, find joy in seeing God use us.

This Week's Teaching Plan

APPROACH TO THE WORD

APPROACH (3-5 minutes)

On the overhead projector or chalkboard write the following descriptions:
"A person who refuses to obey God's Word"
"A person who tries to be obedient to God's Word"

Ask your students to help you list what characteristics each of these people might have. Then ask, **What is the difference between the ways these two people might react to difficult or hard to understand circumstances?** Give students a few moments to discuss this question then say, **The person who tries to obey God's Word will have an understanding of God's involvement and purposes in his or her everyday experiences. This person will have confidence in God and trust that God is using his or her circumstances, whatever they are, for His glory.**

BIBLE EXPLORATION

EXPLORATION (35-50 minutes)

Materials needed: Session 6 Student Worksheet for each student.

Preparation: Read chapters 37,39-50 of Genesis and be ready to add background information as needed to present the sequence of events from Joseph's life story. Keep this information very brief to allow time to cover the lesson material. Letter the headings "Joseph" and "Jesus Christ" on the chalkboard or overhead. The Optional Step 3 requires that a guest come and talk to your students about a time when, because of his or her obedience to God, God used him or her to accomplish His purposes. Listen to your guest's story beforehand to make sure it is applicable to the focus of this session and appropriate for your students' learning experience. Invite your guest several days before class. (Note: If you use the Optional Step 3 you may need to abbreviate the time your class spends on Steps 1 and 2.)

CHRIST **B.C.** | *Joseph* | SESSION **6**

Genesis 37,39–50

A. Joseph	B. Jesus Christ
1. Genesis 37:3	1. Matthew 3:17
2. Genesis 37:18,23,24,28	2. Matthew 26:14-16
3. Genesis 39:6b-9	3. Matthew 4:1; Hebrews 4:14,15
4. Genesis 39:16-20a	4. Luke 23:20-25
5. Genesis 40:1-22	5. Luke 23:32,33,39-43
6. Genesis 41:14,41-43	6. Matthew 28:18; Acts 2:24
7. Genesis 41:55-57	7. John 3:16,17; 6:35; Acts 4:12
8. Genesis 44:16; 45:1-15	8. Colossians 1:22; 1 John 1:9
9. Genesis 45:5-7	9. John 12:27,28; 18:37

Step 1 (20-25 minutes): Distribute the Session 6 Student Worksheets and direct students to open their Bibles to Genesis, chapter 37. Say, **Today we are going to look at the life of Joseph, who was Abraham's great grandson. Joseph is an example of a person who was obedient to God and understood that God was using each of his experiences for His purpose. Let's look at some of the events in Joseph's life and how he responded in each circumstance.** Ask volunteers to share in reading aloud, as indicated in the following outline, the verses listed in column *A* under the heading "Joseph" on their worksheets. As the verses are read, lead a discussion of the verses using the following outline and information from the Teacher's Bible Study. Encourage students to take notes on their worksheets as the discussion progresses. Fill in background information for students as indicated in the outline. As students respond to the questions below, list their ideas on the board or overhead under the heading "Joseph" (see suggested responses in parentheses after each question).

Genesis 37:3
• **How did Joseph's father feel about him?** (Loved by his father.)

Genesis 37:18,23,24,28
• Before having these verses read, briefly describe Jacob's instruction to Joseph to check on his brothers and Joseph's obedience to this instruction.
• Have a volunteer read the verses then ask, **How did Joseph's brothers feel toward him?** (Brothers plotted against him; sold him for 20 shekels of silver—the price of a slave.)

Genesis 39:6b-9
• Before having the verses read, mention that Joseph was sold

to Potiphar, the captain of the guard and an Egyptian official. Describe the circumstances by which Joseph was put in charge of Potiphar's household.
• Have a volunteer read the verses then ask, **What difficult circumstance did Joseph encounter and how did he respond?** (Did not yield to Potiphar's wife's temptation; would not sin against God.)

Genesis 39:16-20a
• **What happened as a result of Joseph's unwillingness to yield to Potiphar's wife?** (Was falsely accused and imprisoned.)

Genesis 40:1-22
• Before summarizing these verses, mention that while in prison the Lord was with Joseph and caused him to prosper despite his captivity.
• Briefly summarize the event described in verses 1-19. Mention that Joseph credited God with his ability to interpret dreams. Then have a volunteer read verses 20-22. Ask, **What did each prisoner receive according to his dream?** (One prisoner received death, the other life.)

Genesis 41:14,41-43
• Before reading verse 14, describe Pharaoh's puzzlement over his dream and the cupbearer's mention of Joseph. Then have verse 14 read.
• Summarize Joseph's interpretation of Pharaoh's dream and the actions Joseph recommended to deal with the famine. Then read verses 41-43. **What did Pharaoh do for Joseph?** (Removed him from prison; gave him all authority in Egypt.)

Genesis 41:55-57
• **In Joseph's position in Egypt, what was he able to do for those who came to him?** (Save them from starvation.)
• Briefly describe the events of chapters 42-44 (through verse 15) by sharing the following: because of the famine the brothers went to Egypt and received food from Joseph; through a series of events Joseph tested his brothers to find out if they had repented of the sin they had committed. Then have a volunteer read the following verses.

Genesis 44:16; 45:1-15
• **How did Joseph's brothers feel about their sin against him and how did Joseph respond to them?** (They admitted their sin; Joseph reconciled his relationship with his brothers and forgave them for their sin against him.)

Genesis 45:5-7
• Have a volunteer reread this verse. Ask, **How did Joseph view all the things that had happened to him?** (He saw that God was with him and that through his life he was fulfilling God's purposes.)

Move to Step 2 by saying, **Joseph is probably the most Christlike of any Old Testament person. Let's look at how his example of faithful obedience to God is a type of Christ.**

Step 2 (5-10 minutes): Ask students to work in pairs or trios to look up the New Testament passages listed in column *B* on their worksheets. Assign one or two of the passages in the column to each pair or trio of students. Make sure each passage has been assigned to a group. Direct groups to write next to their assigned passage(s) how that passage about Jesus compares to what they learned about Joseph in the corresponding passage in column *A*. Allow 4-8 minutes for students to work, then ask for their responses. List their ideas on the chalkboard or overhead under the heading "Jesus Christ." Responses should include: Matthew 3:17—loved by God; Matthew 26:14-16—plot to kill Him and paid for with silver; Matthew 4:1 and Hebrews 4:14,15—did not yield to temptation; Luke 23:20-25—falsely accused and taken prisoner; Luke 23:32,33,39-43—one of two fellow prisoners died in sin, the other received eternal life; Matthew 28:18 and Acts 2:24—released from bondage of death and given all authority and power; John 3:16,17 and 6:35 and Acts 4:12—only one who can save people, give eternal life and provide spiritual nourishment; Colossians 1:22 and 1 John 1:9—reconciles us to God and forgives our sins; John 12:27,28 and 18:37—knew He was fulfilling God's purpose through His life, death and resurrection.

After students have shared ask, **What were the rewards or results of Joseph's obedience to God?** (He had the satisfaction of knowing God's purpose for his life; God was with him and helped him through all his daily circumstances; he was able to help many people survive the famine.) **What were the results of Jesus' obedience to God?** (He fulfilled God's purpose for His life; He made it possible for all of us to receive forgiveness of sins and eternal life.)

If you do not choose to complete the Optional Step 3, move to Step 4.

Optional Step 3 (5-8 minutes): Introduce your guest to your students (see the Preparation). Say, **Today (guest's name) is going to share about a time in his/her life when, because of his/her obedience to God, God used him/her to accomplish His purposes.** Allow 3-5 minutes for your guest to share. Reserve a minute or two for students to ask your guest any questions they may have. Then thank your guest for sharing.

Move to Step 4 by saying, **Let's look at ways we can be obedient to God and consider the results of our obedience.**

Step 4 (10-15 minutes): Divide the class into groups of five to six students each. Provide scratch paper for students to use (they will use the backs of their worksheet in the Conclusion). Give each group the following directions: **As a group decide on a difficult circumstance someone your age might experience. Plan what action a Christian could take in that situation to be obedient to God; then list the results or rewards his or her obedience might have.** Allow 5-8 minutes for groups to work; then ask a representative from each group to share his or her group's work. Optional—groups that feel comfortable doing so may want to act out the situation they have described. Or, in addition to sharing from students, plan ahead of time to present a skit that illustrates a difficult circumstance. Have students discuss possible responses for that situation that would display obedience to God.

Move to the Conclusion by saying, **When we obey God we can be confident that God is using our lives in some way, no matter how difficult or hard to understand our circumstances may seem, to accomplish His purposes and to make a difference in the world. When you feel discouraged, the examples of Joseph and Jesus can be a source of encouragement for you.**

CONCLUSION & DECISION

CONCLUSION (5 minutes)

Direct students to write on the backs of their worksheets a difficult situation they have encountered. Then instruct them to plan one way they can respond in obedience to God should they be confronted with a similar situation in the future. Then allow a few moments for silent prayer so that students can ask for God's help to be obedient to Him, especially in the difficult situations they have described. Close with prayer thanking God that they can rely on God just as Joseph did.

Be available after class to talk with any students who have questions or need help in dealing with a difficult situation. Be sensitive to those students who are experiencing difficulties that require professional help by referring them to a qualified counselor.

Encourage students to read chapter 6 in the student paperback *Christ B.C.* The readings in this chapter explore the theme "obedience."

NOTES:

The Passover

KEY VERSE

"I am the Lord. The blood will be a sign for you on the houses where you are; and when I see the blood, I will pass over you. No destructive plague will touch you when I strike Egypt." Exodus 12:12,13

"For Christ, our Passover lamb, has been sacrificed." 1 Corinthians 5:7

BIBLICAL BASIS

Exodus 3:1—13:16; Matthew 24:42-44; 26:27,28; Mark 14:22; John 1:29; 14:2,3; 1 Corinthians 5:6-8; 2 Corinthians 5:17; Hebrews 9:14

FOCUS OF THE SESSION

Just as the Passover reminded the Israelites of how God delivered them from bondage, Jesus' shed blood reminds us that He can deliver us from the bondage of sin.

AIMS OF THIS SESSION

You and your students will have accomplished the purpose of this Bible study session if you can:

- SUMMARIZE God's instructions for celebrating the Passover as a reminder of His deliverance of Israel from Egypt;
- ANALYZE how the elements of the first Passover symbolize God's deliverance of people today from the bondage of sin;
- DECIDE upon an action that illustrates their response to Christ's sacrifice on the cross.

Teacher's Bible Study

Exodus 12 and 13 gives an account of God instructing Moses and Aaron about how to celebrate the feast of Passover and its adjoining feast of Unleavened Bread. This was a momentous occasion in Israel's history. It was revolutionary in a political sense and defining and prescribing in a spiritual sense. It marked the birth of a special nation and a faith experience.

Nations build their self-identities out of such events. The United States is no exception. It was born in the revolution of 1776 which is remembered July Fourth every year. In 1976 the citizens of the United States celebrated their nation's bicentennial. The ringing of bells, reenactment of the battle on Lexington Green, orations in hundreds of city parks and fireworks in hundreds of stadiums across America reminded citizens of who they were and how their country came to be. Contemporary events have also defined the identity of the United States. The tragic deaths of presidents and social heroes, the glorious joys of the end of two world wars and the celebration of technological achievements such as landing men on the moon have become epochs that define the nation and create patterns for its future national life

For Israel, Passover was the event that gave the nation character and meaning. The Passover had another great meaning: It is a beautiful picture of the coming Messiah.

Israel's Bondage in Egypt

Israel entered Egypt as a family of 70 members (see Gen. 46:27) whose descendants lived there for 430 years (see Exod. 12:40). When liberation came, "six hundred thousand men on foot, besides women and children" (v. 37) plus "many other people" left Egypt (v. 38). During their years in Egypt, the children of Israel went from landowners in the best part of Goshen (Gen. 47:6,11) to slaves under a harsh king. The king said, "Come, we must deal shrewdly with them or they will become even more numerous and, if war breaks out, will join our enemies, fight against us and leave the country" (Exod. 1:10). The king oppressed the Israelites with forced labor and the Egyptians "used them ruthlessly" (v. 14). In addition, the king decreed that, "Every boy that is born you must throw into the Nile, but let every girl live" (v. 22).

It is in this context that we read in Exodus 2 about Moses' birth. To save his life

Moses' mother placed him in a basket and put the basket in the reeds near the bank of the Nile. Baby Moses was discovered by the daughter of Pharaoh and became her son, a member of Pharaoh's household (see v.10). But Moses recognized his Hebrew heritage. In trying to protect "one of his own people" (v. 11), Moses killed an Egyptian and had to flee to Midian to escape Pharaoh's wrath (see v. 15). In the meantime, "the Israelites groaned in their slavery and cried out, and their cry for help because of their slavery went up to God. God heard their groaning and he remembered his covenant with Abraham, with Isaac and with Jacob" (vv. 23,24). God acted on His promise (see Gen. 15:5-7,15,16) and sent Moses to Egypt to bring His deliverance to the Israelites (see Exod. 3:7-10).

The First Passover

The key to Israel's freedom came through the event called the Passover. Exodus 12:1-51 describes in detail what the Passover is and God's instructions to the Israelites concerning its observance. First God told the Israelites, through Moses and his brother Aaron, to prepare a meal. Specific instructions were given as to what was to be prepared, how it was to be prepared and how it was to be eaten. Then God described what action He would take during that first Passover. "On that same night I will pass through Egypt and strike down every firstborn—both men and animals—and I will bring judgment on all the gods of Egypt. I am the Lord. The blood will be a sign for you on the houses where you are; and when I see the blood, I pass over you" (vv. 12,13). Thus the term "Passover" gets it meaning. All the symbols and the annual reenactment of the Passover meal would stand as a reminder to the Jewish people that it was God who had delivered them.

Those difficult years in Egypt, culminating in the Passover, served to develop a singular identity among the Israelites. They had preserved in their memory a record of God's covenant with Abraham, Isaac and Jacob, and when in distress they turned to God for help. They also remembered the oath Joseph had made his brothers take to remember God's covenant. Joseph said, "God will surely come to your aid and take you up out of this land to the land he promised on oath to Abraham, Isaac and Jacob" (Gen. 50:24; also see Exod. 13:19).

Creating an Accurate Memory

Again we see the work of sovereign God doing an impossible thing—from a human point of view. No human effort could have developed and preserved the clear spiritual and cultural identity of Israel while her people were enslaved in a hostile environment. Memories are strange and changeable unless they are actively preserved by deliberate and authentic means. Otherwise they lose their impact upon us and our ability to generate life and meaning from them dies.

We have a tendency to modify memories to remove pain. As time goes by we prefer to recall the pleasant events and suppress the uncomfortable ones. For what other reason do the "good old days" seem to be so good? Why is it that the older a man gets the faster he could run as a boy? We modify our own histories to improve our self-images, to protect ourselves from pain or embarrassment. Sins of the past seem so much more innocent. An event as terrible as the Holocaust in Europe, in which millions of Jews were exterminated, is already being denied by some. Yet we are scarcely a half-century away from the deed. Many Jewish survivors struggle to keep an accurate memory of the horrors of the tragedy alive saying in essence, "We must never forget. We must remember so that such cruelty is not al-

lowed to happen again." Historians agree that unless we remember difficult days and experiences, we are likely to repeat them. As it has often been said, "History repeats itself, especially for those who do not read history."

Israel also had a capacity for memory modification. In the days following the exodus of Israel from Egypt, the difficulties of desert living came upon them and the people began to grumble, asking to be returned to captivity where at least they would not starve to death (see Exod. 16:2,3). Knowing the tendency of the human heart and mind to "forget," God deliberately provided Israel with a celebration that would accurately preserve the impact of the Passover. Exodus 12:14 says that the Passover is "a day you are to commemorate; for the generations to come you shall celebrate it as a festival to the Lord—a lasting ordinance." This feast would become so special and unique that years later children who had no memory of life in Egypt would ask their parents, "What does this ceremony mean to you?" (v. 26). The parents were instructed to reply, "It is the Passover sacrifice to the Lord, who passed over the houses of the Israelites in Egypt and spared our homes when he struck down the Egyptians" (v. 27; also see 13:14-16).

Christ in the Passover

As we have seen, the feast of Passover serves as a reminder of an historical event. But it also stands as a reminder of the coming Redeemer. This historic celebration would make it possible for those faithful Jews who meet the Savior to identify Him as the fulfillment of God's promise established long ago. They would be able to say, "Aha! That's what this is all about. I see it now. Christ is indeed the Passover lamb!" It also serves as a reminder to all Christians of Jesus' life and death. A careful examination of the Passover feast reveals symbols and meaning that apply to the faith experience of the Christian.

The Passover feast was to be held on the tenth day of the month of Abib which is equivalent to our March or April. This month was to mark a new beginning in the Israelites' calendar year (see Exod. 12:1-3; 13:4). Previously the Jews celebrated the new year in the month of Tishri (equivalent to our September or October). The new year would now have a spiritual meaning, indicating the beginning of a new life free from bondage. This freedom is indicative of the Christian's freedom from the bondage of sin. "For we know that our old self was crucified with him so that the body of sin might be done away

with, that we should no longer be slaves to sin—because anyone who has died has been freed from sin" (Rom. 6:6,7).

Freedom is a wonderful experience. The Israelites had longed for freedom and had cried out to God in their misery. God gave them a new beginning, asking only that they show their trust in Him through obedience to His commands (see Exod. 19:3-8). Through Jesus we also can receive a new beginning (see 2 Cor. 5:17). All Jesus asks is that we submit our lives to Him (see Matt. 16:24). Now these requirements of obedience are not qualifications to be met before freedom can be granted. Rather, they are God's way of helping us avoid our human tendency to enslave ourselves again to that from which He has freed us. At first the people of Israel obediently followed Moses out of Egypt. God's deliverance made sense to them because this freedom was what they had prayed for. But when God's actions went beyond their rational understanding and their new freedom appeared to be a liability rather than a benefit (see Exod. 14:10-12), they were tempted to return to their old life of slavery.

This experience illustrates a principle for us: Freedom is often more anxiety-provoking than slavery. We sometimes see this principle enacted in the salvation experience of people today. When they are first set free by Christ they enjoy the headiness of the new experience. But when their faith is challenged and the emotional high has worn off, they are soon tempted to return to old ways. Change is stressful and uncomfortable. Some are not willing to pay the price of change to gain the valuable benefits of freedom in Christ. Or instead of enslaving themselves to their old ways they set up a new realm of enslavement. They create a legal system or institution out of their experience. The change they experience becomes external and nonthreatening rather than personal. They do this rather than live out the rich meaning and adventure of freedom in Christ. Grace experienced can be an unnerving adventure because it forces us into new, unknown areas of faith. But the past, with all its bondages, can provide an unhealthy security that tempts us from time to time.

The Meaning of the Meal

Exodus 12:5 says that the lamb that was to be selected and prepared for the Passover meal must be perfect and without defect. This is clearly typical of Christ. First Corinthians 5:7 states: "For Christ, our Passover lamb, has been sacrificed." God's insistence that the lamb be perfect shows us that we cannot save ourselves from death. We are imperfect and therefore unable to provide for our own salvation (see Rom. 3:10,23). Christ, on the other hand, is perfect and the only one through whom salvation from death is possible (see Acts 4:12; 1 Pet. 1:18,19). Ten thousand times ten thousand angels and the elders in heaven acknowledge the worthiness of Jesus, "the Lamb, who was slain" (Rev. 5:11,12).

Exodus 12:7 tells us that after the Passover lamb was sacrificed by the Israelites, its blood was to be painted over the sides and top of the doorframes of their houses. The spilling of the blood symbolized the blood of Jesus that was later spilled as the final sacrifice for sin. During the Last Supper, which was held at the time of Passover, Jesus "took the cup, gave thanks and offered it to them, saying, 'Drink from it, all of you. This is my blood of the covenant, which is poured out for many for the forgiveness of sins'" (Matt. 26:27,28).

The pouring out of blood meant death had come. Death is the physical and spiritual consequence for all that is imperfect or sinful in the world (see Rom. 3:23; 6:23). Death is the logical conclusion for imperfect people who try to play god in their own lives and reject God's provision for them. Death is the result of humankind's noblest efforts to save themselves. Death is the consequence of all human effort that is moral and good but is done apart from the righteousness of God.

Deliverance from sin can only come through death. Death is the price God demands for sin (see Rom. 6:23). Since we are unable on our own to be all that God wants us to be, only God can make up for our shortfall. On our own, that shortfall leads to spiritual death. But God, in mercy, sent His Son to do the dying for us. Jesus took the consequence for us, sparing us from eternal death (see Rom. 5:8,9). When the Israelites painted their doorframes with blood, they experienced firsthand God's grace in sparing their homes from death (see Exod. 12:13). They depended completely on God's provision for their safety. In a greater way, when we apply Jesus' blood to our lives, He saves us from spiritual death. "How much more, then, will the blood of Christ, who through the eternal Spirit offered himself unblemished to God, cleanse our consciences from acts that lead to death, so that we may serve the living God!" (Heb. 9:14).

God gave the instruction that the Israelites were to roast the Passover lamb whole, as was the practice of wandering shepherds, and eat it with bitter herbs and unleavened bread (see Exod 12:8,9). Traditionally, the bitter herbs have served as a reminder to Israel that their experience in Egypt was bitter. It was important that their memory of the bitterness of Egypt remain accurate and sharp, not softened with the passage of time. Otherwise the impact of the greatness of God's deliverance would become blurred. This was a memory not to be celebrated with cake and ice cream.

It is also important for the Christian to have an accurate picture of the bitterness of life without Christ. Paul referred to his former way of life as a persecutor of Christians in order to show the authenticity of his new life in Christ (see Gal. 1:11-24). Our best witness to others is often the change they see in our lives in words, actions and attitudes. Remembering what we were before Christ redeemed us is also motivation to continue to grow in Him rather than return to our old way of living.

A dominant symbol from the first Passover is that of unleavened bread. It illustrates haste because it tells of the suddenness with which the exodus of the children of Israel from Egypt occurred. "The people took their dough before the yeast was added, and carried it on their shoulders in kneading troughs wrapped in clothing" (Exod. 12:34). The response of the people of Israel to the command to leave was to be instantaneous. No unnecessary activities were to stand in the way of their escape. This brings to mind Jesus' parable of the Great Banquet (see Luke 14:15-24). Everything was ready for the party and the servants were sent out to call the guests. Verse 18 says that "they all alike began to make excuses." The master responded by saying, "Go out to the roads and country lanes and make them come in, so that my house will be full. I tell you, not one of those men who were invited will get a taste of my banquet" (vv. 23,24). Jesus was referring to those who would put off committing their lives to Him. One day He will come again to gather those who have been invited to His wedding feast. For those who are not ready to respond it will be too late.

The Israelites were told to "remove the yeast from your houses, for whoever eats anything with yeast in it from the first day through the seventh must be cut off from Israel" (Exod. 12:15). Unleavened bread is a symbol of the body of Christ (see Matt. 26:26). It is also a symbol of that from which worldly and evil things have been purged. The New Testament describes why we need to remove evil in our lives: "Don't you know that a little yeast works through the whole batch of dough? Get rid of the old yeast that you may be a new batch without yeast—as you really are. For Christ, our Passover lamb, has been sacrificed. Therefore let us keep the Festival, not with the old yeast, the yeast of malice and wickedness, but with bread without yeast, the bread of sincerity and truth" (1 Cor. 5:6-8). In this passage Paul is telling the Corinthians to remove from their fellowship an immoral man. In fact, Paul states that the Corinthian church was proud of this man's presence in their midst. Paul warns the church that this man's immorality, if tolerated, will permeate their whole fellowship like yeast permeates a loaf of bread.

This passage from Corinthians has a broader application. It tell us that our separation from evil and a worldly way of life is to be total and complete. The ways of the world and God's spiritual economy are not compatible.

Some scholars have suggested that the seven days of the Feast of Unleavened Bread (see Exod. 12:15) symbolize the entire life cycle of man. This implies that when we are separated into God's redemptive experience through the blood of Christ, the Passover Lamb, we are committed to a lifetime of grace and spiritual development (see 1 Pet. 2:1-3). We are not to share our lives with evil or worldly pursuits, but rather we are responsible to cleanse our primary environment from these influences. This is reflected in God's command to the Israelites to remove yeast from their houses (see Exod. 12:15).

We are still called to bring the gospel to the world (see Matt. 28:18-20), which will put us in touch with those who are lost in sin and evil ways, but the most significant areas of our lives need to be kept pure so that we can avoid falling into evil. This means that our closest friendships need to support our beliefs, our priorities need to provide time for fellowship with the Lord and His people, our work needs to be done with a clear conscience, our home needs to be a place where we honor God and our stewardship of finances and possessions need to reflect God's values.

Another interesting aspect of the Passover meal is the dress code. "This is how you are to eat it: with your cloak tucked into your belt, your sandals on your feet and your staff in your hand. Eat it in haste; it is the Lord's Passover" (Exod. 12:11). This relates to the point made earlier that, when the Lord calls, we need to be ready to respond instantly. But it also brings to mind another aspect of the Christian life. The life of the believer is a journey, not a territorial occupancy. We are to go through life riding loose in the saddle, rejoicing in the places God leads us knowing that home is yet to come in the presence of God. We are not to find a comfortable spot in life where we can dictate and limit what happens, where we wait out the storm until Jesus comes again. We are to get our feet dirty as we travel in Jesus' footsteps. A look at Jesus' call to His disciples illustrates this point. Matthew 4:18-20 says, "As Jesus was walking beside the Sea of Galilee, he saw two brothers, Simon called Peter and his brother Andrew. They were casting a net into the lake, for they were fishermen. 'Come, follow me,' Jesus said, 'and I will make you fishers of men.' At once they left their nets and followed Him." As you can see, when Jesus called they responded and followed Him "at once." Because of their immediate response they were able to share in the greatest experience a person could possibly have—being part of God's fulfillment of His promises of old (see Luke 4:14-21).

Those who are interested in the Christian life, but refuse to put Jesus' command to follow above their other responsibilities will miss the chance to participate in affecting change in the world for Jesus' sake. Luke 9:61,62 says, "Still another said, 'I will follow you, Lord; but first let me go back and say good-by to my family.' Jesus replied, 'No one who puts his hand to the plow and looks back is fit for service in the kingdom of God." And Matthew 10:37-38 says, "Anyone who loves his father or mother more than me is not worthy of me; anyone who loves his son or daughter more than me is not worthy of me; and anyone who does not take his cross and follow me is not worthy of me." Giving Jesus' call priority has a high cost, but the benefits are beyond measure. To those who take the risk of putting Jesus' call first He promises, "No one who has left home or brothers or sisters or mother or father or children or fields for me and the gospel will fail to receive a hundred times as much in this present age (homes, brothers, sisters, mothers, children and fields—and with them, persecutions) and in the age to come, eternal life" (Mark 10:29-30).

The Passover is a reminder of God's deliverance of the people of Israel from Egypt. It is also a reminder that only through the shedding of the blood of Jesus is deliverance from sin and spiritual death possible. As Jesus celebrated the Passover with His disciples, He established a reminder for us that is based on the symbols of Passover. This reminder, the Last Supper, redefines Passover for us in order to create an accurate memory of what Christ did in order to provide for our freedom. Jesus "took bread, gave thanks and broke it, and gave it to them, saying, 'This is my body given for you; do this in remembrance of me'" (Luke 22:19). The unleavened bread became a symbol of Christ's substitutionary sacrifice on the cross for our sins. It is "given for you" and you are to remember its significance. The cup used in the Passover feast became Jesus' "blood, which is poured out for you" (v. 20). And of course Christ Himself represented the Passover lamb who was about to be sacrificed. Within hours He would be on the cross, shedding His blood to make our redemption from the bondage of sin possible.

This Week's Teaching Plan

APPROACH TO THE WORD

APPROACH (5-7 minutes)

After students have gathered ask, **What happy or important events from your younger years do you remember the best? What people, objects or places remind you of that event?** Allow 3-5 minutes for students to share. Then say, **Often people like to remember, or commemorate, a special event by holding a celebration. Symbols, people or places that remind them of the event are often incorporated into their celebration. Today we are going to look at an important event from the history of the Jewish people. This event, called the Passover, is still celebrated today.**

ALTERNATE APPROACH (8-10 minutes)

Materials needed: Decorations and/or snacks appropriate for commemorating a familiar national holiday.

Preparation: Before class decorate the room as if you are celebrating the holiday you chose. Place snacks where they will be available as students arrive.

As students arrive wish them a "Happy (holiday you are celebrating)" and invite them to help themselves to the food. When all are gathered ask, **What activities and symbols do we use to commemorate this holiday? Why do we, as a nation, feel it is important to remember the event symbolized by this holiday?** Then say, **Today we are going to look at an important event from the history of the Jewish people. This event, called Passover, is still celebrated today.**

BIBLE EXPLORATION

EXPLORATION (30-40 minutes)

Materials needed: Session 7 Student Worksheet for each student. Optional—The following symbols of the first Passover meal: unleavened bread; a piece of lettuce, endive or horseradish; lamb's bone (traditionally Jews use the shank bone as a symbol of the Passover lamb).

Preparation: Make an overhead transparency of the Student Worksheet or copy onto the board or overhead the "God's Instructions" chart from the worksheet.

Optional—You may want to plan a Seder (Passover) meal for your students after completing this session. There are several Christian organizations that minister specifically to Jews who provide helpful resources on this subject. Through Jews for Jesus, located at 60 Haight Street, San Francisco, CA 94102, you may be able to make arrangements for a missionary to present a "Christ in the Passover" demonstration for your students. You can also purchase their *Passover Seder Packet*. The packet contains all the information you need to conduct a Seder meal that presents Christ as the central theme.

Step 1 (2-3 minutes): Briefly summarize the events from the time of Joseph to Moses' encounter with God at the burning bush (see Exod. 1,2). Emphasize the hardships the Israelites experienced as slaves in Egypt and summarize the events surrounding Moses' birth and his flight to Midian.

CHRIST B.C. SESSION **7**

The Passover
Exodus 3:1–13:16

Exodus 3:1-10:

Exodus 3:11–10:29:

Exodus 11:1-10:

God's Instructions

Instructions	Christ in the Passover
1. Date: Exodus 12:1-3;13:4	2 Corinthians 5:17
2. Lamb: Exodus 12:3,5,6,9,10	John 1:29; 1 Corinthians 5:7
3. Blood: Exodus 12:7,13,22,23	Matthew 26:27,28; Hebrews 9:14
4. Bread: Exodus 12:8,15,17-20	Mark 14:22; 1 Corinthians 5:6-8
5. How to Eat: Exodus 12:11	Matthew 24:42-44; John 14:2,3

Step 2 (10-12 minutes): Distribute the Student Worksheets. Direct students to turn in their Bibles to Exodus, chapter 3. Then ask volunteers to share in reading aloud the verses listed under the heading "The Passover" section of their worksheets. As the verses are read, lead a discussion using the following outline and information from the Teacher's Bible Study. Encourage students to take notes on their worksheets as the discussion progresses.

Exodus 3:1-10
• **How did God feel about the Israelites' suffering?** (See v. 7.)
• **How would God deliver the Israelites from bondage? Where would He bring them?** (See vv. 8,10.)
• Mention that following God's command to go to Egypt, Moses was reluctant to obey because he did not feel adequate for the job God had asked him to do. Eventually God persuaded Moses to obey—and Moses went back to Egypt.

Exodus 3:11—10:29
• Mention that because of Moses' feelings of inadequacy, God allowed Moses' brother Aaron to help him.
• Briefly summarize these chapters for your students by stating that Moses met with Pharaoh many times, commanding in the

Lord's name that Pharaoh release the Israelites. Each time Moses confronted Pharaoh, Pharaoh refused to obey and God brought a plague upon the land. This happened ten times and resulted in ten plagues. The first nine plagues were: water turned to blood, frogs, gnats, flies, diseased livestock, festering boils, hail, locusts, then total darkness.

Exodus 11:1-10
• Summarize these verses by saying, **The last plague would take the lives of all the firstborn among the people, Egyptian and Israelite, as well as among the cattle—except for those who followed God's specific instructions on the night the plague came. It was this plague that convinced Pharaoh to release the Israelites. Let's look at God's instructions for escaping this plague.**

Step 3 (10-15 minutes): Divide the class into five groups. Assign each group one element (date, lamb, etc.) from the "Instructions" column of the chart on the worksheet—a different element for each group. (If you have a small number of students, make three groups and give each one two elements from the chart.) Students are to read their assigned verses and write a summary of the instructions described by the verses. The second column of the chart will be completed in Step 4. After 5-6 minutes ask groups to share. Record groups' ideas on the overhead you have made of the worksheet or on the chart you have prepared. Optional—As groups share, pass around the bread, bone and herbs you have brought. Then ask a volunteer to read Exodus 12:24-30. Ask, **What final instruction did God make to the Israelites?** (Observe the Passover yearly as a reminder of God's deliverance from Egypt.) Move to Step 5 by saying, **This event was significant to the Israelites as an historical event, but it also has significance as an indicator of a future deliverance that was to come through Jesus Christ.**

Step 4 (8-10 minutes): Ask volunteers to read aloud the verses listed in the "Christ in the Passover" column of the chart. Use the following information as you discuss the verses to help students understand how God's instructions for the Passover are symbolic of the salvation that Christ offers.
1. **Date observed.** Instruction: Celebration begins on the tenth day of the month; this month (Abib) became a new beginning of their calendar year. Symbolism of Christ: This represents the new beginning that is possible because of salvation through Christ.
2. **Lamb.** Instruction: Lamb without blemish; roast it whole over fire; eat all of it or burn leftovers. Symbolism of Christ: Christ is the Lamb of God, perfect and able to save us from death through His sacrifice.
3. **Blood.** Instruction: Using hyssop branch, spread blood of lamb on the doorframe as a sign. Symbolism of Christ: Blood of the Lamb of God; in the lives of those who have accepted Christ's sacrifice it is a sign of cleansing of sin which leads to death.
4. **Bread.** Instruction: All leaven was to be removed from the house; bread was cooked without yeast; whoever eats yeast will be cut off from Israel. Symbolism of Christ: Represents Christ's body broken on the cross; removing leaven symbolizes purging sin from a person's life;
5. **How to Eat.** Instruction: Dress ready for travel (to Promised Land—see Exod. 12:25); eat in haste. Symbolism of Christ: We need to be ready to respond when the Lord calls and willingly serve Him. The reward is a promised home in heaven.

Move to the Conclusion by asking, **What can Christ, the Passover Lamb, deliver us from? What must we do to experience the deliverance Christ has provided?** or complete the Optional Step 5.

Optional Step 5 (8-10 minutes): Have students return to the groups they were in during Step 3. Have each group think of what elements God might require if the Passover were to occur today. Instruct them to choose elements from today's culture that might carry the same meaning as the elements of the first Passover. After 5 minutes ask groups to share. Students' ideas may include items such as: a perfect pheasant or salmon prepared on the barbecue; broth or gravy (for blood); eat as a picnic lunch on paper plates with plastic tableware; wear tennis shoes and backpack. Move to the Conclusion by saying, **Although the elements from the first Passover are not familiar to us today, their meanings are important. They stand as reminders of the deliverance from sin Jesus Christ has made possible for us.**

CONCLUSION & DECISION

CONCLUSION (3-5 minutes)

Materials needed: Index cards.

Distribute index cards to students. Ask, **What symbol of the Passover best describes for you what Christ did for you when He shed His blood on the cross? Draw or write that symbol on your index card. Now write your response to what Jesus has done. You may want to thank Jesus for dying so your sins can be forgiven and you can live in heaven some day. Or you may want to ask Jesus to cleanse you from sin and commit your life to Him. Write whatever best describes your response.** After allowing a few minutes for students to think and write close in prayer, thanking God that He showed His love for us by substituting His own Son as a sacrifice for our sins. Then say, **Keep your index cards as a reminder of what Christ has done for you and how you want to respond to Him.**

Be available after class to talk with any students who are interested in knowing more about receiving forgiveness for their sins.

Note: If you are holding a Passover Seder for your students, remind them of the time, date and place it will occur.

Encourage students to read chapter 7 in the student paperback *Christ B.C.* The readings in this chapter explore the theme "remembrance."

NOTES:

The Tabernacle Curtain

KEY VERSE

"The Lord spoke to Moses after the death of the two sons of Aaron who died when they approached the Lord. The Lord said to Moses: 'Tell your brother Aaron not to come whenever he chooses into the Most Holy Place behind the curtain in front of the atonement cover on the ark, or else he will die, because I appear in the cloud over the atonement cover.'" Leviticus 16:1,2

"Therefore, brothers, since we have confidence to enter the Most Holy Place by the blood of Jesus, by a new and living way opened for us through the curtain, that is, his body . . . let us draw near to God with a sincere heart in full assurance of faith." Hebrews 10:19,20,22

BIBLICAL BASIS

Exodus 12:35,36; 25:1–27:21; 30:1-10,17-21; 35:4-29; 36:8–38:31; Leviticus 16:1-6; Psalm 99:1; Mark 15:33-38; Romans 8:1-4; Hebrews 9:11,12; 10:12,14; 1 John 1:9

FOCUS OF THE SESSION

The Tabernacle curtain separated an unholy people from God's holy presence. At the moment of Christ's death the curtain tore from top to bottom, symbolizing that through Christ sinners are made acceptable to God.

AIMS OF THIS SESSION

You and your students will have accomplished the purpose of this Bible study session if you can:

- IDENTIFY the characteristics and spiritual function of the Tabernacle curtain;
- DISCUSS how the tearing of the Temple curtain shows that Christ's death on the cross changed the relationship between God and those who love Him;
- PRAY, thanking God that He has made Himself available to you and that you can have an open, intimate relationship with Him.

Teacher's Bible Study

The Tabernacle and Jewish Life

The Tabernacle was the center of Israel's religious experience. In this most revered place God designed a meeting with His people. The Tabernacle with its holy places, priesthood and sacrifices became the most complete type of Christ in the Old Testament. The structure of the Tabernacle illustrates the condition of the relationship between man and God. It marked the beginning of a defined relationship between God and His people. God dwelt in the midst of His chosen people but stood separate and inaccessible, except in limited ways, because of man's sinfulness. Later an event at the Temple in Jerusalem would mark the end of this limited relationship and the establishment of a new order between Christ and His Church. Let's examine some of the facets of the Tabernacle structure and experience and see how the drama of redemption is played out through Israel for us.

From the size and structure of the Tabernacle, it is apparent that it was more than a place of worship. It contained a courtyard where large numbers of people could gather and it was the center of the life of the people. As the Israelites traveled about the Sinai peninsula, they carried the Tabernacle with them (this was possible because its construction was similar to that of a tent). Whenever they stopped to make camp, the tribes of Israel took their assigned place on all four sides of the Tabernacle (see Num. 2:1-34).

In Exodus 25:21 and 40:1-3 we see that the Tabernacle is the place for the ark which held the Ten Commandments or "the Testimony." This indicates that the Tabernacle served a judicial function.

In Exodus 27:21 the Tabernacle is called "the Tent of Meeting," indicating it was the place where God communicated with the people. It was where information and news on a variety of issues was disseminated. When traveling instructions were given to the tribes moving about the Sinai Desert, they were delivered at the site of the Tabernacle (see Num. 10:1-3). When a public health issue existed, God delivered instructions to Moses and the Israelites from the Tabernacle as to how to handle the problem (se Num. 5:1-4).

From this we learn that all of Israel's life was Tabernacle-related or, rather, God-related. There was no distinction or separation between the religious order and the conduct of civic affairs. God was at work in all of Israel's doings and all issues had spiritual significance.

A Freewill Offering

Exodus 25–27 relates the detailed instructions given by God for the construction of the Tabernacle. The first of the insructions is God's request to take a voluntary offering from the people. "You are to receive the offering for me from each man whose heart prompts him to give" (25:2). These offerings, many of which came from articles taken from the Egyptians (see 12:35,36), would make the Tabernacle a place of value and magnificence. Gold, silver and bronze, three colors of yarn and fine linen, goat hair, skins, wood, oil, spices and gems were offered by the people (see 25:3-7).

A principle is illustrated by this giving. We participate in God's divine plans through our willing offerings. Israel did not buy any favor by her gifts because God did not require any payment from His people. It was a gift exchange, illustrating a principle of grace. As Christ gave Himself for us, so we give ourselves freely to Him. As Jesus sent His disciples out to minister

He reminded them that, "Freely you have received, freely give" (Matt. 10:8). We serve Christ as our gift of thanks for His free gift of salvation to us (see Eph. 2:8,9). Because our reconciliation experience with God is not a bartered exchange or the result of bargaining, God is indebted to no one and no human payment can obligate God's favor.

God's instructions for the construction of the Tabernacle were very specific and full of meaning. The Tabernacle consisted of three main sections. The outer court was where the sacrifices were offered. It contained the bronze altar upon which burnt offerings were made and the bronze basin where the priests would purify their bodies by washing their hands and feet. The outer court measured approximately 75 × 150 feet. The inner court, or Tent of Meeting, was divided into two parts: the Holy Place and the Most Holy Place, or Holy of Holies. The Holy Place measured 30 by 15 feet and the Most Holy Place was a perfect square measuring 15 feet on each side. Only the high priest could enter the Most Holy Place—and then only once a year in order to offer a sacrifice for the atonement of the people. Special preparation was required by the high priest for this annual venture into the Most Holy Place. If he did not enter properly prepared, his actions were grievous to God and he would die (see Lev. 16:1,2; also see vv. 3-30). It is said that the priest wore a rope tied to his ankle as he entered. In case he made an error or was improperly prepared and died, he could be pulled out by the priests in the Holy Place.

The Curtain for the Most Holy Place

Each of these sections of the Tabernacle—the outer court, the Holy Place and the Most Holy Place—were separated by curtains. These curtains and the structure of the Tabernacle tell us of the distance between God and His people. The spiritual condition of man prevented his complete access to God.

All members of the Israelite community could pass through the outer curtain and into the outer court surrounding the Tent of Meeting. This curtain had an inner lining of "finely twisted linen and blue, purple and scarlet yarn, with cherubim worked into them by a skilled craftsman" (Exod. 26:1). From this lining the people could recognize that they had entered the house of the Lord of heaven. The outside of this curtain was covered by a curtain of goat hair, then a covering of ram skins dyed red and then by a covering of the hides of sea cows (see vv. 7,14). This curtain gives us a picture of Jesus' earthly body. The lining,

woven with pictures of cherubim, illustrated his divine nature (see Isa. 9:6; John 1:1). The covering of skins reminds us that He was clothed in the flesh of man (see John 1:14).

The second curtain divided the outer court of the Tabernacle from the Holy Place or the entrance to the Tent of Meeting (see Exod. 26:36). Only the priests appointed by God could enter through this curtain (see Heb. 9:6). The curtain was made of "blue, purple and scarlet yarn and finely twisted linen—the work of an embroiderer" (Exod. 26:36). In Jewish tradition, blue is associated with heaven, purple is associated with royalty and scarlet is associated with earthly glory.

This curtain gives us a picture of Jesus' character. John 3:13 says, "No one has ever gone into heaven except the one who came from heaven—the Son of Man." This testifies to Jesus' divinity (blue). Revelation 19:12,13,16 describes Jesus' royalty (purple): "His eyes are like blazing fire, and on his head are many crowns . . . . He is dressed in a robe dipped in blood, and his name is the Word of God . . . . On his robe and on his thigh he has this name written: King of Kings and Lord of Lords." In cruel mockery the Roman soldiers, prior to Jesus' crucifixion, "put a purple robe on him, then twisted together a crown of thorns and set it on him. And they began to call out to him, 'Hail, king of the Jews!' . . . . And when they had mocked him, they took off the purple robe and put his own clothes on him. Then they led him out to crucify him" (Mark 15:17,18,20). Matthew 27:28 describes the robe put on Jesus as being scarlet. Either way, the robe was probably the military cloak of one of the soldiers, and it was used to sarcastically mock Jesus' royalty. The symbolism of scarlet as representing Jesus' earthly glory is obvious when we consider His great work of redemption through the shedding of His blood (see Heb. 9:12). The finely twined linen tells us of Jesus' purity and righteousness (see 2 Cor. 5:21). In Old Testament times, linen was reserved for holy purposes such as the clothing of priests and the Tabernacle curtains (see Exod. 26:1; Lev. 16:4). In Revelation we see that fine linen was associated with the righteous or the saints (see Rev. 19:8).

The third and most significant curtain divided the Holy Place from the Most Holy Place (see Exod. 26:31-33). God's presence rested on the atonement cover of the Ark of the Covenant that was placed behind this curtain. This curtain was like the second that divided the outer court from the Holy Place except that it was embroi-

dered with cherubim. The cherubim indicate the entrance to the throne of God (see Pss. 80:1; 99:1). They symbolize protection of that which is sacred or off limits (see Gen. 3:24; Ezek. 28:14).

The curtain was tightly woven and probably very heavy. It stood as a barrier between God and His people, and access to the Most Holy Place was extremely limited, even to Aaron the high priest. "The Lord spoke to Moses after the death of the two sons of Aaron who died when they approached the Lord. The Lord said to Moses: 'Tell your brother Aaron not to come whenever he chooses into the Most Holy Place behind the curtain in front of the atonement cover on the ark, or else he will die, because I appear in the cloud over the atonement cover'" (Lev. 16:1,2). Aaron was to follow strict guidelines for cleansing before approaching the Most Holy Place, and he was to approach only on God's terms (see vv. 3-14). The reason for this lies in the fact that a holy and perfect God cannot tolerate the presence of imperfect, sinful men. Aaron's cleansing would temporarily make him clean so that he could make a sin offering on the part of the people (see vv. 15,16). This process of cleansing was repeated every year before the annual entrance into God's presence could be made (see v. 34).

Jesus as the Curtain

The New Testament book of Hebrews tells us that this cleansing was symbolic of one who would come who was perfect and who could offer a sacrifice once and for all for the sins of the people. "When Christ came as high priest of the good things that are already here, he went through the greater and more perfect tabernacle that is not man-made, that is to say, not a part of this creation. He did not enter by means of the blood of goats and calves; but he entered the Most Holy Place once for all by his own blood, having obtained eternal redemption" (Heb. 9:11,12).

An imperfect people needs a provision of spiritual purity to gain access to God. People today who have not recognized their need try to make their own way to God. But they cannot bridge the distance between themselves and God by their own goodness or the cleverness of their ideas about God.

This is why it was necessary for God to graphically represent His separation and holiness in the construction of the Tabernacle. It is also why the curtain covering the Most Holy Place is such a beautiful type of Christ. It is only through Him that access to God is possible. This is symbolized for us in a dramatic historical event.

When Jesus, hanging on the cross, breathed His last, the Temple curtain "was torn in two from top to bottom" (Mark 15:38; also see Luke 23:44-46).

By Jesus' day the Tabernacle had been replaced, on God's command, by the Temple in Jerusalem (see 1 Kings 5:3-5). The Temple was a permanent structure with walls of stone instead of curtains. The design of the Temple followed that of the Tabernacle but the materials used were different with one noteable exception: The curtain shielding the Most Holy Place was the only curtain that remained. This curtain probably measured 30-40 feet in height[1] and may have been as thick as 4 inches[2]. The tearing of this large curtain could only have been an act of God. The thickness of the curtain and the fact that it was torn from *top* (30-40 feet above the floor) to bottom indicates a divine act as does the timing of the event to the very moment Jesus died. The sacrifice had been completed; now the way to God was open to all people through Jesus' blood.

Hebrews 10:19-22 describes the curtain as Christ's body: "Therefore, brothers, since we have confidence to enter the Most Holy Place by the blood of Jesus, by a new and living way opened for us through the curtain, that is, his body, and since we have a great priest over the house of God, let us draw near to God with a sincere heart in full assurance of faith, having our hearts sprinkled to cleanse us from a guilty conscience and having our bodies washed with pure water." Jesus' humanity veiled His divine nature, just as the Tabernacle curtain shielded the Most Holy Place from human eyes. From time to time, as in His miracles, Jesus' divinity shown through, and His divine glory was perceived (see Matt. 14:22-33). When the flesh of Christ expired, His divine nature was openly exposed. Even the centurion standing guard at the cross recognized the divine aspect of Jesus' character (see Matt. 27:54; Mark 15:39). As the curtain was torn apart, can you imagine the jolt the high priest must have felt when the Most Holy Place was suddenly exposed? The high priest, no doubt, had some difficult explanations to give.

Perfect in God's Sight

From the point of Christ's death on, the sacrificial system of the Jews was replaced by a new order. The need for continual sacrifices with the blood of bulls and goats was abolished by Jesus. "When this priest had offered for all time one sacrifice for sins, he sat down at the right hand of God . . . . because by one sacrifice he has made perfect forever those who are being made holy" (Heb. 10:12,14). By this sacrifice Jesus has made those who are cleansed by His blood perfect and acceptable to God. Verse 14 says that these people are seen by God as perfect *forever*. From our point of view, we know that Christians are in the process of becoming perfect (see Matt. 5:48). From God's point of view, Christians have already been given His stamp of approval, redeemable when they meet God in heaven (see John 14:2,3; Rom. 8:1-4).

If open access to God is now possible, why are many reluctant to meet Him face to face? Perhaps one reason is that belief is an unveiling process; it requires the initial risk of accepting truth before it is completely understood. God initiated a seemingly strange way for Christians to discover truth. Christians are to believe in what Christ has done and what He claims to be before this truth is personally verified by their experience. This is opposed to the methods of investigation and comprehension taught in our schools and colleges. In the academic community members are very careful not to draw premature conclusions. The evidence must be weighed very carefully and when the evidence is confirmed by experimentation or repeated observation, belief is allowed. The academic leaders assert that all information should be public and all that is true will yield to investigation if we can discover the methods necessary to unveil it.

If academic methods alone were applied to spiritual truth, a moral problem would arise: Only the intelligent person could discover truth and come to a place of full understanding by which belief could then be possible. Because Christians claim that understanding can come only after belief, they are often criticized for blind faith or regarded as gullible. But this is how truth is revealed. The gospel of Christ has been revealed to the simple, and the wise things of God are foolishness to the educated (see Matt. 11:25; 1 Cor. 1:26,27). In fact, intellectuals who deny God's existence are like the Israelites in Moses' day whose minds were veiled from seeing God's glory and understanding His covenant. This is because the veil that limits their understanding of God's plan "has not been removed, because only in Christ is it taken away" (2 Cor. 3:14). But the Lord does not depend on faulty human intellect. He is available to all, wise and foolish. It is by walking in faith that truth is unveiled. Then God can be seen in personal and significant ways. Just as the curtain was the only entrance to the Most Holy Place, so a person must pass *through* Christ before God can be revealed to him or her. Belief must come before full understanding.

A bit of risk accompanies the move to believe before you understand. You are placing your pride on the line, believing that you will be right. You are taking the risk of being wrong. I have known Ph.D.s who have spent years trying to learn enough so they can figure out God without having to believe Him first. They produce some very interesting ideas but still will be blind, unless they first come to God in repentance and faith. Then the veil that blinds them can be lifted and they can begin to understand. "Whenever anyone turns to the Lord, the veil is taken away" (2 Cor. 3:16).

Prideful reluctance is not solely the territory of unbelievers. I find myself constantly wanting to resort to human wisdom. So often I want to know more before I take the risk to exercise faith. But faith in Christ alone provides the way through the veil and allows us to know and relate to God as no other means can. To add to the personal feeling of risk in believing, we are instructed to not only come by faith but to charge in boldly with confidence and "full assurance of faith" (Heb. 10:22; also see v. 19). No inferiority complexes need get in the way. Through Christ, God has esteemed us highly. We are precious to Him and loved as His own children. "How great is the love the Father has lavished on us, that we should be called children of God!" (1 John 3:1). As His children God gladly opens Himself to our simplest and dumbest questions. He is interested in our least concerns. There is no self-improvement program we can embark upon that will bring us to God's throne. The only way is the way He has provided through Jesus (see John 14:6).

This idea prompts a question: Have all your shortcomings been covered by the sacrifice of Christ? The fact is, if you are a Christian God does not see any blemish on you. You are perfect in His sight (see Heb. 10:10,14). Like His own Son who entered the Most Holy Place before you, you can enter His presence *boldly*!

Notes

1. *The Bible Visual Resource Book* (Ventura, CA: Regal Books, 1989), p. 185.

2. Charles E. Fuller, *The Tabernacle in the Wilderness* (Westwood, NJ: Fleming H. Revell Co., 1960), p. 76.

APPROACH TO THE WORD

APPROACH (5-7 minutes)

Briefly discuss with your students the steps involved in being accepted to a prominent university. List these steps on the board or overhead as they are mentioned. Include the following: college entrance exams, completing application forms and sending fees, financial aid forms, entrance interviews and waiting for a letter of acceptance or rejection. Optional—show copies of some of the forms (available from a counselor at your local community college, or write to a prominent school or a college you attended) and read excerpts from the forms' instructions.

Say, **Gaining acceptance to a prominent university often involves a complicated process of filling out forms, paying application fees and waiting. In Old Testament times, gaining access to God was a complicated process of making sacrifices and keeping certain rules. And even then only certain people, usually the high priest, could enter into God's presence. Today we are going to learn how Jesus cut through this process and made it possible for everyone to be accepted by God.**

BIBLE EXPLORATION

EXPLORATION (35-45 minutes)

Materials needed: Session 8 Student Worksheet and a diagram showing the arrangement of the Tabernacle (see the clip art section at the back of this book) for each student.

Step 1 (1-2 minutes): Introduce today's study by saying, **After the Passover, Pharaoh allowed the Israelites to leave Egypt and begin their journey to the land of Canaan, which God had promised to Abraham's descendants. During this time the Israelites turned against God and Moses. God told** them that **because they had disobeyed, they must wander in the desert until the generation of disobedient people had died. Also during this time, God gave the people the Ten Commandments, laws for them to follow to show their obedience. And God gave them instructions for constructing the Tabernacle where the people could worship God and where God would be present among them.**

Step 2 (5-7 minutes): Distribute the Student Worksheets and Tabernacle diagrams. Then direct students to turn in their Bible

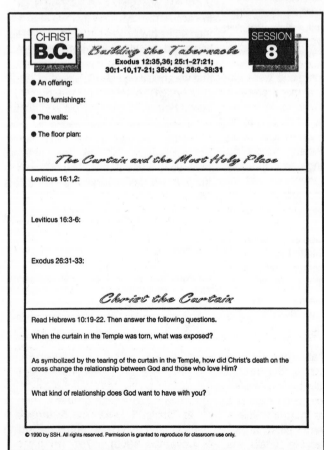

CHRIST **B.C.** — *Building the Tabernacle* — SESSION **8**

Exodus 12:35,36; 25:1–27:21; 30:1-10,17-21; 35:4-29; 36:8–38:31

● An offering:

● The furnishings:

● The walls:

● The floor plan:

The Curtain and the Most Holy Place

Leviticus 16:1,2:

Leviticus 16:3-6:

Exodus 26:31-33:

Christ the Curtain

Read Hebrews 10:19-22. Then answer the following questions.

When the curtain in the Temple was torn, what was exposed?

As symbolized by the tearing of the curtain in the Temple, how did Christ's death on the cross change the relationship between God and those who love Him?

What kind of relationship does God want to have with you?

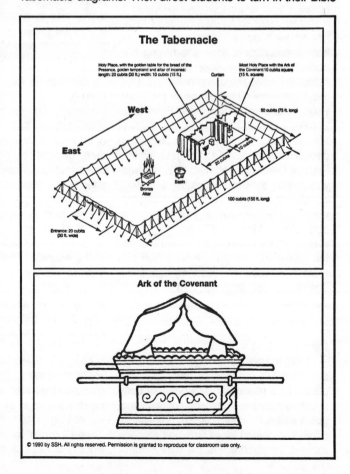

The Tabernacle

Holy Place, with the golden table for the bread of the Presence, golden lampstand and altar of incense; length: 20 cubits (30 ft.) width: 10 cubits (15 ft.)

Most Holy Place with the Ark of the Covenant: 10 cubits square (15 ft.)

Curtain

West

East

50 cubits (75 ft. long)

20 cubits

10 cubits

Bronze Altar

Basin

100 cubits (150 ft. long)

Entrance: 20 cubits (30 ft. wide)

Ark of the Covenant

to Exodus, chapter 35. Present a brief lecture describing the construction of the Tabernacle (see Exodus 25–27; 30:1-10,17-21; 35:4-29; 36:8–38:31). Encourage students to take notes on the "Building the Tabernacle" section of their worksheets and refer to their diagrams as you present your material.

Mention the following points in your presentation:

- The materials for making the Tabernacle came from a freewill offering made by the people. (Then read aloud Exod. 37:1-7.) These materials were probably given to the Israelites by the Egyptians before they left Egypt (read aloud Exod. 12:35,36).
- Among other furnishings, the Tabernacle contained an altar for burnt sacrifices, a basin for washing and a box, called the Ark of the Covenant, to hold the Ten Commandments.
- The walls of the Tabernacle were made of woven curtains and skins so that it could be disassembled and carried with the Israelites where ever they went.
- The structure of the Tabernacle consisted of three main sections: an outer courtyard where all the people could enter; the Holy Place, a room that only the priests could enter; and the Most Holy Place, the room beyond the Holy Place, where the Ark of the Covenant was placed. No one except the high priest was allowed in the Most Holy Place, and then only once a year.

Step 3 (12-14 minutes): Say, **There is so much we can discuss about all the parts and pieces of the Tabernacle that we can't possibly cover everything in one session. So today we are going to focus on one part, the curtain that covered the entrance to the Most Holy Place where the Ark of the Covenant was kept.**

Ask volunteers to share in reading aloud the verses listed on their worksheets under the heading "The Curtain and the Most Holy Place." As the verses are read, lead a discussion of the verses using the following outline and information from the Teacher's Bible Study.

Leviticus 16:1,2

- **What was special about the Most Holy Place?** (It was where God appeared.)

Leviticus 16:3-6

- **Under what conditions could the high priest enter the Most Holy Place?** (He had to wear sacred garments, bathe and offer a sacrifice for his and his household's sins.)
- State that the sacrifice the high priest made for his sin made him temporarily acceptable to God so he could enter God's presence and offer a sacrifice for the sins of the people of Israel. Each year this sacrifice was repeated before the high priest passed behind the curtain to the Most Holy Place.

Exodus 26:31-33

- After reading these descriptions of the curtain, ask students to suggest each of its individual characteristics. List their suggestions on the board or overhead. Your list should include: blue, purple, scarlet, fine linen, embroidered with cherubim, separates the Holy Place from the Most Holy Place, hung with gold hooks on wood posts with silver bases.

- **What spiritual function did the curtain serve?** (It separated sinful man from holy God.)
- Then share Dr. Lloyd Ahlem's comments (see the Teacher's Bible Study section titled "The Curtain for the Most Holy Place") concerning the traditional meaning for the Jews of the linen (reserved for holy purposes such as priests' clothing), the colors blue, purple and scarlet (heaven, royalty and earthly glory) as well as the symbolism of the cherubim (the divine; God's throne—have a volunteer read Ps. 99:1).

Step 4 (10-12 minutes): Say, **The New Testament book of Hebrews talks about Christ as the curtain. Let's discuss how each characteristic of the Tabernacle curtain illustrates a characteristic of Christ.** Lead a brief discussion including the following points: fine linen describes Christ as our holy high priest—see Hebrews 8:1,2; blue tells us that Jesus came from and returned to heaven—see John 3:13; purple tells us about Jesus' status as King of Kings—see Revelation 19:12-16; scarlet tells us of how Jesus was glorified on earth through His death on the cross—see John 12:27,28 and 13:31,32; cherubim tell us that Jesus is divine and sits at the right hand of the throne of God—see Hebrews 12:2.

Ask, **What does Jesus' role as the curtain tell us about the way God can be approached?** (Access to God is only possible through Christ.) Then say, **The curtain is a picture of Christ, but Christ also serves in the role of the high priest who can pass behind the curtain.** Then read Hebrews 9:11,12 and 10:12. Ask, **How is Jesus different from the high priest described in Exodus?** (He does not have to repeat His sacrifice; it provides eternal redemption for the sins of the people.) Read 1 John 1:9. **Who can receive forgiveness because of Jesus' sacrifice?** (Those who confess their sins to Him.)

Step 5 (7-10 minutes): Say, **We have seen how the Tabernacle curtain is a symbol of Christ, the only One through whom God can be approached. We have also seen that as the High Priest, Jesus' sacrifice for the sins of the people only had to be made once and therefore can provide eternal redemption for those who come to Him. Now let's look at a New Testament event that changed forever the relationship between God and those who put their faith and trust in Him.**

Move the class into groups of three to five students. (If your class is small in number, group students in pairs or trios.) Read aloud Mark 15:33-38. Then direct the groups to complete the assignment in the "Christ the Curtain" section of their worksheets. Then ask students to share their responses to the questions on the worksheet. Responses might include: the Most Holy Place where God's presence was appeared was exposed; when the curtain was torn there was no longer any barrier between man and God; all people can have access to God; God wants us to come into His presence with confidence, faith and a sincere heart; God wants to cleanse our lives of sin and have an open, intimate relationship with us.

CONCLUSION & DECISION

CONCLUSION (5-8 minutes)

Say, **On the back of your worksheet draw or write a short description of how you see yourself—your appearance, your personality traits, your abilities.** Give students several minutes to work. Then read Romans 8:1-4 and Hebrews 10:12,14. Say, **Now draw or write a description of how God**

sees anyone who has committed his or her life to Him through faith in Jesus' sacrifice on the cross. After a couple minutes ask, **How different are your two descriptions?** Then say, **Through Jesus Christ's death on the cross, God has made many things possible. One of the exciting things God has given Christians is acceptance. When we as Christians** approach God, He accepts us, sees us as perfect and wants to have an open, intimate relationship with us.

Close in prayer, asking God to help each person see him- or herself through God's eyes. Then thank God that He has made it possible for each person to have access to Him and establish a loving relationship with Him.

Encourage students to read chapter 8 in the student paperback *Christ B.C.* The readings in this chapter explore the theme "reconciliation."

NOTES:

The Ark of the Covenant

KEY VERSE

"Make an atonement cover of pure gold . . . . And make two cherubim out of hammered gold at the ends of the cover . . . . The cherubim are to face each other, looking toward the cover. Place the cover on top of the ark and put in the ark the Testimony, which I will give you." Exodus 25:17,18,20,21

"For all have sinned and fall short of the glory of God, and are justified freely by his grace through the redemption that came by Christ Jesus. God presented him as a sacrifice of atonement, through faith in his blood." Romans 3:23-25

BIBLICAL BASIS

Exodus 25:10-22; Leviticus 16:1,2,11,15,16,34; 1 Samuel 4:4; Psalm 99:1; Romans 2:5,6; 3:25; 5:8-10; Hebrews 2:17; 1 John 4:9,10

FOCUS OF THE SESSION

The Ark of the Covenant is a picture of Christ dwelling in our midst, providing atonement and mercy to all who come to Him in faith.

AIMS OF THIS SESSION

You and your students will have accomplished the purpose of this Bible Study session if you can:

- DISCUSS ways in which the Ark of the Covenant is a type of Christ and His sacrifice of atonement;
- SHARE ways in which God expresses His mercy to people today;
- EXAMINE ways in which you can respond to God's mercy and the consequences of your responses.

Teacher's Bible Study

The Ark

The Ark of the Covenant was a simple box. The size of it gives no clue to its significance. It was only 3¾ feet long, 2¼ feet wide and 2¼ feet high (see Exod. 25:10). God had given special instructions for its making (see vv.10-16) because He intended to symbolize by its construction His relationship to man. It was made of acacia wood, a strong enduring material common in the desert in which Israel traveled while on route to the Promised Land. The wood was overlaid with pure gold—no doubt part of the treasure looted from Egypt (see 12:35,36).

These materials, wood and gold, are generally believed to symbolize the human and divine character of Jesus Christ. Gold is repeatedly used as a symbol for the enduring character of the kingdom of God. The New Jerusalem as described in the book of Revelation is adorned with gold (see 21:18). Gold was the most decay-proof material known to man and represents permanence—Christ's eternal, heavenly character. The wood, an impermanent substance, represents Jesus' human body, and our human condition: perishable. It is interesting that God had the

ark built out of a common wood readily available in the desert, rather than cedar from Lebanon or oak from Palestine. A long difficult journey would have been required to obtain these fancier woods. In the same way, God sent His Son to earth as a man, with common flesh like ours, rather than sending someone like an angel. Like the wood growing in our midst, Jesus is readily available to us (see Rev. 3:20).

The Atonement Cover

After giving instructions for making the ark God said, "Make an atonement cover of pure gold" (Exod. 25:17). No wood was to be used on the cover because this was where God's holy presence would rest and where His work of atonement for the sins of the people of Israel would be carried out (see Lev. 16:15,16). In the same way, it is through Jesus' divinity, His triumph over death, that our sins can be forgiven (see 1 Cor. 15:55-57; 2 Tim. 1:10).

Then God instructed that two cherubim be hammered out of gold and made to stand facing each other on top of the atonement cover (also called the mercy seat). Their wings were "spread upward,

overshadowing the cover" (Exod. 25:20) and their faces were looking down, focused on the cover. The presence of the cherubim symbolizes that on the atonement cover God sat enthroned (see Ps. 99:1). God told Moses, "There, above the cover between the two cherubim that are over the ark of the Testimony, I will meet with you and give you all my commands for the Israelites" (v. 22).

It is also on the cover that Aaron was directed to sprinkle the sacrificial blood that was spilled in atonement for the sins of the people (see Lev. 16:15,16). During the Passover in Egypt God's judgment passed over the homes where blood had been painted on the doorposts (Exod. 12:23). In the same way, the offering of blood made by the high priest was sufficient to spare the people from judgment and restore their broken relationship with God. Yet, unlike Christ's sacrifice, this atonement sacrifice by Aaron had to be repeated each year. The sacrificial system was imperfect in terms of effectively removing sin; it only covered it. Yet it served as a perfect introduction for the picture of the perfect sacrifice that was to come through Jesus. Jesus' sacrifice would perfectly replace this imperfect covering for sin by providing for the permanent removal of sin from people's lives (see Gal. 3:23-25; Heb. 10:8-10).

God in Our Midst

The ark was the holiest of all the furnishings in the Tabernacle. On this small box, settled into the innermost part of the Tabernacle, dwelt the glory of God (see Lev. 16:2). When the Tabernacle was moved, the ark was covered by the curtain and other heavy cloths that shielded the radiance of the presence of God from the people (see Num. 4:5,6). This radiance is called the Shekinah Glory of God (God's glory manifested); it has a magnificence so powerful that anyone who stood in its presence would die, unless perfectly atoned for by blood sacrifice. Even then God's glory had to be shielded from view. When Aaron prepared to enter the Most Holy Place where the ark stood he was instructed by God to "take a censer full of burning coals from the altar before the Lord and two handfuls of finely ground fragrant incense and take them behind the curtain. He is to put the incense on the fire before the Lord, and the smoke of the incense will conceal the atonement cover above the Testimony, so that he will not die" (Lev. 16:12,13). The awesomeness of God's glory is obvious as is the division, caused by sin, between God and people. Because of this division the people of the Old Testament were limited in their access to God.

Today, through Christ's sacrifice, we have free access to God. Charles E. Fuller stated that: "This Shekinah Glory was a local manifestation of the very presence of God, and since this presence was located between the Cherubim over the place where the shed blood was applied, we see once again the fact that it is impossible to come into the presence of God unless one comes to the Cross of Christ, humbly admitting his sin, his inability to save himself, and trusting completely in the finished work of Christ."[1] It is through atonement—initiated and designed by God—that entrance into His presence and mercy through His grace are possible (see Eph. 2:13; Col. 1:19,20). In this sense the ark is a symbol of God's gift of atonement through Christ.

What if God had let man design the ark, the place where God and man would meet? What would it have looked like? Most likely it would have been some magnificent structure such as is a cathedral. It has been my privilege to visit some of the great cathedrals of the world: St. Paul's in London, Notre Dame in Paris and St.

Isaac's in Leningrad. Each is a grand structure, far beyond my ability to design. Each is rich in symbolism. The symbolism is conveyed through architectural design and stained glass windows that are artistically and superbly crafted. Many of these cathedrals were designed to reproduce the awesomeness of entering God's presence—of being in heaven. The efforts of the designers and builders are to be praised, but the buildings do not represent how God chooses to relate to man. We do not have to enter heaven to meet with God; God has come to us through His Son Jesus who is called "'Immanuel'—which means, 'God with us'" (Matt. 1:23). For the Israelites God chose to come by the means of a little box, housed in a temporary, moveable structure. He dwelt in their midst, traveled with them and communicated with them. And as He did so His glory was evident to the people. "So the cloud of the Lord was over the Tabernacle by day, and fire was in the cloud by night, in the sight of all the house of Israel during all their travels" (Exod. 40:38).

Today we continue to create great structures, great ideas and theologies about God, yet miss the point. By building a picture showing only God's greatness, we put Him at a distance—out of reach. We also have a tendency to do the opposite. We dwell on Jesus' human character, His goodness and His wise teachings. We call Him our "friend," yet we do not always remember to call Him "Lord." God came to Israel in a small box, the ark. He came again in a simple manger in Bethlehem. He did this without losing any of His greatness or glory. Rather He voluntarily set aside His equality with God in order to reach us on our level (see Phil. 2:5-8). Today He finds His way into our midst, in the small places of our lives, without losing one particle of His awesomeness and power. God's glory and greatness cannot be separated from His accessibility and presence in our midst.

Mercy and Wrath

God dwelling in the midst of the Israelites is certainly a picture of Christ and His mercy and grace. Christ humbly left His exalted position in heaven to take on the flesh of a man. John 1:14 says, "The Word became flesh and made his dwelling among us. We have seen his glory, the glory of the One and Only, who came from the Father, full of grace and truth." Christ did this to fulfill God's plan to provide complete and perfect atonement for humankind's sin. Through Christ, undeserving people can receive mercy and escape the wrath of God which they have duly

earned. Romans 3:25,26 describes how God, in His mercy, withholds His wrath in order to provide sinners with an opportunity for repentance and faith. These verses state, "God presented him as a sacrifice of atonement, through faith in his blood. He did this to demonstrate his justice, because in his forbearance he had left the sins committed beforehand unpunished—he did it to demonstrate his justice at the present time, so as to be just and the one who justifies those who have faith in Jesus."

The ark contained three special objects (see Heb. 9:4) that stood as expressions of God's mercy toward the Israelites and His involvement in their lives. These three objects were the Ten Commandments carved on stone tablets (see Exod. 31:18; 40:20), the rod of Aaron that had budded, bloomed and bore almonds (see Num. 17:8-10) and a pot of manna that was Israel's food during the sojourn through the desert. These are symbolic of the fact that God's truth, God's direction and God's sustenance are available to His people and are the means by which His people should make their way through life. To do otherwise would result in experiencing God's wrath.

The wrath of God is the natural result of not living in obedience or conformity to the spiritual principles of God (see Gal. 6:7,8). God's wrath is a permanent and consistent attitude of a holy and just God who is confronted by sin and evil. This is not to say that God's wrath is a process of cause and effect that operates in the world at large. It is, rather, a personal trait of God expressed in response to man's sin.[2] For example, if I choose to organize my life around my own self-pleasure, I'm going to run into trouble. I was created to organize my life with God at the center (see Matt. 22:37,38). If I place ego in the central position, I have replaced God with myself. If I go against God's guidelines for faith and conduct I will suffer spiritual, and sometimes physical and emotional, consequences. And in many instances I may cause others to suffer also. By myself, and under my own direction, I am terribly short-sighted, selfish and vain. There is neither pleasure nor spiritual health in vanity. My own desires are unfulfillable and my ambitions are empty. The evidence of the wrath of God operating in my life may be a miserable, lonely existence of trying to play God for myself and failing. What amazes me most is that I persist, even though I know better. But I am truly grateful for forgiveness and mercy and the opportunity for a new start. I may still suffer physical and emotional consequences because of my actions and I may need to repair broken relationships, but in the light of eternity I have, through repentance, been cleansed from all unrighteousness (see 1 John 1:9) and have been saved from God's wrath. "God's wrath is always tempered with mercy,"[3] especially for the redeemed (see Rom. 5:10; 1 Thess. 1:10).

In several incidents the Israelites experienced God's mercy when they were deserving of His wrath. In Numbers 13,14 we read that they did not trust God's promise to lead, sustain and provide for them in the land God had provided. Instead they grumbled and cried, asking to return to Egypt. They disobeyed and refused to enter the land and they paid the consequences for their disobedience—forty years of wandering homeless in the desert.

Even in their disobedience Israel experienced God's mercy. God could have turned His anger on them and destroyed them. But in His mercy and faithfulness to His promises to give the land to Abraham's descendants, God held back His anger, allowed the Israelites to experience the consequences of their rebellion (see 14:17-25) and gave them the opportunity to turn back to Him. As they wandered in the desert God went with them, dwelt in their midst and met with them in the Most Holy Place over the Ark of the Covenant.

This experience is also true of many Christians who rebel against God. They remove God from a position of primary importance in their lives and try to assume that position themselves. These Christians may experience pain as a direct result of their actions and they create a spiritual chasm between themselves and God. They may also inflict pain on others—especially other Christians with whom they are close. Many times these people, like the Israelites, repent and turn back to God. They find that He has, in His mercy, never left them. When they begin to reorder their lives with God at the center they receive spiritual healing, relief and the strength to deal with any unresolved consequences of their sin. As we seek first to do God's will and place ego in orbit around the leadership of God, we find mercy and grace. When God is in charge, we find healing in our values, priorities become well ordered and our needs are satisfied (see Ps. 37:4; Matt. 6:33).

It is a struggle to let go and rely on God to direct and sustain our lives. Yet it is encouraging to know that whenever we turn to God through faith in Christ Jesus He is with us, in our midst, ready to guide us in obedience. We deserve to be cast out of His presence, but in His mercy He allows us to come to Him through the blood sacrifice of His Son, Jesus Christ.

Notes

1. Charles E. Fuller, *The Tabernacle in the Wilderness* (Westwood, NJ:Fleming H. Revell Co., 1960), p.82.

2. J.D. Douglas, ed., *New Bible Dictionary* (Grand Rapids: Wm. B. Eerdmans Publishing Co., 1962), p. 1341.

3. *New Bible Dictionary*, p. 1341.

This Week's Teaching Plan

APPROACH TO THE WORD

APPROACH (5-8 minutes)

Before class letter the words "Mercy is . . . " on a large sheet of paper and post it where students can easily reach it. As students arrive, ask them to write a definition or describe a situation that illustrates the meaning of the word mercy.

When all students have gathered, read aloud what students have written about mercy. Then read the following definition of the word: "compassion or forbearance shown especially to an offender or to one subject to one's power" (see *Webster's Ninth New Collegiate Dictionary*). Move to the Exploration by saying, **Today we are going to look at the Ark of the Covenant and Christ's death, both of which illustrate God's mercy toward sinful people.**

BIBLE EXPLORATION

EXPLORATION (35-45 minutes)

Materials needed: Session 9 Student Worksheet for each student, dictionary. Optional— an object made of wood and one made of gold.

Step 1 (10-15 minutes): Introduce your study of the Ark of the Covenant by briefly reviewing the situation of the Israelites in the desert and God's instructions to build the Tabernacle. Then say, **One of the furnishings of the Tabernacle was the Ark of the Covenant. The ark was kept in the innermost room of the Tabernacle where only the high priest could enter.** Distribute the Session 9 worksheets to students and direct them to turn in their Bibles to Exodus, chapter 25. Ask volunteers to share in reading aloud the verses listed in the "Ark of the Covenant" section of their worksheets. As the verses are read, lead a discussion of the verses using the following outline and information from the Teacher's Bible Study. Encourage students to take notes on their worksheets as the discussion progresses.

Exodus 25:10-16

• Say, **These measurements equal approximately 3³/₄-feet long, 2¹/₄-feet wide and 2¹/₄-feet tall. The word "ark," in this instance means "box" or "chest."**

• Optional—show the gold and wood objects you have brought. Ask, **If these objects were thrown into a fire, what would happen to the wood?** (It would be destroyed.) **What would happen to the gold?** (It may melt, but it would not be destroyed. It would still retain the worth of the gold it is made of.) Then say, **If we look at the ark as a type of Christ, what would the wood used in the ark represent?** (Jesus' perishable body—see John 1:14; 4:6.) **What would the gold represent?** (Jesus' divine nature—see 1 Tim. 1:17.)

55

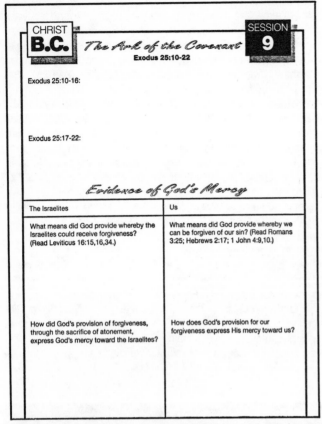

CHRIST B.C.

The Ark of the Covenant
Exodus 25:10-22

SESSION 9

Exodus 25:10-16:

Exodus 25:17-22:

Evidence of God's Mercy

The Israelites	Us
What means did God provide whereby the Israelites could receive forgiveness? (Read Leviticus 16:15,16,34.)	What means did God provide whereby we can be forgiven of our sin? (Read Romans 3:25; Hebrews 2:17; 1 John 4:9,10.)
How did God's provision of forgiveness, through the sacrifice of atonement, express God's mercy toward the Israelites?	How does God's provision for our forgiveness express His mercy toward us?

- **Acacia wood came from the local trees growing in the desert. What form did Jesus take when He came to live on earth?** (A common man rather than a king, official or supernatural being—see Phil. 2:5-8.)

Exodus 25:17-22

- **What do you think the word "atonement" means?** After students give several suggestions, give the dictionary to a volunteer and ask him or her to look up and read the definition for "atonement," or give the following definition: Reconciliation; the reconciliation of God and man through the sacrificial death of Jesus Christ. Mention that the atonement cover has also been called the "mercy seat."

- Read Leviticus 16:1,2,11,15,16. Briefly explain that during the time before Jesus' coming to earth, atonement was made possible on a temporary basis. Each year, after making a sacrifice for his own sins, the high priest would enter the room that held the ark and make a sacrifice of atonement to obtain forgiveness for the sins of the Israelite people. For this sacrifice the high priest would slaughter a goat then take its blood into the room where the ark was kept and sprinkle the blood on the atonement cover and in front of it. This sacrifice had to be repeated once every year.

- **Why do you think it's significant that only gold was used and not wood also to make the atonement cover for the ark? What is it about Jesus' character, symbolized by the gold in the atonement cover, that makes it possible for Him to repair the relationship between sinful people and God?** (The fact that He is divine—has power over death—means He has the power to bring people back into relationship with God—read aloud Rom. 5:10.)

- Read 1 Samuel 4:4 and Psalm 99:1. **What do the cherubim tell us about the ark?** (It is holy; it represents the throne of God.)

- **What did God say would occur over the ark?** (See Exod. 25:22.)

Move to Step 2 by saying, **We have looked at the structure of the ark and the characteristics of Christ symbolized by its structure. Now let's look at the role of the ark and how this role points to God's involvement in people's lives today.**

Step 2 (12-15 minutes): Move the class into two groups (or a multiple of two). Refer to the definition for mercy shared during the Approach. Then direct students to the "Evidence of God's Mercy" chart on their worksheets and assign half the class to complete "The Israelites" column and the other half of the class to complete the "Us" column of the chart. Allow 5-8 minutes for groups to work. Circulate around the room, answering questions or giving added direction as needed.

Ask volunteers to share their findings. As necessary to enhance student's understanding, ask the following questions: **How was God's presence among the Israelites an expression of His mercy?** Mention that instead of abandoning the Israelites when they were disobedient God gave them the opportunity to return to Him and find forgiveness. **How is Jesus present with Christians today? How is the presence of the Holy Spirit in the heart of a Christian an expression of mercy toward him or her? What is the difference between the atonement the Israelites received and the atonement we can have through Christ?** (See Heb. 10:11-14.) **How has God's mercy affected the lives of His people?**

Step 3 (13-15 minutes): Ask, **Why do you think God extends His mercy to us?** After giving students a few moments to share their thoughts, read Lloyd Ahlem's comments from the Teacher's Bible Study section titled "Mercy and Wrath" beginning with the words "Christians may experience pain as a direct result of . . . " (see the sixth paragraph of this section) and continuing to the end of the paragraph. Then, in light of these comments, ask volunteers to summarize for the group reasons why God is merciful. Clarify as necessary any information shared.

Then ask, **When are some times God may express mercy today?** Because this is a difficult concept to grasp, share an illustration from your own life that when you deserved to experience God's wrath, but because you repented of your sin and turned to Him for help you experienced mercy instead of wrath. If this is uncomfortable for you, or if you cannot think of a suitable example, use the example of Christ's encounter with Zacchaeus (see Luke 19:1-10). Then encourage students to share possible situations where if they respond to the opportunity God has given them, God may respond toward them in mercy. Ask, **Why might God express mercy in that situation?** List their suggestions on the board or overhead. Situations may include: Being invited to a Bible study so I can learn about Jesus and eternal life then responding by becoming a Christian; giving me a Christian friend who is willing to tell me when I am headed into sin then responding by trying to do what God wants; showing me how sin has messed up others' lives then responding by deciding that I don't want to follow their example; helping me realize how a sinful action of mine has hurt others then responding by apologizing and not continuing to commit that sin; allowing me to have a Bible where I can read about what God has done and how he wants me to live then responding by applying what I have learned.

Move to the Conclusion by reading Romans 2:5,6 and 5:8-10. Then say, **Sometimes it seems as if evil people are left unpunished by God. These verses tell us that all people will someday be judged for their deeds. Those who belong to Christ will be saved from the day of God's wrath and will receive eternal life. Those who have rejected Jesus will experience God's wrath and will not go to heaven.**

CONCLUSION & DECISION

CONCLUSION (3-5 minutes)

On the back of his or her worksheet, direct each student to write a description of a time when he or she was shown mercy by God. Then direct each student to write his or her response to God because of His mercy in that situation—repentance and thankfulness, indifference, anger or giving him- or herself credit for God's action, etc. If students need help, refer to the list made during Step 3.

Close in prayer thanking God that He has given each student in your class today an opportunity, by listening to God's Word, to respond to His mercy and express repentance, find forgiveness and begin a new life with Jesus' Spirit living in him or her.

Encourage students to read chapter 9 in the student paperback *Christ B.C.* The reading in this chapter explores the theme "mercy."

NOTES:

The Bronze Snake

KEY VERSE

"The Lord said to Moses, 'Make a snake and put it up on a pole; anyone who is bitten can look at it and live.' So Moses made a bronze snake and put it up on a pole. Then when anyone was bitten by a snake and looked at the bronze snake, he lived," Numbers 21:8,9

"Just as Moses lifted up the snake in the desert, so the Son of Man must be lifted up, that everyone who believes in him may have eternal life." John 3:14,15

BIBLICAL BASIS

Numbers 21:4-9; John 1:12; 3:14-17; 14:26; Acts 4:12; Romans 3:23; 5:6,8; 6:5-10,23; 2 Corinthians 5:21; Hebrews 9:14; 1 John 1:9

FOCUS OF THE SESSION

As the bronze snake lifted up by Moses saved all who looked at it from death, so Jesus offers salvation to all who look to Him.

AIMS OF THIS SESSION

You and your students will have accomplished the purpose of this Bible study session if you can:

- COMPARE the bronze snake lifted up by Moses to Christ's death and resurrection;
- DISCUSS God's solution for sin found only through Christ's death and resurrection;
- PRAY, as the Holy Spirit leads, to accept salvation through Christ.

Teacher's Bible Study

Today's study focuses on a strong type of the salvation available to us because of Christ's death on the cross, resurrection and ascension into heaven. This colorful type is created through a bronze snake made by Moses.

Grumbling Israelites

The Lord told Moses to "make a snake and put it up on a pole; anyone who is bitten can look at it and live" (Num. 21:8). The background to this event is important. The Israelites had struggled in their meanderings. They had come to Edom and the Edomites had refused them passage through their land (see 20:14-21). Thus they had to follow a circuitous route around Edom. During this time Aaron died and the office of high priest was passed to his son Eleazar (see vv. 22-29). When they reached Arad in the Negev desert they were attacked by the local king's forces (see 21:1). Although the Lord gave the Israelites complete victory (see v. 3), the business of being aliens was taking its toll. The people grew impatient, began to gripe and "spoke against God and against Moses, and said, 'Why have you brought us up out of Egypt to die in the desert? There is no bread! There is no water! And

we detest this miserable food!'" (v. 5). In response God sent poisonous snakes through their area. This experience was God's way of chastising them for defaming His character and all He had done to provide for their needs. It was also God's way of establishing a symbol that would point to Christ, as we will soon see.

Among the Israelites multitudes were bitten. The snakes had completely infiltrated the encampment and a great cry went up to Moses for relief from the plague. "We sinned when we spoke against the Lord and against you. Pray that the Lord will take the snakes away from us," (v. 7) the people pleaded. Many had died painfully and the survival of Israel may have been at stake. When Moses prayed for the people, God directed him to fashion a snake and lift it high upon a pole so that it might be clearly seen (see v. 8). Then the instruction was given that whoever "was bitten by a snake and looked at the bronze snake" would live (v. 9).

God's snake was not intended to be an object of worship. Worship of the bronze snake would have gone directly against God's commandment, "You shall not make for yourself an idol in the form of anything in heaven above or on the earth beneath

or in the waters below" (Exod. 20:4). The purpose of the bronze snake was to point the people toward God, the one who could heal their affliction and the one deserving of their worship. But when Hezekiah became king of Judah, approximately 700 years later, the people are reported to have been worshiping Moses' brazen serpent. As well as abolishing other images of idolatry, Hezekiah destroyed the snake by breaking it into pieces (see 2 King 18:4).

Lessons for Life

Several lessons emerge from this experience relating to the bronze snake. First, it is God who is to be adored, not the symbols that represent Him. The reason for this is obvious: The symbol has no power; God is the source of power represented by the symbol. John 3:13,14 tells us that the symbol of the snake lifted up by Moses is also a symbol of Christ lifted up: "Just as Moses lifted up the snake in the desert, so the Son of Man must be lifted up, that everyone who believes in him may have eternal life." For the Israelites, the result of looking to the serpent was restored health and continuing life on earth. For those who look to Christ and put faith in Him the result is cleansing from sin and eternal life (see Rom. 6:23; 1 John 1:7). Therefore we worship Christ; we do not worship the cross. The cross is a symbol pointing us to Christ, the deserving object of our awe, praise and devotion.

I remember the story of a missionary to India who was challenged by an Indian intellectual. The Indian said, "Why do you bring all your theology with you? Why don't you just do the good works missionaries are known to do and leave the religious stuff alone?" The Indian was making an argument for the integrity of local religions and found Christian teaching upsetting to him. The missionary was clear in his reply, "By themselves these good things we do call attention only to themselves. We must point you to Christ who is the author and source of the good works."

A lesson related to idolatry and worship is this: The means by which we obtain our knowledge of salvation must not become an idol that we substitute for the God of our salvation. We must not adore the experience or the person who led us to the Lord more than the Lord. The Lord is eternal and He is a jealous God; He will not take a back seat to anything or anyone.

I heard a preacher once say that people are incurably worshipful and that they become like that which they worship. People also have the nasty habit of inventing diminutive gods out of their own experiences, as Israel has illustrated. If this is so, then it is incumbent upon us to be careful of what and who we worship. I have come to believe that each of us will worship something. It is not a matter of worshiping or not worshiping; it is a matter of our choice of where we will direct our worship. This is not an entirely religious idea. Nonreligious people worship as well. Their object of worship may be money, their outward image or possessions, an intimate relationship or a celebrity. They may not identify their adorations and devotions as worship, but indeed they worship. But God, who is the Creator of all, is the only legitimate object of our worship. And, in the Israelites' situation, He was also the source of healing from the plague.

The second lesson that can be learned from the picture of the bronze snake is this: In order to be saved, each person had to look upon the serpent for him- or herself. It was a requirement of "anyone who is bitten" (Num. 21:8). It would not do for the head of a household to take a look and report to his family that he had seen the serpent image and then expect the ill in his family to be made well. Nor would it do for Israel to cast a vote to affirm the validity of the healing process and then ex-

pect, as a result, that all of the people of Israel would be saved. Unless individuals took advantage of healing by viewing, the result was death from the sting of the viper. The requirement, "looking," was so simple that every individual had the opportunity to receive healing—from the small child to the elderly grandmother. The fact that the snake was raised up on a pole where it could be seen easily, even by the desperately ill, reinforces this fact (see v. 8). So it is with us in relation to Christ. We must come to Him individually. It will not do to belong to a church that affirms Christ; we must individually acknowledge Christ as our Savior and Lord before He can cleanse us from our sin. No one can experience His saving grace on our behalf. Although many people in the same setting may accept Christ at the same time, essentially coming to Christ is not a group phenomenon or cultural tendency. It is personal.

The third lesson we can learn comes from the fact that all Israel was affected by the plague. Scripture does not say that each and every person was specifically bitten by a serpent, but so many had been poisoned that the survival of the nation may have been in question (see vv. 6,7). Humanly speaking, the demise of Israel was imminent and with it the representation of God to humankind. The point is not to argue that part of the people may not have been bitten, but that the need for salvation from the plague was universal. This tells us that the notion that some people are exempt from the need for redemption through Christ is inconsistent with clear Bible teaching. Romans 3:23 tells us that "all have sinned."

People who conclude that they are exempt from the need for God's transformation and forgiveness do interesting things. Often their primary goal is to make themselves the center of their religious and psychological experience and worship their humanity. Such is the case with present-day humanism. Humanists believe that people are basically good and are to be affirmed as such. They admit that people have made some awful mistakes, but people have within them the intelligence and capacity to right their wrongs and create a better world. The humanist manifestos that have been written make this abundantly clear. Some of the great people of our time—some of our most learned scholars and a number of religious people—have signed some of these manifestos. These people clearly declare that no outside force, such as a concept of God who is external to human experience, is necessary. All that people need is built

into their natures. Of course they don't know where this "built-in" nature came from, but they vouch for its existence. Those humanists who acknowledge a spiritual side to existence do so without including God. They involve themselves in New Age philosophies that deify themselves and their spiritual experiences.

The fourth lesson we can learn from this type of Christ is that the means for healing is singular. Either look upon the serpent or no healing will take place. Ada R. Habershon has a good line to this effect: "It would have been no use for the bitten Israelites to bathe their wounds, or to put ointments or plasters on them, or to bandage them up; but there are many who try to get rid of their sins in this way. They bathe their wounds with tears of repentance; they put on the ointment of good works, or plasters of good resolutions, and bandage themselves with doing their best; but the bites of sin get no better with this sort of treatment; a look at the Crucified One is what they need, and all they need."[1] Moses did not go from tent to tent prescribing one kind of medicine for one person and another kind for others. He did not send some to the local psychiatrist for release of emotional tensions and another to the herbal medicine man for an exotic cure. Nor did he form small groups to discuss the matter so they could report their findings to the whole congregation. Healing came by a singular means. To be healed meant one had to face the one who was lifted up.

The term "lifted up," *hupsosen*, used in John 3:14 is from the same term Jesus used to describe Himself being lifted up on the cross (see John 8:28; 12:32). This term is also used in Acts 2:33, 5:31 and Philippians 2:9 in reference to Jesus' ascension to heaven. In these verses it is often translated as "exalted."

Crucifixion and ascension are tied together with the same language. One cannot look to the crucifixion without looking to Christ's resurrection and ascension. As Paul says in 1 Corinthians 15:17, "If Christ has not been raised, your faith is futile; you are still in your sins." It is by Jesus' death *and* resurrection that we are saved from our sins (see Rom. 5:9-11; 6:5-10; 10:9).

The fifth lesson we can learn comes from the understanding that the serpents that bit the people of Israel are symbolic of Satan and sin. This symbol for Satan is used several times in Scripture (see Rev. 12:9; 20:2). Not only have we all been infected with the poison of sin that comes from Satan, but control of our natures is being battled for by Satan, an evil fallen being (see 2 Cor. 4:4; 1 Thess. 3:5; 1 Pet. 5:8).

There is a tendency among Christians to regard God as personal and goodness as godly, and at the same time regard sin as impersonal and not under anyone's control in particular. We need to clearly understand that evil is personally dominated by Satan and that he will be dealt with personally by God. This is a battle that we are in the middle of and must undertake with God's direction (see Eph. 6:10-18). Even though we continue to battle with Satan and sin, we do know that God has already won this war with Satan. He did this, of course, through the sacrifice of His Son, Jesus Christ (see Col. 2:15).

Through Jesus' sacrifice on the cross, "God made him who had no sin to be sin for us, so that in him we might become the righteousness of God" (2 Cor. 5:21). Christ took upon Himself that which afflicts us all and has made it possible for us to be healed of this affliction and stand as righteous in the midst of Satan's scheming. All we need to do is look to Christ (see John 10:7-10; Acts 2:21; Rom. 10:9). This picture of Christ becoming sin for us explains why God directed Moses to make an image of a snake, rather than providing some other means of healing. What was afflicting the people became a symbol of healing from that affliction. Christ became sin for us in order that we might find healing and forgiveness.

An Illustration of Grace

The spiritual warfare that we are engaged in against Satan as well as the tendency in human beings to create false gods reemphasize for us the role of the bronze snake and the cross in our experience. Their purpose is to point us to God and to illustrate for us His grace. It is by the means of Christ lifted on the cross and

Christ exalted in heaven as Lord that we can be reconciled to God. It is purely by God's grace that this means is made available to us (see Eph. 2:8,9). Like the Israelites who were afflicted and dying, we are unable to save ourselves from sin. We are only able to call out to God for healing. "You see, at just the right time, when we were still powerless, Christ died for the ungodly . . . . But God demonstrates his own love for us in this: While we were still sinners, Christ died for us" (Rom. 5:6,8). This is grace in a nutshell. With this picture in mind, how offensive to God and utterly ridiculous are misplaced worship and false gods. Also, like the Israelites, after receiving salvation we need to fight our tendency to demote the Lord and put ourselves in the center of our lives in His place. Thankfully grace again reigns and we can turn back to God, and with His help we can resubmit ourselves to Him as Lord.

To evaluate my life in terms of false worship there are several questions I can ask. If, as a result, I am able to turn my focus back upon the Lord, I will find grace and peace. These questions include the following:

1. What dominates my thought life—my fantasy life? That dominating theme is a good clue to what is most important and most adored in my personal purposes. I may be in love with increasing my financial status. I may be captivated by my physical image or seek to improve my appearance by wearing lavish clothes and jewelry. Any of these things may be competing for my worship. Read Philippians 4:8 for God's viewpoint on your thought life.

2. What consumes my emotional and physical energy? How am I expending myself in this world? Am I fighting for the preservation of the environment, for the acquisition of possessions and cash, for the security of my family, for the defense of

the nation or for the preservation of a particular religious dogma? Some of these are worthy causes, but they are not to consume my emotions and activities. If they do they may become objects of worship.

3. What or who commands most of my behavior? To be sure, I'm stuck with certain accommodations in life. But can I identify who ultimately calls the shots in my life?

4. What is my primary reason for living? Do I feel that I am merely a biological accident of my parents, or have I assumed responsibility for the life God has given me and submitted its management to God and His service?

The need to worship is so dominating a force in psychological and spiritual life that it will be met, even if it is not met in completely rational ways. That is why we see intelligent, rational people latch onto spellbinding political and religious leaders and follow them to their demise. Remember that coming to Christ in humble worship and submission brings healing to both mind and soul (see Heb. 10:19-22). Growing in knowledge of Christ will correct faulty perceptions and shatter false gods in your life. Experiencing Christ will bring peace to a troubled emotional experience. Believing in Christ places the outcome of our earthly lives in divine hands and assures us of eternal life with God the Father in His place prepared for us. "In him we have redemption through his blood, the forgiveness of sins, in accordance with the riches of God's grace that he lavished on us with all wisdom and understanding" (Eph. 1:7,8). Because of his grace we are able to receive healing and salvation.

Note

1. Ada R. Habershon, *Hidden Pictures in the Old Testament* (Grand Rapids: Kregel Publications, 1916), pp. 90,91.

This Week's Teaching Plan

APPROACH TO THE WORD

APPROACH (3-5 minutes)

Bring a snakebite kit, complete with instructions, to class (available at your local pharmacy). Talk with your students about the consequences of being bitten by a poisonous snake. Include a description of the symptoms a person would experience as well as a prognosis for his or her recovery if he or she does not

receive immediate treatment (see instructions with the kit). Mention that some snakebites are lethal within minutes. Then say, **Today we are going to learn about an Old Testament incident where the Israelites were afflicted by snakebites. We are also going to talk about something equally deadly that afflicts every person and the only cure for this affliction.**

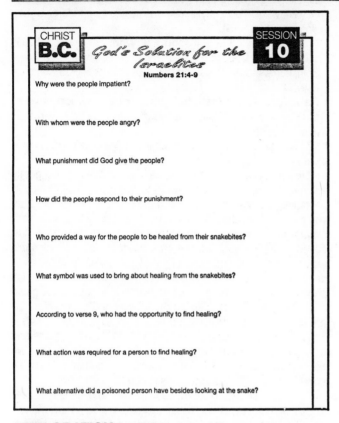

CHRIST B.C.
God's Solution for the Israelites
SESSION 10
Numbers 21:4-9

Why were the people impatient?

With whom were the people angry?

What punishment did God give the people?

How did the people respond to their punishment?

Who provided a way for the people to be healed from their snakebites?

What symbol was used to bring about healing from the snakebites?

According to verse 9, who had the opportunity to find healing?

What action was required for a person to find healing?

What alternative did a poisoned person have besides looking at the snake?

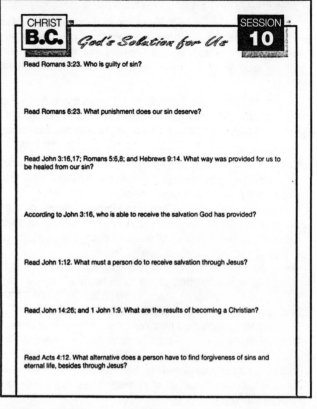

CHRIST B.C.
God's Solution for Us
SESSION 10

Read Romans 3:23. Who is guilty of sin?

Read Romans 6:23. What punishment does our sin deserve?

Read John 3:16,17; Romans 5:6,8; and Hebrews 9:14. What way was provided for us to be healed from our sin?

According to John 3:16, who is able to receive the salvation God has provided?

Read John 1:12. What must a person do to receive salvation through Jesus?

Read John 14:26; and 1 John 1:9. What are the results of becoming a Christian?

Read Acts 4:12. What alternative does a person have to find forgiveness of sins and eternal life, besides through Jesus?

EXPLORATION (30-40 minutes)

Materials needed: One copy of each Session 10 Student Worksheet for each student. Optional—8½X11-inch sheets of plain white paper; metal paper fasteners; fine point felt pens in a variety of colors; photocopies of clip art illustrating kids talking together, praying (from clip art books you have); glue sticks; scissors (see the Optional Step 4 for details).

Preparation: Optional—make a sample evangelism tract as directed in the Optional Step 4.

Note: If you chose to use the Optional Step 4 you may need to shorten the time you spend on Steps 1-3, or you may want to skip the Approach activity.

Step 1 (3-5 minutes): Briefly describe the setting in which the incident described in Numbers 21:4-9 took place. Include the following points in your description: the Israelites were still wandering in the desert as a result of their refusal to enter the land God had promised to give Abraham's descendants; The Edomites had refused to let them pass through their land, so the Israelites had to take a circuitous route into the Negev desert; Aaron, the high priest and one of their key leaders died; in the desert they were attacked by a local king's forces; they were victorious over the king's attack, but the business of being aliens was taking its toll and the Israelites began to become impatient and grumbled against Moses and God.

Step 2 (12-15 minutes): Distribute Session 10 Student Worksheet titled "God's Solution for the Israelites." Direct students to turn in their Bibles to Numbers, chapter 21. Then ask a volunteer to read the story from Numbers 21:4-9. After the passage is read, use the following outline and information from the Teacher's Bible Study to discuss the questions listed on the worksheets. Encourage students to take notes on their worksheets as the discussion progresses.

Numbers 21:4-9

- **Why were the people impatient?** (They were tired of wandering in the desert with only the water and food God provided for them—see v. 5.)
- **With whom were the people angry?** (God and Moses.)
- **What punishment did God give the people?** (He sent poisonous snakes in their midst. They bit many people and many of the Israelites died because of them.) Mention that this is not the first time the Israelites had expressed ungrateful feelings toward God, even though God had delivered them from slavery in Egypt and had provided for their needs as they wandered in the desert. Underline the fact that the people could have already entered the land God had promised them, but they had refused. Their wandering in the desert was a consequence of their own disobedience, not a hardhearted act of God.
- **How did the people respond to their punishment?** (They repented of their sin and asked Moses to pray to God on their behalf—see v. 7.)
- **Who provided a way for the people to be healed from their snakebites?** (God.) **What symbol was used to bring about healing from the snakebites?** (An image of a snake.) Mention that the snake symbolized the problem that was afflicting the people—the poisonous snakebites as well as the people's sin. A snake is a common Bible symbol for Satan and sin. Say, **When we look at the bronze snake as a type of Christ you will see why this symbolism is important.**
- **According to verse 9, who had the opportunity to find healing?** (Anyone.)
- **What action was required for a person to find healing?** (The person must look at the bronze snake.)
- **What alternative did a poisoned person have besides looking at the snake?** (None.)

Take a moment to answer any further questions students may have about this passage of Scripture. Then move to Step 3 by saying, **Let's look at the New Testament event that the bronze snake illustrates.**

Step 3 (15-20 minutes): Read aloud John 3:14,15. **What event do these verses refer to when they say Jesus was "lifted up"?** (His death on the cross.) Mention that the term "lifted up" also refers to Jesus' resurrection and ascension into heaven.

Distribute the "God's Solution for Us" worksheet. Ask volunteers to share in reading the verses. Lead a discussion of the verses and questions using the following outline and information from the Teacher's Bible Study as a basis for your discussion.

- **Read Romans 3:23. Who is guilty of sin?** (Every person who has ever lived, except for Jesus—see Heb. 4:15—has been disobedient to God and sinned.)
- **Read Romans 6:23. What punishment does our sin deserve?** (Death.) Mention that this means more than physical death. It includes spiritual death or eternal separation from God and not being allowed to enter heaven.
- **Read John 3:16,17; Romans 5:6,8; and Hebrews 9:14. What way was provided for us to be healed from our sin?** (God gave His own Son, Jesus, to die on the cross in our place and take the punishment for our sin. It is by Jesus' death that God has made cleansing from our sin possible. We are unable to save ourselves from sin.) Mention that the reason God made this sacrifice of His Son Jesus, is because of His great love for us. God also raised His Son from the dead so that we can experience eternal life in heaven. (Read Rom. 6:5-10 to your students.)
- Say, **God directed Moses to make an image of a snake, an image of the very thing that was afflicting the people.** Read 2 Corinthians 5:21 to your students. Then say, **The bronze snake is a type of Christ because it illustrates the fact that Christ became sin, the very thing that afflicts us, so that we can find healing from sin.**
- **According to John 3:16, who is able to receive the salvation God has provided?** (Any person who believes in Jesus, God's Son.)

- **Read John 1:12. What must a person do to receive salvation through Jesus?** Explain that receiving Jesus means asking Him to take control of your life and being willing to live the way He wants you to. This includes asking Him to forgive your sins (see Acts 3:19).
- **Read John 14:26 and 1 John 1:9. What are the results of becoming a Christian?** (Our sins are forgiven and God's Spirit comes to live in us and help us know how God wants us to live.)
- **Read Acts 4:12. What alternative does a person have to find forgiveness of sins and eternal life, besides through Jesus?** (None.)

Move to the Optional Step 4. Or if you do not choose to complete the Optional Step 4, move to the Conclusion.

Optional Step 4 (10-15 minutes): Spend 3-5 minutes briefly summarizing with your students the basic principles involved in becoming a Christian. Show them the sample evangelism tract you prepared or other literature you have brought to help them simplify these principles into several short sentences. Write the summary on the board. Make sure the following principles are included in the summary: everyone has sinned and deserves death—eternal separation from God; because God loves us He provided His Son, Jesus Christ, to die on the cross in our place so that we can find forgiveness for our sins and eternal life—we are unable to find forgiveness on our own; to receive the salvation God has provided we must ask God to forgive our sins and take control of our lives; when we receive Christ into our lives we become members of God's family and His Spirit lives in us; we now have a place reserved for us in heaven with God.

Direct the students to form pairs or trios. Distribute materials to groups then say, **Using the principles we've listed, make a booklet that you could use to explain to a friend what is involved in becoming a Christian.** Students may cut the paper into four equal pieces to make pages and secure the pages along one edge using two metal paper fasteners. They may then write and illustrate on the pages the principles listed on the board or overhead. Encourage students to put these principles into their own words. Allow students about 10 minutes to work, then move to the Alternate Conclusion. Students who did not finish their booklets may do so after class or at home.

CONCLUSION & DECISION

CONCLUSION (5-8 minutes)

Say, **We have learned that the only way to find healing for our sins is through Jesus Christ. Let's summarize the steps involved in finding forgiveness and new life through Jesus.** With students' help, list steps on the board or overhead. Include the following in your list: everyone has sinned; the penalty for sin is death—eternal separation from God; God has provided forgiveness for sin and eternal life through the death of Jesus; to receive forgiveness and eternal life we must ask God to forgive us and take control of our lives; When we receive Christ we become members of His family and His Spirit lives in us.

Then say, **If you are a Christian, prayerfully review these steps and thank God for coming into your life. If you are not a Christian, consider what it means to be a Christian. If you want to talk more about forgiveness and eternal life, I'll be glad to talk to you after class.**

ALTERNATE CONCLUSION (5-8 minutes)

Say, **You can use your booklet to help you if someone asks you what it means to be a Christian.** Optional—have students or leaders role-play a situation where the evangelism tract is used to share the gospel with a friend. Then say, **If you are a Christian, this booklet will help you understand the decision you have made to commit your life to Christ. If you are not a Christian, this booklet will help you understand how to become a Christian if that is what you decide to do.** Then close in audible prayer, thanking God that through Jesus' death and resurrection, we can have the opportunity to have our sins forgiven and receive eternal life.

Be available after class to speak with any students who want to know more about receiving forgiveness and eternal life.

Encourage students to read chapter 10 from the student paperback *Christ B.C.* The readings in this chapter explore the theme "grace."

Prophesies of the Messiah

KEY VERSE

"But you, Bethlehem Ephrathah, though you are small among the clans of Judah, out of you will come for me one who will be ruler over Israel, whose origins are from of old, from ancient times." Micah 5:2

"So Joseph also went up from the town of Nazareth in Galilee to Judea, to Bethlehem the town of David, because he belonged to the house and line of David. He went there to register with Mary, who was pledged to be married to him and was expecting a child. While they were there, the time came for the baby to be born." Luke 2:4-6

BIBLICAL BASIS

Psalm 16:9-11; 68:18; Isaiah 7:14; 11:1; 52:14; 53:1-12; Micah 5:2; Malachi 3:1; Matthew 1:1,6,20-23; 8:16,17; 13:53-58; 27:12,27-31,38; Mark 14:55,56; 15:43-46; Luke 2:4-7; 7:24-27; 22:37,54; John 19:34; Acts 1:10,11; 2:22-28; Romans 10:16; 15:8,12; Ephesians 4:7-9; Hebrews 7:25; 1 Peter 2:21-25; Revelation 5:6

FOCUS OF THE SESSION

The amazing accuracy of prophecies foretelling Jesus' birth, ministry, death and resurrection reaffirms for us that the Bible is trustworthy. The Bible is not just history or literature; it is truth.

AIMS OF THIS SESSION

You and your students will have accomplished the purpose of this Bible study session if you can:

- MATCH Old Testament prophecies about Jesus with their New Testament fulfillments;
- DISCUSS the role of faith in understanding the truth contained in God's Word;
- IDENTIFY a doubt you may have concerning Jesus and PLAN one step to take in resolving that doubt.

Teacher's Bible Study

Prophecy and Faith

As a young high schooler, I entered a speaking contest that set me on a course that was sponsored by the churches of my denomination. For me the most important aspect of the entire tournament was reading a book that had been recommended to me. It has long since gone out of print, but it had a marked effect upon my thinking as a young Christian.

The book was titled *The Credentials of Jesus* by a Swedish pastor named Hjalmar Sundquist. He clarified for me answers to a number of questions that I had pondered a good deal. The questions were, "How do I know that the Bible is true?" and "How do I know that Jesus Christ is the only way to know God?" Pastor Sundquist developed a line of reasoning that has, to this day, satisfied these questions for me and helped me a great deal in taking the leap of faith in Jesus Christ and in God's Word. Sundquist's method was called the Christo-centric approach.

Sundquist states, "The Christo-centric approach . . . is in full accord with the words of the master himself who said, 'I am the way, the truth, and the life: no one cometh unto the Father, but by me' [John 14:6].

"As Christ himself is the center of our faith—its 'author and perfecter' [see Heb. 12:2]—so he is also the center of the Bible. Throughout the Old Testament we are constantly being led forward to him, who came in 'the fulness of time,' [Gal. 4:4] and the New Testament is brim full of him from beginning to end. As he, in his own person and in what he was wrought, has amply authenticated himself as the Son of God, so he has also authenticated the Scriptures, wherein he has made himself known to us, as the word of God. If we take Jesus at his word and accept him as the one he claims to be, we need have no difficulty in accepting and believing any of the details in his life and work. Why should we have any difficulty in accepting the miracles if we have already accepted the greatest miracle of them all, Jesus Christ himself with all his claims of one-ness with God?"[1]

So as you study Messianic prophecies, ask yourself whether you believe in Jesus Christ because He was prophesied accurately or whether you believe in the prophesies because of the nature and character of Christ. I have come to believe in the Bible because of Christ more than because of all the demonstrated literary analyses and logical reasonings that many good men have offered. These analyses and reasonings greatly reinforce my faith in Christ, but they are not the source of my faith. There are people who withhold belief in Jesus as the Son of God because they have doubts about Scripture. I suspect that such withholding is a dodge, a means of avoiding the leap of faith. Their understanding of Scripture is limited to the rational and devoid of the spiritual. So often they claim that Jesus was a great man, but don't dare trust their lives and eternal destinies to Him. They would like to measure Christ by their own intellects and create doubts about Scripture to keep from surrendering in faith. I remember a missionary who stated that he believed in Jesus Christ, not because of the fact of the virgin birth of Christ, but that he believed in the virgin birth because of the fact of his personal relationship with Christ. His point was that it is possible to let questions of faith keep us from faith when we use them to dodge the question of our relationship with Christ.

Christ and Scripture are validating of each other. Christ affirms the Scripture and the Scripture affirms Him. Jesus was the Word of God incarnate: "The Word became flesh and made his dwelling among us. We have seen his glory, the glory of the One and Only, who came from the Father, full of grace and truth" (John 1:14). Scripture is the active, life-changing Word of God in written form (see 2 Thess. 2:15; 2 Tim.3:16,17; Heb. 4:12). Both are essential to our fully developed faith. I have suggested the previous ideas to get you to consider whether or not you have erected some intellectual barrier to a full understanding of and commitment to Jesus.

Jesus Fulfills God's Plan

Prophecy is history written beforehand. It has been suggested that a history of Jesus Christ and His purchase of our salvation could have been written entirely from the prophecies concerning Him. First Corinthians 15:3,4 illustrates this: "For what I received I passed on to you as of first importance: that Christ died for our sins according to the Scriptures, that he was buried, that he was raised on the third day according to the Scriptures." The Old Testament is laced with prophetic material, from early in the book of Genesis to its very last books. The gospel of Christ must be the fulfillment of prophecy; it must be consistent with God's plan proclaimed throughout history, or it is false. Many religious movements such as Mormonism and the Jehovah's Witnesses have been established on some new revelation that is not consistent with Scripture. These religions are false and their adherents are eternally lost unless they turn to Christ and believe the truth of the gospel.

Jesus fulfilled God's plan presented in the Old Testament to give evidence of His divinity and His authenticity as the promised Messiah. He quoted generously from the Old Testament to point His followers to His accurate fulfillment of Scripture and to counter challenges from the religious leaders of His day (see Matt. 21:13-16,42-46; 22:15-22,41-46; 26:51-54,59,60; Mark 7:6-13; 9:11-13; 14:55,56; Luke 20:17-19). Yet despite their exposure to Christ and His teachings, most of these leaders missed the Messiah and sought to destroy His influence on the Jewish community.

Isaiah 53: An Illustration of Christ

The greatest sweep of prophecy concerning Jesus is found in the book of Isaiah. Isaiah was a man, inspired by God, who spoke boldly to the problems of his day as well as to future events. This great prophet lived more than 600 years before the birth of Christ, at a time when the kingdom of Israel had been divided in two and the northern kingdom had been swallowed by Assyrian hordes (see 2 Kings 17:7-23). At the beginning of Isaiah's ministry, King Ahaz came to power in the southern kingdom and openly turned to idolatry (see 2 Kings 16:1-4). During this time Isaiah predicted the Assyrian invasion of Israel (see Isa. 8:6-8). At the same time the prophet saw an end to Israel's troubles in the coming of the Messiah (see 7:14; 8:13-15; 11:1-5,10-12).

Later on in Isaiah's ministry, after Ahaz had died, Isaiah recorded what is now considered the largest concentration of messianic prophecy in the Bible. These prophecies are found in Isaiah, chapters 40–66. They can be read in a single sitting of an hour or so and this should be done to get the scope of Isaiah's message. These chapters tell us of both the restoration of Israel (see 49:8-26) and the coming of the Messiah. The focus on the Messiah becomes sharpest in Isaiah 53. With Bible in hand, let's take a walk through Isaiah 53 and compare each verse to New Testament verses about Christ.

Isaiah 53:1: "Who has believed our message and to whom has the arm of the Lord been revealed?" This verse is quoted in Romans 10:16 and refers to the fact that many of the Jews rejected Jesus' message of good news.

Isaiah 53:2: "He grew up before him like a tender shoot, and like a root out of dry ground. He had no beauty or majesty to attract us to him, nothing in his appearance that we should desire him." This reference here to "a tender shoot" refers to the fact that Jesus would be born of the house and lineage of David, a shoot "from the stump of Jesse" (11:1). Jesus' genealogy is listed in Matthew, chapter one. It includes King David, the son of Jesse. Romans 15:8,12 confirms that Jesus is the Promised One: "For I tell you that Christ has become a servant of the Jews on behalf of God's truth, to confirm the promises made to the patriarchs so that the Gentiles may glorify God for his mercy . . . . Isaiah says, 'The Root of Jesse will spring up, one who will arise to rule over the nations; the Gentiles will hope in him.'" The "root out of dry ground" (Isa. 53:2) is believed by scholars to be a reference to Jesus' humble beginnings (see Luke 2:6,7). The lack of beauty and majesty in Jesus' appearance is thought to be a reference to Jesus' final days of suffering when He was beaten, humiliated and mocked. Isaiah describes His appearance at this time as "so disfigured beyond that of any man" (52:14; also see Luke 18:31,32).

Isaiah 53:3: "He was despised and rejected by men, a man of sorrows, and familiar with suffering. Like one from whom men hide their faces he was despised, and we esteemed him not." The beginning of this verse describes the event in Luke 4:16-29 where Jesus was rejected by the people in whose midst He grew to manhood. The references to His suffering and rejection also bring to mind the description of Jesus being beaten and mocked by the soldiers before being led away to be crucified (see Matt. 27:29-31).

Isaiah 53:4-6: "Surely he took up our infirmities and carried our sorrows, yet we considered him stricken by God, smitten by him, and afflicted. But he was pierced for our transgressions, he was crushed for our iniquities; the punishment that brought us peace was upon him, and by his wounds we are healed. We all, like sheep, have gone astray, each of us has turned to his own way; and the Lord has laid on him the iniquity of us all." These verses graphically describe the reason for Jesus' suffering and the purpose behind His death on the cross. Christ died for us, a sinful people who had turned our backs on Him. Count the number of times you see the words "our," "we" and "us" repeated in these verses. Jesus' purpose in dying was clearly for our sake and we are certainly undeserving of such a sacrifice. (For further study read Matt. 8:16,17; John 19:33-37; Rom. 4:25; 1 Pet. 2:24.)

Isaiah 53:7-9: "He was oppressed and afflicted, yet he did not open his mouth; he was led like a lamb to the slaughter, and as a sheep before her shearers is silent, so he did not open his mouth. By oppression and judgment he was taken away. And who can speak of his descendants? For he was cut off from the land of the living; for the transgression of my people he was stricken. He was assigned a grave with the wicked, and with the rich in his death, though he had done no violence, nor was any deceit in his mouth." These verses are direct references to Jesus' trial, death and burial. First Jesus is referred to as a lamb, willingly giving His life (see v. 7). This is supported by the words of John the Baptist, "Look, the Lamb of God" (John 1:29,36); the words of Revelation 5:6; and by Phillip as he explained these verses and their reference to Christ to the Ethiopian eunuch (see Acts 8:26-35). Isaiah 53:7 describes Christ as silent before His oppressors. Matthew 27:12 says, "When he was accused by the chief priests and the elders, he gave no answer" (also see

Mark 14:60,61; 15:4,5; Luke 23:8,9; and John 19:8,9). Isaiah 53:8, "Who can speak of his descendants?" points to the fact that Jesus had no physical children. Verse 9 indicates that Christ was given an unfair trial. This is supported by the accounts of false witnesses in Jesus' trial before the chief priests and Pilate's inability to find fault with Him (see Mark 14:55,56; Luke 23:4). Isaiah 53:9 also describes Jesus' crucifixion between two criminals (see Matt. 27:38) and continues by saying, "and with the rich in His death." Jesus was buried in the tomb of Joseph of Arimathea, a prominent member of the Jewish Council and a wealthy man as evidenced by the sort of tomb He had prepared for himself (see Matt. 27:57-60: Mark 15:43-46). Finally, Isaiah 53:9 refers to Jesus as sinless, there was no "deceit in his mouth." Jesus' example throughout the gospels supports this as an obvious trait of the Son of God. First Peter 2:21, in speaking of Jesus, quotes this verse, "He committed no sin, and no deceit was found in his mouth."

Isaiah 53:10-12: "Yet it was the Lord's will to crush him and cause him to suffer, and though the Lord makes his life a guilt offering, he will see his offspring and prolong his days, and the will of the Lord will prosper in his hand. After the suffering of his soul, he will see the light of life and be satisfied; by his knowledge my righteous servant will justify many, and he will bear their iniquities. Therefore I will give him a portion among the great, and he will divide the spoils with the strong, because he poured out his life unto death, and was numbered with the transgressors. For he bore the sin of many, and made intercession for the transgressors." The most obvious theme of these verses is that Jesus died for our sins as a part of God's plan to redeem us from sin. The phrases "cause him to suffer," "makes his life a guilt offering," "will bear their iniquities," "poured out his life unto death" and "bore the sin of many" all testify to Jesus' saving sacrifice on the cross. First Peter 2:23-25 supports this in saying, "When they hurled their insults at him, he did not retaliate; when he suffered, he made no threats. Instead, he entrusted himself to him who judges justly. He himself bore our sins in his body on the tree, so that we might die to sins and live for righteousness; by his wounds you have been healed. For you were like sheep going astray, but now you have returned to the Shepherd and Overseer of your souls." Isaiah 53:11, "He will see the light of life," is a reference to Jesus' resurrection. Luke 22:37 quotes Isaiah 53:12, "And he was numbered with the transgressors," in reference to Jesus' arrest as a fulfillment of prophecy. Lastly, Isaiah 53 makes reference to the fact that Jesus makes "intercession for the transgressors" (v. 12). Hebrews 7:25 repeats this role of Christ in saying, "Therefore he is able to save completely those who come to God through him, because he always lives to intercede for them."

Other Prophecies of the Messiah

There we have it. The whole of the gospel enveloped in a single chapter of Old Testament prophecy. What assurance that the Bible is truth and the claims of Christ are trustworthy! But this is only a small slice of Old Testament prophecy concerning Jesus Christ. To supplement what is written in Isaiah 53, you may want to read the following Old Testament prophecies concerning Jesus' birth, ministry, death and resurrection as well as their corresponding New Testament fulfillments.

The Event	The Prophecy	The Fulfillment
The way prepared	Isaiah 40:3-5	Luke 3:3-6
Preceded by John	Malachi 3:1	Luke 7:24-27
Born in Bethlehem	Micah 5:2	Luke 2:4-7
Born of a virgin	Isaiah 7:14	Luke 1:26-31
Slaughter of children by Herod	Jeremiah 31:15	Matthew 2:16-18
Flight to Egypt	Hosea 11:1	Matthew 2:14,15
Taught in parables	Psalm 78:2-4	Matthew 13:34,35
Betrayed by a friend	Psalm 41:9	Luke 22:47,48
Forsaken by the Father	Psalm 22:1	Matthew 27:46
Resurrection from death	Psalm 16:10	Mark 16:6,7; Acts 2:22-28
Ascension into heaven	Psalm 68:18	Ephesians 4:7-9

The Truth about Jesus

Old Testament prophecies cover a full sweep of Jesus Christ's life, death, resurrection and ascension. Each significant event is set forth in the Old Testament and confirmed in the New. The apostle Peter describes the important role prophecy plays in undergirding and reinforcing our faith in Christ: "Concerning this salvation, the prophets, who spoke of the grace that was to come to you, searched intently and with the greatest care, trying to find out the time and circumstances to which the Spirit of Christ in them was pointing when he predicted the sufferings of Christ and the glories that would follow. It was revealed to them that they were not serving themselves but you, when they spoke of the things that have now been told you by those who have preached the gospel to you by the Holy Spirit sent from heaven. Even angels long to look into these things" (1 Pet. 1:10-12).

The words of prophecy are holy and grounded in the Spirit of Christ. They are not empty phonics, belching out catechisms and creeds. We can repeat these great mysteries to the point that they become meaningless monosyllables, or we can find in them strength for our faith and a renewed awe of God and what He has done in Christ.

Malcolm Muggeridge in his book *Jesus Rediscovered* describes his life-changing encounter with God. Muggeridge says, "What can be said with certainty is that, once the confrontation has been experienced—the rocky summit climbed, the interminable desert crossed—an unimaginably delectable vista presents itself, so vast, so luminous, so enchanting that the small ecstasies of human love, and the small satisfactions of human achievement, by comparison pale into insignificance."[2]

The testimony of faith of Muggeridge is humble and gentle. C.S. Lewis makes the point more sharply; having encountered the claims of Jesus and the validity of the prophecies about Him Lewis says, "I am trying here to prevent anyone saying the really foolish thing that people often say about Him: 'I'm ready to accept Jesus as a great moral teacher, but I don't accept His claim to be God.' This is the one thing we must not say. A man who was merely a man and said the sort of things Jesus said would not be a great moral teacher. He would either be a lunatic—on a level with the man who says he is a poached egg—or else he would be the Devil of Hell. You must make your choice. Either this man was, and is, the Son of God: or else a madman or something worse. You can shut Him up for a fool, you can spit at Him and kill Him as a demon; or you can fall at His feet and call Him Lord and God. But let us not come with any patronizing nonsense about His being a great human teacher. He has not left that open to us. He did not intend to . . . . He was neither a lunatic nor a fiend; and . . . unlikely as it may seem, I have to accept the view that He was and is God. God has landed on this enemy-occupied world in human form."[3]

Note

1. Hjalmar Sundquist, *The Credentials of Jesus* (Chicago: The Covenant Book Concern, 1930), pp. 95,96.

2. Malcolm Muggeridge, *Jesus Rediscovered* (Wheaton, IL: Tyndale House Publishers, 1974), p. 49.

3. C.S. Lewis, *Mere Christianity* (New York: The MacMillan Company, 1960). p. 55,56.

This Week's Teaching Plan

APPROACH TO THE WORD

APPROACH (5-8 minutes)

Preparation: Write on the board or overhead the steps listed below that are used by scientists to test if a theory or hypothesis is true. Keep these steps out of your students' sight until you are ready to share them.

Ask your students, **What criteria do scientists use to prove if something is true or not?** After giving students a moment to think and give suggestions, share the following steps used in the scientific world to test a theory or hypothesis (a tentative formula or explanation for a principle operating in nature):

1. A scientist begins with a preliminary observation as to what he or she thinks may be true.
2. The scientist then decides what information is needed in order to prove if his or her preliminary observation is true.
3. Then an experiment must be devised by which the scientist's preliminary observation can be tested.

4. The experiment is conducted several times and the results are weighed against the preliminary observation. If necessary, the observation is revised to reflect the results of the experiment.

5. The experiment must be repeated several times with the same results supporting the observation in order for the observation to be accepted as true.

Move to the Exploration by saying, **Today we are going to look at Old Testament prophecies of Jesus' birth, life on earth, death, resurrection and ascension into heaven. These prophecies were written long before Jesus was born and they predicted that specific things about Jesus would be true. Let's compare these prophecies to events concerning Jesus and see how accurate they are.**

BIBLE EXPLORATION

EXPLORATION (35-50 minutes)

Materials needed: Session 11 Student Worksheet for each student. Optional—rewards for the winning team of the contest described in Step 1 (coupons or munchies work well).

Step 1 (15-20 minutes): Distribute the Session 11 worksheets to students. Divide the class into two or more groups and give them the following instructions: **Work with your group to complete the "Prophecies of Jesus" assignment on your worksheets. On your page you will see both New Testament and Old Testament references. First, match each Old Testament prophecy with its New Testament fulfillment. Then list next to each prophecy and fulfillment everything about Jesus that the prophecy predicted.** Allow 10 minutes for students to work then ask groups to share their work. Compile a list on the board or overhead of each prophecy of Jesus that came true. (Step 2 provides you with a list of the corresponding Old and New Testament passages and a description of the events they refer to.)

Optional—offer a reward to the group that can identify and list the most things, as described by the Scriptures on their page, that came true about Jesus. When you have allowed 10 minutes for research, have each group total its list of true things. Then have the group with the highest total read its list. Eliminate from the list any incorrect items. Have other groups do the same for any items mentioned that are not correct. Then ask other groups to share any true things they found that have not been shared. Have groups count their final totals and declare the winning group. After class distribute the rewards you have brought to the group that finished with the highest total.

Step 2 (10-15 minutes): Go over the list made in Step 1 and add to it any points that may have been missed. Briefly discuss the list and share any needed information about the prophecies. Use the following as a basis for completing and discussing your

list (also refer to the "Isaiah 53: An Illustration of Christ" section of the Teacher's Bible Study).

CHRIST B.C.	*Prophecies of Jesus*	SESSION 11

Prophecies

Micah 5:2	Isaiah 53:4-6
Isaiah 7:14	Isaiah 53:7,8
Isaiah 11:1	Isaiah 53:9
Malachi 3:1	Isaiah 53:10-12
Isaiah 53:1	Psalm 16:9-11
Isaiah 53:3a	Psalm 68:18
Isaiah 52:14 and 53:3	

Fulfillments

Matthew 8:16,17; John 19:34; 1 Peter 2:24	Matthew 27:38; Mark 14:55,56; 15:43-46; 1 Peter 2:21-23	Luke 22:37,54; Hebrews 7:25; 1 Peter 2:23-25
Matthew 27:12; Revelation 5:6	Matthew 1:1,6; Romans 15:8,12	Acts 1:10,11; Ephesians 4:7-9
Acts 2:22-28	Matthew 27:27-31	Matthew 1:20-23
Luke 7:24-27	Luke 2:4-7	Matthew 13:53-58
	Romans 10:16	

- **Micah 5:2/Luke 2:4-7**—Jesus was born in Bethlehem.
- **Isaiah 7:14/Matthew 1:20-23**—a virgin gave birth to Jesus.
- **Isaiah 11:1/Matthew 1:1,6;Romans 15:8,12**—Jesus' earthly ancestry came from the lineage of Jesse, King David's father.
- **Malachi 3:1/Luke 7:24-27**—Jesus was preceded by a messenger, John the Baptist.
- **Isaiah 53:1/Romans 10:16**—Many Jews rejected Jesus' message.
- **Isaiah 53:3a/Matthew 13:53-58**—Jesus was rejected by His own people.
- **Isaiah 52:14 and 53:3/Matthew 27:27-31**—Jesus suffered greatly, especially during the time between His trial and death on the cross. He was beaten, flogged, mocked, insulted and then crucified. Optional: If time permits, read the account of Jesus' crucifixion from Luke 23:32-49.
- **Isaiah 53:4-6/Matthew 8:16,17; John 19:34; 1 Peter 2:24**—Jesus healed the sick and possessed; after He had died on the cross, Jesus was pierced in the side by a soldier's sword; Jesus died for our sins; Jesus bore our sins so that we can be healed of sin.
- **Isaiah 53:7,8/Matthew 27:12; Revelation 5:6** (you may also want to refer to Acts 8:26-35)—Jesus is the Lamb of God who was slain for our sins; He was silent before His accusers.
- **Isaiah 53:9/Matthew 27:38; Mark 14:55,56; 15:43-46; 1 Peter 2:21-23**—Jesus was falsely accused and found faultless; He was crucified between two criminals and buried in the tomb of a wealthy man; He committed no sin.
- **Isaiah 53:10-12/Luke 22:37,54; Hebrews 7:25; 1 Peter 2:23-25**—Jesus was arrested and crucified as a criminal; He rose from the dead to intercede for (speaks to God on the behalf of) those who come to Him in faith; He died for our sins as part of God's plan of salvation for the world.
- **Psalm 16:9-11/Acts 2:22-28**—God raised Jesus from the dead. If time permits, read the account of the empty tomb from John 20:1-18.
- **Psalm 68:18/Acts 1:10,11; Ephesians 4:7-9**—Jesus ascended into heaven.

Move to Step 3 by saying, **We have discussed the various** prophecies concerning Jesus' birth, life, death, resurrection and ascension to heaven. Now let's explore how these facts and faith work together.

Step 3 (10-15 minutes): As outlined in the Approach, refer to the criteria by which scientists establish something to be true. Then ask the following questions and discuss possible answers (refer to the "Prophecy and Faith" section at the beginning of the Teacher's Bible Study for additional information):
- **In evaluating spiritual matters to see if they are true, what problems do you see in applying only a scientific approach to your study of Scripture?** (Spiritual matters cannot be tested and proven by scientific means.)
- **In what ways can a scientific approach to studying Scripture help you in understanding some facts about the Bible?** (A rational comparison of prophecies and fulfillments can help in reinforcing what you believe about Jesus. It can also help you identify things you believe that may not be true according to what the Bible teaches.)
- What areas of Scripture cannot be understood scientifically? (Those things that cannot be observed physically—for example: God, Devil, faith.)
- **What are some ways you can evaluate if your understanding of something in the Bible is correct?** (You can study the Bible to see if your understanding is supported by Scripture as a whole, or if it is based on Bible verses taken out of context.)
- **At what point do you think a person needs to place faith in Christ in order to understand what the Bible says?**
- **In what ways does faith in Christ help a person understand what God is saying in His Word?** (A person who has a personal relationship with Christ has the wisdom of the Holy Spirit by which he or she can understand the Bible.)

After several minutes of discussion, share Lloyd Ahlem's comments in the section of the Teacher's Bible Study titled "Prophecy and Faith" concerning the Christo-centric approach to Scripture. Do this by reading the paragraph that begins with the words, "So as you study the messianic prophecies . . . " Then move to the Conclusion.

CONCLUSION & DECISION

CONCLUSION (3-5 minutes)

On the back of their worksheets, instruct students to write one thing about Jesus that they have difficulty believing. Then instruct them to write one thing they can do to understand God's Word better as it applies to the doubts they have. If students are having difficulty thinking of steps they can take to deal with their doubts, suggest the following: with some friends and the help of a mature, older Christian do a Bible study of the subject you are having difficulty with—you may discover that what you thought was true is not, or you may come to a point where you can accept in faith that it is true; pray that God's Holy Spirit will guide you as you seek to study and understand His Word and pray that He will help you deal with your doubts—then begin studying; put your faith in Christ as the only one who can save you from your sins and help you know God and understand His Word.

Close in prayer thanking God that He has given us so much evidence to assure us that Jesus is the Savior promised in the Old Testament. Ask God to help each student put his or her faith in the truth that He has given in His word.

Encourage your students to read chapter 11 of the student paperback *Christ B.C.* The readings in this chapter explore the theme "truth."

NOTES:

The Suffering Servant

KEY VERSE

"Surely he took up our infirmities and carried our sorrows." Isaiah 53:4

"The next day John saw Jesus coming toward him and said, 'Look, the Lamb of God, who takes away the sin of the world!'" John 1:29

BIBLICAL BASIS

Isaiah 42:2,3,6,7; 49:1; 50:6; 52:14; 53:1,2,4,9; Matthew 8:16,17; 12:15-21; 26:59-61; 27:12-14,27-30; Mark 7:31-36; Luke 9:34,35; Hebrews 2:18

FOCUS OF THE SESSION

The prophet Isaiah foretold the suffering Jesus would experience. Because Jesus understands pain and suffering, He understands our needs and our suffering.

AIMS OF THIS SESSION

You and your students will have accomplished the purpose of this Bible study session if you can:

- DETERMINE Jesus' qualifications for the role of Savior of the world;
- LIST reasons why Jesus, as the Savior, is able to understand human suffering;
- EXAMINE a painful experience in your life and WRITE a response you can make to your experience because of Jesus' understanding of your pain.

Teacher's Bible Study

In this session you will be looking at the prophecies of Isaiah that are commonly called the "Servant Songs." Through an examination of these prophecies and their New Testament fulfillments, you and your students will clearly see why Jesus is completely qualified to serve as the Savior of the world.

Qualifications for Leadership

Often election campaigns are circuses. They are theater and politics all wrapped into one big brazen show of human ostentation. Candidates announce themselves as the answer to all the problems of the world. Promises that the difficult issues associated with international affairs and the welfare of the nation will all be resolved if only the correct candidates are elected are abundant. Candidates' war records, college records and medical records are all closely inspected and broadcast by the media. Much of this becomes ludicrous, but apparently all the hype and baloney has become a necessary part of getting a candidate elected. This is the means by which leaders are sometimes promoted as qualified for serving in a public office in our world today.

What a contrast to Christ's qualifications for leadership and to His methods of service as outlined in the Old Testament.

They are listed in Isaiah, illustrating the character of the One God has appointed as our Savior and Lord. (See Isa. 42:1-7; 49:1-7; 50:4-11; 52:13–53:12.)

The Unacceptable Image

The obedient, suffering servant of Isaiah would never have fulfilled the concept of a leader in our world. So also Christ, the king-on-a-donkey, did not fulfill the Jews concept of the Messiah. Isaiah 53:1 says, "Who has believed our message and to whom has the arm of the Lord been revealed?" John 12:38 repeats this verse in reference to Jews who, after witnessing many miraculous signs done by Jesus, refused to believe in Him. Jesus' image was unacceptable to them; it didn't fit their misconception.

Another area in which Jesus would probably be considered lacking, in human terms, was His outward appearance. In Isaiah He is described as one who "had no beauty or majesty to attract us to him, nothing in his appearance that we should desire Him" (53:2). During the time before His death, after he had been flogged and tormented (see 50:6; Matt. 27:29), His outward image must have been hideous. Isaiah 52:14 says that "there were many who were appalled at him—his appearance was so disfigured beyond that of any man and his form marred beyond human likeness." To the nonbeliever His image was that of a criminal.

Isaiah 42:2 describes another aspect of Jesus' image. He would "not shout or cry out, or raise his voice in the streets." Often in the Gospels Jesus makes a point not to draw attention to His deeds. After healing a deaf and mute man, Jesus commanded the people who had witnessed the miracle "not to tell anyone" (Mark 7:36). Christ works quietly and unobtrusively. He accomplishes His task without a public relations consultant, political advisor or flashy diplomacy. This is a definite contrast to the TV splashes our leaders make. If the Madison Avenue professional campaigners were to set standards for leadership for God to follow, then His Son Jesus would be out of the running!

God's Concept of the Messiah

Obviously God's standards are different from worldly standards. It is not His method to launch some great political campaign to deal with the problems of suffering in society. It is His way to work from the inside out—to initiate change within people, one person at a time. Then change and help for the suffering will come to our society. For this task Jesus is uniquely qualified.

The picture of the servant described in Isaiah illustrates Jesus' unique qualifications as the Messiah. He is one who will reach out to people where they are to comfort them in their hurts and encourage them in their weaknessess. Isaiah 42:3 says, "A bruised reed he will not break, and a smoldering wick he will not snuff out. In faithfulness he will bring forth justice" (also see Matt. 12:15-21). God's appointed Messiah is gentle. He mends broken lives and will not put out the struggling fires of faith that burn in us. He has put ministering to our needs for healing in a position of importance. Bringing healing for sin is His primary purpose.

Isaiah 42:6,7 tells us that Jesus came to be "a covenant for the people and a light for the Gentiles, to open eyes that are blind, to free captives from prison and to release from the dungeon those who sit in darkness." Isaiah 53:4 says, "Surely he took up our infirmities and carried our sorrows." These prophecies were fulfilled both in the miracles of physical healing that Jesus wrought as well as in the spiritual light He has brought to searching souls. Matthew 8:16,17 tells us that both the spiritually oppressed—the demon possessed—and the physically sick were healed by Jesus. Jesus did all this to "fulfill what was spoken through the prophet Isaiah: 'He took up our infirmities and carried our diseases'" (v. 17). Again a contrast can be drawn between the servant leadership of Christ and the privileged existence worldly leaders may expect. Political leaders are often so far removed from the hurting and oppressed that they have to take special tours and talk to consultants to find out how the "other half" lives; Jesus is personally acquainted with grief and suffering and therefore perfectly empathizes with our hurt.

Another characteristic of the Messiah is that He was chosen by God. Isaiah 49:1 says, "Before I was born the Lord called me." God's identification of Jesus as His chosen One is repeated on the mount of transfiguration. In the presence of Peter, John and James, God proclaimed of Jesus: "This is my Son, whom I have chosen; listen to him" (Luke 9:35). Jesus does not beg, coerce, campaign or request our acceptance of Him as Savior. He is Savior despite any acknowledgement on our part. He has no competition because He is the only authentic means of salvation for us. Jesus said, "I am the way and the truth and the life. No one comes to the Father except through me" (John 14:6). Jesus can never be demoted, voted out of office or replaced by any means. He stands forever as the only Savior of the world.

From time to time elected officials break the law or rules for ethical conduct. In a democratic society, special prosecutors may be appointed and committees named to hold hearings on such conduct. Usually elaborately constructed defenses exalting the virtues of the accused are promoted. Opposing witnesses may parade before the panels presenting contradictory views. Efforts to get media exposure for each one's biases are strenuously made. When the proceedings are concluded, no one has admitted guilt and questions of truth and falsehood linger unresolved.

What a contrast to the servant of Isaiah who "had done no violence, nor was any deceit in his mouth" (Isa. 53:9). He required no defense, because all accusations against Him were false. In Matthew 27:13,14 we read, "Then Pilate asked him, 'Don't you hear the testimony they are bringing against you?' But Jesus made no reply, not even to a single charge—to the great amazement of the governor."

We also may be accused falsely at times. It is a comfort to know that Christ can empathize intimately with such suffering. Sometimes we will see God's vindication for the wrong done to us, but often we will not. We are to be examples, providing justice and mercy to our world, but vengeance is not our affair (see Mic. 6:8; Rom. 12:19). Only God can repay such wrong. Such examples are a rarity in our self-oriented world and may result in amazement in others.

In being falsely accused, Jesus was labeled as a felon and died a felon's death—crucifixion. Crucifixion was how Romans executed political and the most undesirable of their prisoners. Isaiah says, "He was assigned a grave with the wicked" (53:9), and so Jesus died painfully, hanging on a cross between two criminals (see Matt. 27:38). Jesus' disciples were afraid of being associated with their crucified leader. Such an association would not only endanger them, it would also taint them with the reputation of a despised, dangerous person.

Jewish believer Moishe Rosen, in his book Y'Shua, tells of the days after his conversion to Christ. He was enthusiastic about his faith and determined to tell everyone of his fellow Jews about his experience. But in his culture he soon realized that, by committing his life to Christ, he had likewise been tainted by association with a despised person. His people, once his friends, now dug up every real and imagined fault of his past and made them common lore concerning him. With Jesus

he had been assigned to the ranks of those held in contempt.

As a result of his loyalty to Jesus, Rosen had one particularly challenging and eventually rewarding discussion with a neighbor. The neighbor was so elated at defeating the arguments and testimony of Rosen that he sought out a rabbi to direct him in further study of Isaiah 53. The rabbi felt that the passage was not regarded by Jews as a messianic passage. But as the neighbor read carefully he saw the messianic message. Eventually the neighbor had to conclude that Jesus was the subject of Isaiah 53 and surrendered to Him as the Messiah. The neighbor was happy to tell of his pilgrimage later when Rosen was addressing the church where the neighbor was now a deacon.[1]

Jesus' experience of death adds the final qualification to His job description as Savior of the world. Raised up on the cross as a felon, Jesus took the sins of the world, our sins, upon Himself and experienced the pain of separation from God. In darkness and aloneness Jesus cried out, "My God, my God, why have you forsaken me?" (Matt. 27:46; also refer to 2 Cor. 5:21). Jesus identifies with us when we are separated from God, crushed by the burden of our sin. Jesus also identifies with our physical pain because He experienced the ultimate in physical suffering—a painful torturous death.

Unlike Any Human Idea

Our concept of what we need in order to solve the problems in our world can be colored by many influences. We may think that we need a highly visible savior, with the political clout and material resources to relieve suffering and combat sin in society. We may think we need programs that will reach the masses and lift them out of their misery and into a better life. We may look for a defense attorney to fight for justice on our behalf. Often people readily accept, even cling to, those who seem to have answers or promise to bring improvement. Many of these people may accomplish good things, but their efforts, at best, are imperfect and incomplete solutions. When expectations placed on these people are not met, their followers may feel that a solution for our world's problems is too tall of an order for anyone to fill.

The inadequacy of humans to resolve world problems points to the fact that our real needs are deeper and have a spiritual source. The world needs the Savior, Jesus Christ, who chose to change the world one person at a time. Christ could have wielded His power in its fullness and destroyed evil with a blink of the eye (and knowing the human condition, not one of us would have survived such a display of power). But He did not. He came personally and, by changing human hearts, has and is changing the world in great ways.

Our ideas about what is needed to deal with sin, pain and suffering are limited compared to God's insight. An illustration of this comes from the difficulty many Jews had accepting Jesus as the promised Messiah. They had expected the Messiah to come as a political figure who would break the yoke of Roman oppression. Because of this misconception they did not recognize Jesus. Human ideas such as these have a number of predictable characteristics that, without the guidance of God's insight, will lead people to fail in recognizing Jesus' Lordship. These characteristics include the following:

1. Human ideas are colored by human preconceptions. We bring our limitations and biases to all we think.
2. Human ideas are inevitably limited to human comprehension and logic. God is above logic; logic is a human invention to help us think clearly within human limitations.
3. Human ideas measure attributes and abilities in terms of our own needs for those attributes and abilities. What is desirable reflects what we want to see in our own lives. What is weak is like that which we do not want to be. What is beautiful is that which appeals to our limited senses and that which we are persuaded to think of as attractive.
4. Human ideas, without divine light, are inevitably self-centered. We value that which seems good to us in our very short-sighted vision.
5. Human ideas about God inevitably diminish God to mere human character and size. Thus a God who could be a man, a God who could suffer, a God who could die, a God who was of unattractive appearance is not desired or recognized by anyone who has a human vision of grandeur in mind.

Many people today feel that, as a point of freedom of religion in a pluralistic society, no one should be able to tell them if their concepts about Jesus are wrong. To them it becomes a matter of "open-mindedness" to be able to form a personal belief. The problem is, Jesus isn't an elected official and God's kingdom isn't a democracy. Jesus is the Savior and He does not work according to personal agendas. If we cannot recognize Him as Lord then we are lost.

Prophecy gives us a basis by which we can identify Jesus as the Christ. It is by God's authority and with His insight that the prophets spoke. Second Peter 1:20,21 declares, "Above all, you must understand that no prophecy of Scripture came about by the prophet's own interpretation. For prophecy never had its origin in the will of man, but men spoke from God as they were carried along by the Holy Spirit."

All of the prophecies foretelling the coming of the Messiah to earth have been fulfilled in Jesus. In reading them we have learned that the Messiah is one who has suffered for the sake of our sins and through whose suffering we can find healing for our souls. Because of His suffering, we have a Savior who can truly care for us and meet our needs for redemption from sin, for compassion in times of pain and for assurance of ultimate triumph over death (see Heb. 2:14-18).

The Question of Suffering

It is difficult to describe Jesus as a suffering servant without raising the question asked by people who challenge the fact that God is loving. The question is this: If God is loving why does He allow suffering? The world is filled to the brim with suffering and to some there doesn't seem to be a God to abate it. If this question comes up during your class discussion, the following points may help them.

1. It is important to establish that it is in God's nature to love. If this were not so, Christ would never have come into the world. In loving us, God set us free so that we can choose to love Him in return. God loves us willingly and wants us, of our free will, to return His love and express love to others. (See Matt. 22:37; 1 John 4:7-12.)

2. In freedom, we have the right to refuse God's love, to disobey His Word and to follow our own designs. Adam and Eve illustrate this point for us. They chose to play God for themselves and to serve themselves (see Gen. 3:1-24). Given their limited human aptitude and vision they made some bad choices. Pain and death resulted. At this point the reality of physical and spiritual death entered the world, and with it all its trappings: separation from God, disease, enmity between people. Death has a ripple effect, touching lives indiscriminately. We experience pain oftentimes because we live in a fallen world. (See Rom. 5:12.)

3. As people it is our tendency to put ourselves first, to play God. In doing so we discover that others are trying to do the same. Because we cannot play God and have our wishes thwarted, we will experience conflict with others who are also seeking their own ends and will probably inflict pain to preserve our wills. Thus our pain sometimes finds its source in the selfish will of another—whether we deserve it or not. (See Jas. 3:16,17; 1 Pet. 2:19.)

4. In order to deal with the problem of pain, God became one of us and suffered with us. No god invented by man could do this. God, out of the depths of His love, has responded to the pain that exists in our fallen world because of sin. He has personally identified with all that we suffer through Christ's experience on earth. Hebrews 4:15 says, "For we do not have a high priest who is unable to sympathize with our weaknesses, but we have one who has been tempted in every way, just as we are—yet was without sin." Only a suffering servant could bring salvation to our broken hearts and identify with our human needs.

5. As Christians, our question should not be so much "Why do we suffer?" as it should be "How can my suffering be used to God's glory?" Hopefully one of the greatest differences between godly people and the ungodly is how they suffer. Like the apostle Paul we can regard our suffering as not worthy of comparison to the wonderful things we will experience in eternity (see Rom. 8:18). It has been said that pagans waste their pain because they see no meaning in their suffering. When we understand that in the light of eternity our suffering is inconsequential, then we will stand as witnesses to nonbelievers. When we see our suffering as a means of identifying ourselves with Christ's suffering for our sake then we become part of the great drama of salvation. Only a loving God would both love us and suffer for us as one of us. (See Luke 21:12-19; 2 Cor. 1:3-11; 12:7-10.)

Notes

1. Moishe Rosen, *Y'Shua* (Chicago: Moody Press, 1982), pp.66-68.

For further study on the topic of suffering, you or your students may want to read one of the following resources:

Lewis, C.S. *The Problem of Pain*. London: Fontana Books, 1957.

Yancy, Phillip, *Where Is God When It Hurts?* Grand Rapids, MI: Zondervan Publishing House, 1977.

APPROACH TO THE WORD

APPROACH (5-8 minutes)

Before class letter the words "Qualifications for a Great Political Leader" on a large sheet of paper and post it within reach of students. As students arrive encourage them to write what attributes the world identifies as important for a person to have who is in a position of great influence over others.

After students have had an opportunity to write their ideas ask, **Why did you choose these attributes?** After several students share say, **Today we are going to look at the One God appointed to fill the position of Savior and Lord of all people: Jesus Christ, God's only Son. We are going to do this by looking at several Old Testament passages of Scripture that foretold Jesus' character.**

BIBLE EXPLORATION

EXPLORATION (35-50 minutes)

Materials needed: Session 12 Student Worksheet for each student.

CHRIST B.C. / SESSION 12

The Suffering Servant

Isaiah 50:6; 52:14; 53:1,2/Matthew 27:27-30:

Isaiah 42:2/Mark 7:31-36:

Isaiah 42:3/Matthew 12:15-21:

Isaiah 42:6,7; 53:4/Matthew 8:16,17:

Isaiah 49:1/Luke 9:34,35:

Isaiah 53:9/Matthew 26:59-61;27:12-14:

Jesus Understands Our Pain

Review the events from Jesus' life on earth that you have studied today. In one or two sentences write a description of the ways in which Jesus suffered.

Read Hebrews 2:18. List as many reasons as you can why Jesus is able to understand people's suffering.

Step 1 (15-20 minutes): Distribute Session 12 worksheets to students. Ask volunteers to share in reading aloud the verses listed in "The Suffering Servant" section of their worksheets. As the verses are read, lead a discussion of the verses using the following outline and information from the Teacher's Bible Study. Encourage students to take notes on their worksheets as the discussion progresses. As appropriate, refer to the characteristics listed on the poster made during the Approach. Introduce this study by saying, **The Old Testament prophecies of Jesus that** we are going to look at today are commonly called the "Servant Songs." They foretold events that would happen during Jesus' life on earth. They also give us a clear picture of the character of Jesus. Then begin your discussion.

Isaiah 50:6; 52:14; 53:1,2/Matthew 27:27-31

• Mention that Isaiah 53:2 describes Jesus' everyday outward appearance. The other verses describe Him during the time right before His death when He was badly beaten. Ask, **How is this picture of Jesus' appearance and circumstances different from what the world looks for in a person of authority?** Reread Isaiah 53:1. Mention that this verse is repeated in John 12:37,38 in reference to the many Jews who, after witnessing many miraculous signs done by Jesus, still refused to believe in Him. Jesus was not what they expected the Messiah (God's promised Savior) to be like, so they didn't recognize Jesus for who He was. In the eyes of these unbelievers Jesus was a criminal.

Isaiah 42:2/Mark 7:31-36

• Say, **Often Jesus made a point of not drawing attention to His deeds. Many believe He did this in order to prevent His rising popularity from heightening tension with the religious leaders before He had fulfilled His purpose for coming to earth. How is Jesus' attitude of shunning untimely attention different from the attitude commonly held by a person seeking a position of power today?** Share Lloyd Ahlem's comments at the end of "The Unacceptable Image" section of the Teacher's Bible Study. Begin with the words "Christ works quietly and unobtrusively . . . " and continue to the end of the paragraph.

Isaiah 42:3/Matthew 12:15-21

• **What things do these verses say are part of Jesus' purpose as the Messiah? What kinds of people do you think the words "smoldering wick" and "bruised reed" are describing?** (Those with a flickering, fragile faith or damaged lives.)

Isaiah 42:6,7; 53:4/Matthew 8:16,17

• **What needs did Jesus minister to in these verses?** (Both spiritual and physical oppression or illness.)

Isaiah 49:1/Luke 9:34,35

• **What do these verses tell you about Jesus? By what authority has Jesus been appointed as the Messiah or Savior?** (He is chosen by God and has the authority to speak for God.) Mention that, although both Jesus and the prophets

71

spoke with God's authority, Jesus alone is God in human form.

- **What do these verses tell you about those who try to compete with Christ for the position of Messiah or Savior?** Refer to false religions such as Mormonism and the Jehovah's Witnesses who have redefined Jesus' character to the point that they do not ascribe to Him the authority of God, the Creator of the world and the author of all life. Share Lloyd Ahlem's comments from the fourth paragraph of the "God's Concept of the Messiah" section of the Teacher's Bible Study concerning Jesus as the only authentic means of salvation.

Isaiah 53:9/Matthew 26:59-61; 27:12-14

- **What do these verses say about Jesus' character?** (He is without fault or corruption; He maintains His integrity in the face of false accusations and oppression.)
- **Why do you think integrity is a crucial attribute for the Messiah to have?**

Step 2 (5-8 minutes): Help your students summarize what they have studied by asking the following question: **How are God's qualifications for Jesus as Savior and Lord different from what people might think are necessary qualifications?** Then share Lloyd Ahlem's characteristics of human ideas as outlined in the "Unlike Any Human Idea" section of the Teacher's Bible Study.

Move to Step 3 by saying, **We have looked at how God's qualifications for the Savior are different from what people** expect from rulers of worldly kingdoms. We have also seen through the book of Isaiah how Jesus, God's Son, fulfilled what God had planned for the Savior to do and be while living on earth. Now let's look at how Jesus' experience of suffering while He lived on earth has qualified Him to understand our suffering and help us in times of painful need.

Step 3 (5-10 minutes): Move students into pairs or trios. Say, **The passages in Isaiah you have been studying portray Jesus as one who suffered greatly. Because of these verses, Jesus is often referred to as the "Suffering Servant of Isaiah."** Direct groups to complete the "Jesus Understands Our Pain" section of the worksheet.

Step 4 (10-12 minutes): After about five minutes regather into the larger group and ask volunteers to share their work. Then say, **One question that many people ask is, "If God is loving, why does He allow suffering?" How would you respond to a person who asked you this question?** Allow students several moments to share their thoughts. Mention that this is a complex question that has no easy answers. Then share Lloyd Ahlem's points addressing this question. As you share, make sure you read the verses Dr. Ahlem has listed with each point. It is important for your students to hear what God's Word says concerning such a sensitive issue. Refer students to any resources that deal with this topic that you feel will benefit those who wish to study the topic further.

CONCLUSION & DECISION

CONCLUSION (3-5 minutes)

On the back of their worksheets, direct students to individually complete the following sentences as you read them aloud (you may want to write these sentence starters on the overhead or board for students to refer to):

"A painful experience for me was . . . "

"Jesus can understand my pain because . . . "

"Because Jesus understands my pain, I can . . . "

After completing these sentences, allow time for silent prayer so students can speak with Christ about the pain they have experienced in their lives. Then close in audible prayer, thanking God that we are not alone in our pain because He has provided One who can truly understand the difficult things we experience.

Before students leave, tell them that in your next session you'll be discussing a very different side of Jesus' character—His role as mighty victorious king. Then encourage them to read chapter 12 in the student paperback *Christ B.C.* The readings in this chapter explore the theme "compassion."

NOTES:

The Victorious King

KEY VERSE

"The Lord will be king over the whole earth. On that day there will be one Lord, and his name the only name." Zechariah 14:9

"The kingdom of the world has become the kingdom of our Lord and of his Christ, and he will reign for ever and ever." Revelation 11:15

BIBLICAL BASIS

Genesis 2:8,9; Isaiah 63:1-3; Jeremiah 29:8,9,11; Daniel 10:5,6; Zechariah 14:9; Matthew 10:29; 24:24,36,42-51; 28:16-20; Luke 21:25-28; Romans 8:1; 1 Corinthians 1:8,9; 2:9,10; 15:24,25,58; Philippians 2:10,11; 2 Peter 2:1-6; Revelation 1:12-18; 11:15; 19:13-16; 21:1-8; 22:1-6

FOCUS OF THE SESSION

For God's people, the end of history is the beginning of a glorious eternity with Jesus as their Victorious King.

AIMS OF THIS SESSION

You and your students will have accomplished the purpose of this Bible study session if you can:

- EXAMINE principles for considering the future from God's point of view and DISCUSS what will happen when Jesus returns from heaven;
- IDENTIFY tasks assigned to Christians as they wait for Jesus' victorious return;
- PLAN how they will respond to the promise of Jesus' return.

Teacher's Bible Study

This session is more than a discussion of the complete fulfillment of God's plan for the world as presented in Old and New Testament apocalyptic Scripture. The chronology of events and interpretation of specific details and symbols will not be discussed. The point is not to examine the tree, but to get a picture of the whole forest. It is the purpose of this study to present a basis for hope in the future where the end of human history will be the beginning of a glorious eternity for God's people, and Jesus Christ will reign as the victorious, eternal King.

History: A Divine Drama

In my sophomore year in high school we were required to take a course in world history. World War II was plunging ahead and our teacher did not know if he would be drafted into military service. He was obviously asking questions about his own life's meaning and the meaning of the events of war and their part in the flow of history. His concern lent a lot of spirit to his teaching. From time to time he writhed in anguish over the horrors of war and his possible involvement in combat. But occasionally he looked hopefully ahead to an end to despotism from Nazi rule and Japanese militarism. He was a strange mixture of fear and hope. I can't say that I learned a great deal from the history book that semester, but I have one vivid memory from the class. It is the conclusion my teacher drew from the events of the time: "History is up for grabs and will be made by whomever seizes its making."

The teacher was from a religious background, but that did not figure strongly in his thinking. He had been educated in a university that was obviously Christian, but no concept of God's involvement in history was evident in his perception of events. Christianity was an addendum to his life, not a structure of personal faith upon which to build a reason for living or a basis for reasoning. Faith was peripheral and impersonal, not central and vital. As a result, his conclusion that history is up for grabs reflected his lack of faith.

This illustrates one of the essential differences between Christian and humanist thought in regard to the outcome of history. Christians face the future with the certainty that a divine drama is being played out. Humanists on the other hand, regard history as something to be created. Positive humanists live with a hope that what they create will be wholesome and helpful. Negative humanists structure their lives around avoidance—seeking to prevent the worst that people can do. Negative humanists would support the position that the best we can hope for is to build on the firm ground of despair in the hope that we won't repeat destructive behavior.

Hope for the Future

Jeremiah 29:11 gives God's point of view on the issue of history. In writing to the Jews exiled from Jerusalem to Babylon, Jeremiah's message from God was, "'For I know the plans I have for you,' declares the Lord, 'plans to prosper you and not to harm you, plans to give you hope and a future.'" Jesus also gave a message of hope concerning the future to His followers. It is recorded in John 14:3,4. He said, "And if I go and prepare a place for you, I will come back and take you to be with me that you also may be where I am going. You know the way to the place where I am going." These passages from both the Old and New Testaments apply to us as well because they express truth concerning God's view of history and the future. This concept of history is quite different from the one propounded by my high school teacher. To be a Christian is to take a radical view of history: that is, history is in the hands of God and the future is both certain and of His making.

In Jeremiah's declaration to the exiles there are several principles we can learn from as we look through God's eyes to the future and the end of human history. The first principle is a warning against false prophets. There was a false prophet, named Hananiah who was spreading the lie that their captivity would be short and an early relief from Babylonian oppression was coming (see 28:10-17). God told Jeremiah that the actual time of captivity would last for a couple of generations (see 29:5-9). Through Jeremiah the Lord said to the captives, "Do not let the prophets and diviners among you deceive you. Do not listen to the dreams you encourage them to have. They are prophesying lies to you in my name. I have not sent them." (vv. 8,9).

We also need to be on guard against false prophets. In describing the signs of the end of the age Jesus said, "At that time if anyone says to you, 'Look, here is the Christ!' or, 'There he is!' do not believe it. For false Christs and false prophets will appear and perform great signs and miracles to deceive even the elect—if that were possible" (Matt. 24:23,24; also refer to 2 Thess. 2:1-4).

The second principle from Jeremiah by which we must look at prophecies of the future is this: Because the future is in God's hands, His faithful children can live in hope, not despair. Through Jeremiah the Lord was honest in warning that their exile would not be quickly over and of the difficulty to come to those who did not listen to the Lord, but He also spoke words of hope to those whose hearts were faithful. The Lord said, "'Then you will call upon me and come and pray to me, and I will listen to you. You will seek me and find me when you seek me with all your heart. I will be found by you,' declares the Lord, 'and will bring you back from captivity. I will gather you from all the nations and places where I have banished you'" (Jer. 29:12-14). In the difficult days of estrangement from their homeland, God would be close at hand ministering to them. Ultimately, God fulfilled His promise and delivered the Jews from captivity.

In the same way Jesus was honest about and discussed at length the extreme difficulties and fearful upheaval that will occur at the end of the age (see Matt. 24:1–25:46; Mark 13:1-37; Luke 21:5-36). Yet for the faithful, upon recognizing the signs of these difficult times, there is hope. Jesus says, "Do not be frightened" (Luke 21:9), "make up your mind not to worry beforehand" (v. 14) and "by standing firm you will gain life" (v. 19). Jesus also says, "When these things begin to take place,

stand up and lift up your heads, because your redemption is drawing near" (v. 28). We have not been abandoned as we watch and wait for evidence of the fulfillment of God's plans for the end of history. In leaving the world, Jesus reassured his disciples saying, "I am with you always, to the very end of the age" (Matt. 28:20). Throughout history God has been faithful to His promises; in the future He will continue to be faithful.

Promises for the Future

The prophecies that you will focus on today are those depicting Christ as victorious King. In these passages we will see the complete fulfillment of God's plan for the salvation of the world and the source of our hope for the future.

There are several Old Testament passages that picture Christ as King and the final victor over Satan and evil. A phrase often used in conjunction with this picture is "the day of the Lord" (2 Pet. 3:10). This speaks of the time when Christ will return and all things will be put into submission to Him. The Old Testament prophet Zechariah said, "The Lord will be king over the whole earth. On that day there will be one Lord, and his name the only name" (14:9). This prophecy is consistent with the words of Philippians 2:10,11, "that at the name of Jesus every knee should bow, in heaven and on earth and under the earth, and every tongue confess that Jesus Christ is Lord, to the glory of God the Father" and the words of 1 Corinthians 15:24,25, "The end will come, when he hands over the kingdom to God the Father after he has destroyed all dominion, authority and power. For he must reign until he has put all his enemies under his feet."

The confirmation of these declarations is found in the book of Revelation. It describes seven trumpets sounded by seven angels. The sounding of the first six trumpets results in various disasters reminiscent of those described by Jesus as signs of the end of the age (see Rev. 8:6–9:21; also see Matt. 24:1-51; Mark 13:1-37; Luke 21:1-36). The sounding of the seventh trumpet points to Christ fully assuming His role as victorious, eternal king. When this trumpet is sounded voices will declare, "The kingdom of the world has become the kingdom of our Lord and of his Christ, and he will reign for ever and ever" (Rev. 11:15).

There are many Old Testament prophecies that describe Christ as victorious king. The most obvious is in Daniel 10:5,6. In these verses Daniel describes a vision of a man "dressed in linen, with a belt of the finest gold around his waist. His body

was like chrysolite, his face like lightning, his eyes like flaming torches, his arms and legs like the gleam of burnished bronze, and his voice like the sound of a multitude." This man, who Daniel refers to as "my lord" and in whose presence Daniel is overwhelmed (see v. 17), strengthens Daniel and tells him "what will happen to your people in the future, for the vision concerns a time yet to come" (v. 14). Daniel's response to this man expresses submission as to a powerful king. The description of events the man in Daniel's vision gave includes the destruction and establishment of many earthly kingdoms (see Daniel 11). These conflicts are accompanied by spiritual battles between the divine and the demonic (see 10:12,13). The book of Daniel concludes by describing the end times when deliverance will come to the righteous (see 12:1-13).

Revelation 1:12-16 gives us a vision similar to Daniel's. This vision is seen by John and consists of someone "like a son of man." Like Daniel, John was also overwhelmed and then encouraged by the Son of Man (see v. 17). This is obviously a vision of Jesus. His description of Himself as the "First and the Last" (v. 17), identifies Him as equal with the Lord God who proclaimed, "I am the Alpha and the Omega . . . who is, and who was, and who is to come, the Almighty" (v. 8). Like Daniel, the book of Revelation also describes the rise and destruction of many kingdoms. Revelation concludes with a description of the final judgment and the establishment of the "Holy City, the New Jerusalem" (21:2) where man and God will dwell together perfectly. In our day we see evidence of the political upheaval described in Revelation—especially in the Mideast. Although tragedy accompanies such experiences, we can be reassured by them that the time of peace in God's presence is that much closer.

In Revelation 19:16 Jesus is called by the title "King of kings and Lord of lords." As such He is "dressed in a robe dipped in blood" (v. 13) and "He treads the winepress of the fury of the wrath of God Almighty" (v. 15; also see 14:19). This description was also given long ago by Isaiah, "His garments stained crimson . . . . 'I have trodden the winepress alone; from the nations no one was with me. I trampled them in my anger and trod them down in my wrath; their blood spattered my garments'" (63:1,3). These vivid verses describe Jesus as King, dispensing judgment.

We must live knowing judgment is coming, thankful that if we are Christians we will be spared and vindicated. We must also respond to the need of our neighbors who do not know the Lord. We should share Jesus' desire that all people submit to Him. "He is patient with you, not wanting anyone to perish, but everyone to come to repentance. But the day of the Lord will come like a thief. The heavens will disappear with a roar; the elements will be destroyed by fire, and the earth and everything in it will be laid bare." (2 Pet. 3:9,10). The non-Christian's opportunities to turn to the Lord are quickly diminishing. Time will someday, unexpectedly run out.

Knowing that God will fully establish Jesus as eternal, victorious king is cause for joy among God's faithful. With Jesus as absolute reigning king, Satan will be bound, the problem of sin will be obliterated and life as God intended it will be recaptured. Revelation 22:2 describes the tree of life growing in the New Jerusalem. The symbolism here is of the reestablishment of a perfect relationship between God and His servants. "Now the dwelling of God is with men, and he will live with them. They will be his people, and God himself will be with them and be their God. He will wipe every tear from their eyes. There will be no more death or mourning or crying or pain, for the old order of things has passed away" (Rev. 21:3,4). What a reason for joy and hope among those who belong to God!

Today's Situation

Yet many struggle with putting their faith in God's words of prophecy. These people, and any serious readers of prophecy, are confronted with two challenges. The first is, "Am I willing to believe that the prophetic message is true?" A step of faith and a knowledge that many biblical prophecies have already been fulfilled should lead us to affirm that God does not lie, that His word is true and that we can interpret our newspapers and experiences in light of Scripture. We must dare to believe that in doing so we are on solid biblical and intellectual grounds. The second challenge is, "How is my belief reflected in the way I make life decisions and respond emotionally to my personal circumstances?" I know Christians who affirm their belief in biblical prophecy and God's sovereignty

over people's affairs, yet plan and react to events as if God is sitting in heaven biting His nails, wondering what on earth people will do next. The certainty that God's promises are true has not made an emotional or practical impact on their lives.

Right now we live in a time between prophecies of Christ's ultimate reign as victorious King and their complete fulfillments. As we interpret events of our day in the light of Scripture we can see evidence of God's plan unfolding. We can also participate in bringing hope to others who currently stand outside of the joy God has designed for His people by sharing the gospel with them. As we do this we must realize that Satan is actively working to keep as many souls out of God's hand as he can (see 2 Cor. 4:4; 1 Pet. 5:8).

Throughout Scripture efforts to thwart God's plans have had the smell of Satan's involvement. At one time, the lineage from which the Messiah would be born was threatened by Jezebel's daughter, Athaliah (see 2 Kings 11:1-21). Years later Herod tried to eliminate the Messiah by massacring all the boys in Bethlehem who were two years old or younger (see Matt. 1:13-18). During Jesus' sojourn in the desert, Satan tried to tempt Jesus to follow his plans instead of God's (see Matt. 4:1-11; Mark 1:12; Luke 4:1-13). At the Last Supper, Satan entered Judas, participating in the betrayal of Jesus (see John 13:27). What irony that, in attempting to cancel God's plan of redemption, Satan participated in its fulfillment. At Calvary Satan might have thought he had finally succeeded in his battle with God. Yet Colossians 2:15 says, "And having disarmed the powers and authorities, he made a public spectacle of them, triumphing over them by the cross."

Every generation, from Bible times until today, has been subject to an effort to disclaim the promises of God. It is Satan's purpose to hold as many people in unbelief as possible. The Christian's battle is to remain faithful to the gospel, share it with others and watch for Christ's coming (see Matt. 24:42-44; 28:16-20; 1 Pet. 5:9). This is difficult in a world filled with the allure of lust; the rationalization of human evil into normal behavior; theories of human behavior and personality that proclaim that a

fulfilled person is a person who is in control of his or her life; and the onslaughts of Satan against public Christian personalities. Under such conditions nominal Christians often abandon their faith for New Age movements and eastern mysticism or often resort to a stand for atheism. All of these are symptoms of Satan desperately struggling to overcome an enemy he can never defeat: God.

As Christians, in these times of international stress, nuclear threat and the undermining of positive moral values, our response to historic and current events must be built on a strong basis of faith and knowledge of God's Word—not on human perceptions. Negative humanists deal only in human perceptions and not in Christian hope. They dismiss this hope as implausible. Positive humanists create false hopes in their message. They look at man, ignore his lawlessness and carnage, and pronounce hope without dealing with man's spiritual condition.

By His Spirit

On the day I was married a pastor friend sent my new wife and me a telegram. In it he quoted 1 Corinthians 2:9,10. This passage speaks of the wisdom that God gives to those who have His Holy Spirit. It is a wisdom by which Christians can understand God's ways. It says, "However, as it is written: 'No eye has seen, no ear has heard, no mind has conceived what God has prepared for those who love him'—but God has revealed it to us by his Spirit. The Spirit searches all things, even the deep things of God." It is through the Spirit of Christ living in our hearts that we can face the future with a true hope. As we are obedient to the Holy Spirit and seek to understand and identify God's control in human events, we will be rewarded with insight and a vision for the future. We will be like the servants in the parable who are dressed and ready to respond, watching for the moment the master returns (see Luke 12:35-40). Our waiting and watching must consist of our work at the tasks He has appointed us (see Matt. 24:45,46; Mark 13:34-37), knowing that once He appears it will be to late for such things. "It will be good for those servants whose master finds them watching when he comes" (Luke 12:37).

NOTES:

This Week's Teaching Plan

APPROACH TO THE WORD

APPROACH (3-5 minutes)

Before students arrive, letter the following heading on a large piece of paper or on the chalkboard: "The Future." Under this heading add two more headings: "Hopes" and "Fears."

As students arrive, encourage them to list under the "Hopes" and "Fears" headings what comes to mind when they consider their future (both immediate and distant future). When all students have gathered, read both lists aloud. Then say, **All of us have certain hopes for the future, and all of us struggle with fears of not knowing what will happen in the future. Today we are going to look at history as well as the future through God's eyes.**

BIBLE EXPLORATION

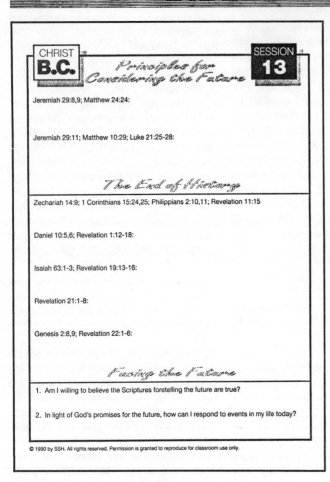

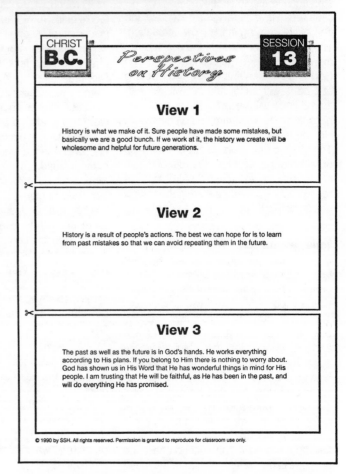

EXPLORATION (40-50 minutes)

Materials needed: Session 13 Student Worksheet for each student; the Session 13 "Perspectives on History" sheet.

Preparation: Before class cut the "Perspectives on History" sheet along the dotted lines. Write the two assignments listed in Step 4 on the board or overhead transparency. Keep the assignments covered until you reach Step 4.

Step 1 (7-8 minutes): Move students into three groups. Give each group one view from the "Perspectives on History" sheet. Then ask each group to answer this question: **Based on the quote I gave you, what words would you use to describe this view of the outcome of history?** Allow four to five minutes for groups to work. Then regather into the large group and ask volunteers who evaluated View 1 to share their group's findings. Then ask groups who worked on View 2 and View 3 to share. As necessary, share Lloyd Ahlem's comments from the "History: A Divine Drama" section concerning the characteristics of the positive and negative humanist views of the outcome of history. Optional—have each group briefly present an argument supporting the point of view it was given. Allow time for groups to debate each argument.

Move to Step 2 by saying, **Two of these quotes, View 1 and View 2, represent views of historic and future events that are held by many people in our society today. View 3 repre-**

sents God's point of view of history. Let's take a closer look at what God says about the future.

Step 2 (8-10 minutes): Distribute Session 13 Student Worksheets to students. Direct students to the "Principles for Considering the Future" section of the worksheet and say, **God gives us two important principles to follow when considering the future and the end of history.** Ask volunteers to read Jeremiah 29:8,9 and Matthew 24:24. **What principle for examining events through God's eyes do you see in these verses?** (Be careful about believing what others say about the future; measure the words of people against God's Word. Be aware that people will come making predictions for the future with the intention of deceiving others.) **How could a false prophet confuse a person's insight into God's plans for the future?** (Inaccurate, but convincing, opinions about the future can make it difficult for the person who is not familiar with God's Word to know what is true; this person may not recognize God's actions as His plans for the future are fulfilled.) Mention that groups such as the Jehovah's Witnesses and Mormons claim that certain things will happen in the future. They also claim that their beliefs contain additional information based on, but in addition to, the Bible. What they say may contain Christian-sounding words, but they are definitely not supported by our only written source of information for God's point of view: the Bible.

Then ask volunteers to read Jeremiah 29:11; Matthew 10:29; Luke 21:25-28. Ask, **What principle do these verses give us about how we should view God's involvement in what will happen in the future?** (Because the future is in God's hands, those who belong to Him can have hope, not despair.) Mention that Jesus was honest in sharing difficult things that will happen as signs of the end of history, but He also promised to be with those who love Him to the end (read Matt. 28:20). Say, **The end of history is often referred to as "the end of the age."** Move to Step 3 by saying, **Now that we have some insight into God's engineering of events, let's take a look at several prophecies about Jesus and what He will accomplish at the end of history.**

Step 3 (15-20 minutes): Direct students to "The End of History" section of their worksheets. Ask volunteers to share in reading the verses listed in this section. As the verses are read, lead a discussion of the verses using the following outline and information from the Teacher's Bible Study. Encourage students to take notes on their worksheets as the discussion progresses.

Zechariah 14:9; 1 Corinthians 15:24,25; Philippians 2:10,11; Revelation 11:15

- Mention that the phrase "day of the Lord" is another term often used to refer to the time when Jesus will return and all things will be put into submission to Him. **What titles are used for Jesus in these verses?** (Lord, King.)
- **How will people everywhere show they recognize Jesus as the Lord?** (They will bow to Him and verbally acknowledge His authority over everything.)
- **What do these verses say will happen when Jesus fulfills His role as Lord and King?** (Put His enemies under His feet by destroying their authority, power and influence in the world; reign forever.)
- **Who are Jesus' enemies?** (Satan, evil and those who have rejected Him—see Matt. 10:32,33; John 3:20,21.)

Daniel 10:5,6; Revelation 1:12-18

- Tell students that these verses describe Jesus as He is in heaven. Ask students to suggest as many adjectives describing Jesus from these verses as they can. List their suggestions on the board or overhead. Then ask, **What overall impression do these descriptions give you about Jesus?**

- Say, **The prophecies following these descriptions include accounts of the rise and destructions of many earthly kingdoms as well as spiritual battles. The Bible clearly states that the events leading up to Jesus' ultimate return as King will be difficult and often accompanied by tragedy.** Then ask, **How can knowing these are signs of Jesus' return and knowing that God has control of history affect the way a person looks at current events or his or her personal experiences?**

Isaiah 63:1-3; Revelation 19:13-16

- **What do these verses say Jesus will accomplish when He returns?** (He will dispense judgment for sin that the world deserves.)
- Read 2 Peter 2:1-6 and then Romans 8:1 and 1 Corinthians 1:8,9. Ask, **When He returns, how will Jesus respond to the ungodly?** (He will judge them and give them the punishment they deserve.) **How will He respond to those who belong to Him?** (They will not be condemned; they will be blameless before God.)

Revelation 21:1-8

- **When Jesus has returned and sin and evil have been taken care of, what will be the situation of those who belong to God?** (They will be in God's presence; they will no longer experience death, pain, sadness, thirst or other hurts that we experience in our world today.)

Genesis 2:8,9; Revelation 22:1-6

- **What was present in the garden of Eden that will also be present in God's future, eternal kingdom?** (The tree of life.) Mention that, in the garden of Eden, Adam and Eve were free to eat from the tree of life, but did not do so. Genesis 3:22 implies that eating from the tree of life would result in experiencing eternal life.
- Say, **At the beginning of time when God created the world, everything was perfect. Sin had not entered into human experience and Adam and Eve enjoyed a close relationship with God. When Adam and Eve committed the first sin, the perfect relationship between God and the people He had created was broken. Death was the penalty. Adam and Eve were cast out of the garden of Eden in order to prevent them from eating from the tree of life and so avoid the penalty of death** (see Gen. 3:22,23). **At the end of history, after sin has been taken care of, the perfect relationship God had intended to have with people will be restored** (ask a volunteer to reread Rev. 21:3). **The presence of the tree of life in God's eternal kingdom, referred to as the New Jerusalem, is symbolic of the restoration of a perfect relationship between God and people. Those who belong to God will live forever, enjoying the relationship with Him that was originally intended in Eden.** Mention that a significant difference between Eden and the New Jerusalem is that in the future, when Satan and evil have been obliterated, the possibility of sin will no longer exist.

Move to Step 4 by saying, **Those who belong to God have many wonderful things to look forward to. But until that time comes to pass, we still have to deal with living today.**

Step 4 (10-12 minutes): Move the class into groups—three to four students in each group. Reveal the two assignments listed on the board or overhead. Give half of the groups assignment 1 and the other half assignment 2.

1. Read 1 Corinthians 2:9,10. What has God given to help us understand current and future events? How can a person have access to this gift from God?
2. Read Matthew 24:36,42-51. While we are waiting for Christ to

return, what are we instructed to do? What are some ways we can do this?

Allow 5 minutes for groups to work; then ask volunteers who worked on assignment 1 to share their work. Then ask groups who worked on assignment 2 to share. Make sure the following is shared for each assignment: (1) The wisdom to understand current and future events comes from God's Spirit. Mention that access to the wisdom of God's Spirit only comes through a personal relationship with God; (2)We are commanded to be watchful and to be faithful servants in the tasks Jesus has given us to do. Have volunteers read Matthew 28:16-20 and 1 Corinthians 15:58. After the verses are read ask, **What tasks do these verses say have been assigned to Christians?** (Telling others about Jesus; standing firm in faith; serving the Lord.)**What are some specific ways you can accomplish these tasks?**

Move to the Conclusion by saying, **A Christian's response to historic, current and future events must be based on a knowledge of God's Word, not human perceptions alone. A Christian who is obedient to God's Word and nurtures his or her relationship with God can face the future with hope, knowing that the outcome of history is certain and is in God's hands.**

CONCLUSION & DECISION

CONCLUSION (5-8 minutes)

Direct students to individually complete the questions in the "Facing the Future" section of their worksheets. After students have had 3-5 minutes to work, close in prayer thanking God that He is in control of the future and that those who belong to Him do not need to be afraid of what the future may bring. Also pray that those who do not belong to the Lord will consider what the future holds for them and the opportunity they have for hope in the future if they accept the salvation God has provided through Jesus Christ.

Encourage students to read chapter 13 of the student paperback *Christ B.C.* The readings in this chapter explore the theme "victorious future."

NOTES:

Student Worksheets
The following pages are the reproducible student worksheets for this course.

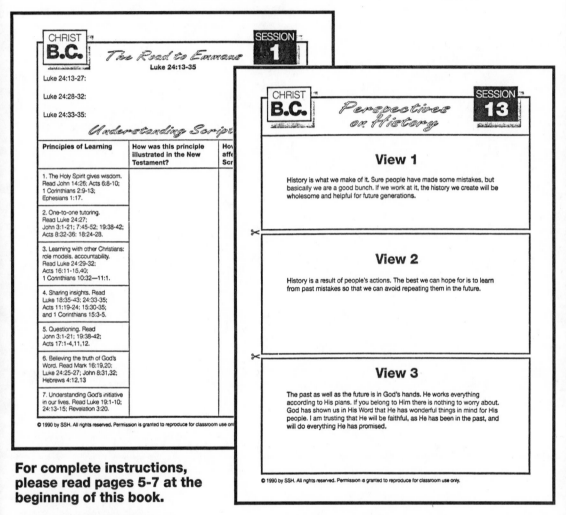

For complete instructions, please read pages 5-7 at the beginning of this book.

A Helpful Note:
It is not necessary for you to reproduce every Student Worksheet for each week's session!

● Many Student Worksheets contain only a sentence or two of information. This has been included for your convenience, primarily for making overhead projector transparencies. You can avoid copying these by handing out blank paper to your students and simply **reading** the instructions aloud or writing them on the chalkboard.

● We at the Light Force recognize that to much of a good thing—even Student Worksheets—can be too much. Seek variety in your teaching times. Spice up your classes with a guest speaker, or show a good Christian film for discussion. Even a trip to the donut shop can give you an opportunity to disciple your students!

CHRIST **B.C.**

The Road to Emmaus
Luke 24:13-35

Luke 24:13-27:

Luke 24:28-32:

Luke 24:33-35:

Understanding Scripture

Principles of Learning	How was this principle illustrated in the New Testament?	How can this principle affect your study of Scripture?
1. The Holy Spirit gives wisdom. Read John 14:26; Acts 6:8-10; 1 Corinthians 2:9-13; Ephesians 1:17.		
2. One-to-one tutoring. Read Luke 24:27; John 3:1-21; 7:45-52; 19:38-42; Acts 8:32-36; 18:24-28.		
3. Learning with other Christians: role models, accountability. Read Luke 24:29-32; Acts 16:11-15,40; 1 Corinthians 10:32—11:1.		
4. Sharing insights. Read Luke 18:35-43; 24:33-35; Acts 11:19-24; 15:30-35; and 1 Corinthians 15:3-5.		
5. Questioning. Read John 3:1-21; 19:38-42; Acts 17:1-4,11,12.		
6. Believing the truth of God's Word. Read Mark 16:19,20; Luke 24:25-27; John 8:31,32; Hebrews 4:12,13		
7. Understanding God's initiative in our lives. Read Luke 19:1-10; 24:13-15; Revelation 3:20.		

God Covers Adam and Eve's Nakedness

Genesis 3:1-21

Genesis 3:1-6:

Genesis 3:7-11:

Genesis 3:12,13:

Genesis 3:14-19:

Genesis 3:20,21:

Excuses, Excuses

CHRIST B.C.

Noah Finds Refuge in the Ark
Genesis 6:1–8:22

Genesis 6:1-7,11-13:

Genesis 6:8,9:

Genesis 6:14-22:

Genesis 7:1–8:22:

It Pays to Prepare

CHRIST B.C.

Stormy Times

On a scale of 1 to 5, rate each experience listed according to how stressful or difficult an experience it would be.

		A breeze				Very difficult
		1	2	3	4	5
1.	Pressure to drink, take drugs or have sex.					
2.	A family member or close friend dying.					
3.	Wearing the wrong thing to a social gathering.					
4.	Being abused.					
5.	Deciding what to do after graduation.					
6.	Developing a serious health problem.					
7.	Having a pet named Fred.					
8.	Being criticized behind your back by a friend.					
9.	Parents divorcing.					
10.	Breaking off a relationship.					
11.	Not having a boyfriend/girlfriend					

Refuge in Christ

Group 1
Write a newspaper article describing a person who can find refuge in Christ. Use these verses as a basis for your article: Genesis 6:9,22; 7:5; Psalm 32:6; 91:14; 1 John 5:3-5.

Group 2
Write slogans or one-word descriptions that illustrate what refuge in Christ is like. Use these verses as a basis for your descriptions: Genesis 6:21; 7:11-13,16,23; Psalm 32:7; 57:1-3; 91:2,4,5; Isaiah 40:28-31; Matthew 11:28-30; Philippians 4:6,7.

Group 3
List the "top ten" influences in the world from which you need protection. Use these verses as a basis for your list: Deuteronomy 7:25; Luke 12:15; 1 Corinthians 6:18-20; 2 Timothy 4:17,18; 1 Peter 5:8; 2 Peter 2:1-3; 17-19.

Genesis 14:1-16:

Genesis 14:17-20; Hebrews 7:1-3:

Where Am I Seeking Redemption?

5

Abraham and Isaac

Genesis 12:1-4; 18:9-12; 22:1-18

Genesis 12:1-4; 18:9-14:

Genesis 22:1,2:

Genesis 22:3-10:

Genesis 22:11-18:

A New Testament Parallel

Use the following verses to make a comparison between the story of Abraham and its New Testament counterpart.

Luke 2:30-35:

John 19:17:

John 3:16 and Romans 8:32:

Romans 6:23 and Hebrews 9:14:

Hebrews 4:14-16 and 10:21,22:

Romans 5:6-8:

© 1990 by SSH. All rights reserved. Permission is granted to reproduce for classroom use only.

A. Joseph	B. Jesus Christ
1. Genesis 37:3	1. Matthew 3:17
2. Genesis 37:18,23,24,28	2. Matthew 26:14-16
3. Genesis 39:6b-9	3. Matthew 4:1; Hebrews 4:14,15
4. Genesis 39:16-20a	4. Luke 23:20-25
5. Genesis 40:1-22	5. Luke 23:32,33,39-43
6. Genesis 41:14,41-43	6. Matthew 28:18; Acts 2:24
7. Genesis 41:55-57	7. John 3:16,17; 6:35; Acts 4:12
8. Genesis 44:16; 45:1-15	8. Colossians 1:22; 1 John 1:9
9. Genesis 45:5-7	9. John 12:27,28; 18:37

CHRIST B.C.

The Passover

Exodus 3:1–13:16

Exodus 3:1-10:

Exodus 3:11–10:29:

Exodus 11:1-10:

God's Instructions

Instructions	Christ in the Passover
1. Date: Exodus 12:1-3;13:4	2 Corinthians 5:17
2. Lamb: Exodus 12:3,5,6,9,10	John 1:29; 1 Corinthians 5:7
3. Blood: Exodus 12:7,13,22,23	Matthew 26:27,28; Hebrews 9:14
4. Bread: Exodus 12:8,15,17-20	Mark 14:22; 1 Corinthians 5:6-8
5. How to Eat: Exodus 12:11	Matthew 24:42-44; John 14:2,3

● An offering:

● The furnishings:

● The walls:

● The floor plan:

The Curtain and the Most Holy Place

Leviticus 16:1,2:

Leviticus 16:3-6:

Exodus 26:31-33:

Christ the Curtain

Read Hebrews 10:19-22. Then answer the following questions.

When the curtain in the Temple was torn, what was exposed?

As symbolized by the tearing of the curtain in the Temple, how did Christ's death on the cross change the relationship between God and those who love Him?

What kind of relationship does God want to have with you?

Exodus 25:10-16:

Exodus 25:17-22:

Evidence of God's Mercy

The Israelites	Us
What means did God provide whereby the Israelites could receive forgiveness? (Read Leviticus 16:15,16,34.)	What means did God provide whereby we can be forgiven of our sin? (Read Romans 3:25; Hebrews 2:17; 1 John 4:9,10.)
How did God's provision of forgiveness, through the sacrifice of atonement, express God's mercy toward the Israelites?	How does God's provision for our forgiveness express His mercy toward us?

CHRIST B.C.

God's Solution for the Israelites

Numbers 21:4-9

Why were the people impatient?

With whom were the people angry?

What punishment did God give the people?

How did the people respond to their punishment?

Who provided a way for the people to be healed from their snakebites?

What symbol was used to bring about healing from the snakebites?

According to verse 9, who had the opportunity to find healing?

What action was required for a person to find healing?

What alternative did a poisoned person have besides looking at the snake?

Read Romans 3:23. Who is guilty of sin?

Read Romans 6:23. What punishment does our sin deserve?

Read John 3:16,17; Romans 5:6,8; and Hebrews 9:14. What way was provided for us to be healed from our sin?

According to John 3:16, who is able to receive the salvation God has provided?

Read John 1:12. What must a person do to receive salvation through Jesus?

Read John 14:26; and 1 John 1:9. What are the results of becoming a Christian?

Read Acts 4:12. What alternative does a person have to find forgiveness of sins and eternal life, besides through Jesus?

Prophecies of Jesus

Prophecies

Micah 5:2	Isaiah 53:4-6
Isaiah 7:14	Isaiah 53:7,8
Isaiah 11:1	Isaiah 53:9
Malachi 3:1	Isaiah 53:10-12
Isaiah 53:1	Psalm 16:9-11
Isaiah 53:3a	Psalm 68:18
Isaiah 52:14 and 53:3	

Fulfillments

Matthew 8:16,17; John 19:34; 1 Peter 2:24	Matthew 27:38; Mark 14:55,56; 15:43-46; 1 Peter 2:21-23	Luke 22:37,54; Hebrews 7:25; 1 Peter 2:23-25
Matthew 27:12; Revelation 5:6	Matthew 1:1,6; Romans 15:8,12	Acts 1:10,11; Ephesians 4:7-9
Acts 2:22-28	Matthew 27:27-31	Matthew 1:20-23
Luke 7:24-27	Luke 2:4-7	Matthew 13:53-58
	Romans 10:16	

Isaiah 50:6; 52:14; 53:1,2/Matthew 27:27-30:

Isaiah 42:2/Mark 7:31-36:

Isaiah 42:3/Matthew 12:15-21:

Isaiah 42:6,7; 53:4/Matthew 8:16,17:

Isaiah 49:1/Luke 9:34,35:

Isaiah 53:9/Matthew 26:59-61;27:12-14:

Jesus Understands Our Pain

Reveiw the events from Jesus' life on earth that you have studied today. In one or two sentences write a description of the ways in which Jesus suffered.

Read Hebrews 2:18. List as many reasons as you can why Jesus is able to understand people's suffering.

Jeremiah 29:8,9; Matthew 24:24:

Jeremiah 29:11; Matthew 10:29; Luke 21:25-28:

The End of History

Zechariah 14:9; 1 Corinthians 15:24,25; Philippians 2:10,11; Revelation 11:15

Daniel 10:5,6; Revelation 1:12-18:

Isaiah 63:1-3; Revelation 19:13-16:

Revelation 21:1-8:

Genesis 2:8,9; Revelation 22:1-6:

Facing the Future

1. Am I willing to believe the Scriptures foretelling the future are true?

2. In light of God's promises for the future, how can I respond to events in my life today?

View 1

History is what we make of it. Sure people have made some mistakes, but basically we are a good bunch. If we work at it, the history we create will be wholesome and helpful for future generations.

View 2

History is a result of people's actions. The best we can hope for is to learn from past mistakes so that we can avoid repeating them in the future.

View 3

The past as well as the future is in God's hands. He works everything according to His plans. If you belong to Him there is nothing to worry about. God has shown us in His Word that He has wonderful things in mind for His people. I am trusting that He will be faithful, as He has been in the past, and will do everything He has promised.

Clip Art

The following pages contain all sorts of Bible artwork. Use the art on hand outs, bulletins and overhead projector transparencies. Cut 'em out, paste 'em up, and there you have it!

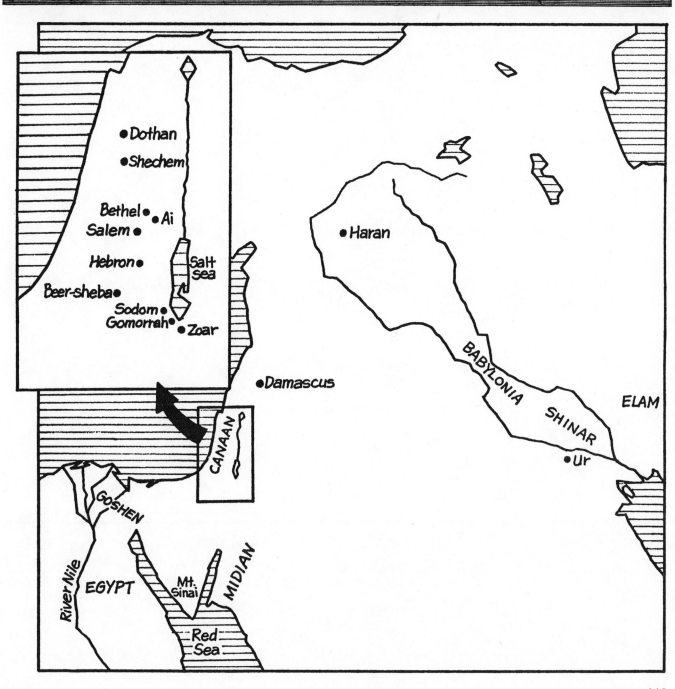

Bible Chronology

1 1/4 inches (3.125 cm) = 400 years

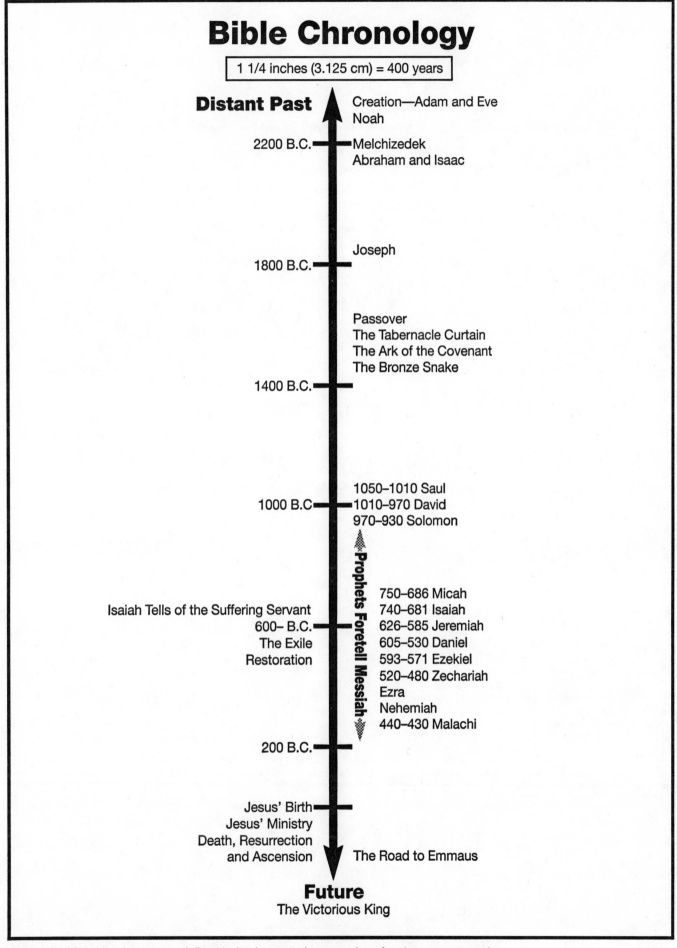

Distant Past

Creation—Adam and Eve
Noah

2200 B.C. — Melchizedek
Abraham and Isaac

Joseph

1800 B.C.

Passover
The Tabernacle Curtain
The Ark of the Covenant
The Bronze Snake

1400 B.C.

1050–1010 Saul
1000 B.C. — 1010–970 David
970–930 Solomon

Prophets Foretell Messiah

750–686 Micah
740–681 Isaiah
Isaiah Tells of the Suffering Servant
600– B.C. — 626–585 Jeremiah
The Exile
605–530 Daniel
Restoration
593–571 Ezekiel
520–480 Zechariah
Ezra
Nehemiah
440–430 Malachi

200 B.C.

Jesus' Birth
Jesus' Ministry
Death, Resurrection
and Ascension   The Road to Emmaus

Future
The Victorious King

The Tabernacle

Holy Place, with the golden table for the bread of the Presence, golden lampstand and altar of incense: length: 20 cubits (30 ft.) width: 10 cubits (15 ft.)

Most Holy Place with the Ark of the Covenant:10 cubits square (15 ft. square)

Curtain

West

East

50 cubits (75 ft. long)

10 cubits

20 cubits

Basin

Bronze Altar

100 cubits (150 ft. long)

Entrance: 20 cubits (30 ft. wide)

Ark of the Covenant

THE HIGH PRIEST